How I Escaped from *Gilligan's Island*

A RAY AND PAT BROWNE BOOK

Series Editors
Ray B. Browne and Pat Browne

How I Escaped From
Gilligan's Island

And Other Misadventures of
a Hollywood Writer-Producer

William Froug

THE UNIVERSITY OF WISCONSIN
POPULAR PRESS

The University of Wisconsin Press
1930 Monroe Street
Madison, Wisconsin 53711

www.wisc.edu/wisconsinpress/

3 Henrietta Street
London WC2E 8LU, England

1   3   5   4   2

Printed in the United States of America

Library of Congress Cataloging-in-Publication Data
Froug, William.
How I escaped from Gilligan's Island :
and other misadventures of a Hollywood writer-producer /
William Froug.
p.   cm.
"A Ray and Pat Browne book."
Includes index.
ISBN 0-87972-873-6 (cloth: alk. paper)
1. Froug, William.
2. Television writers—United States—Biography.
3. Television producers and directors—United States—Biography.
I. Title.
PN1992.4.F73A3   2005
808.2′25—dc22   2005005442

For
CHRISTINE MICHAELS, SUZY ALLEGRA,
NANCY EARTH, LISA FROUG-HIRANO, and
JONATHAN FROUG
whose love and support have kept me afloat
through many tempestuous and perilous seas.
My love and gratitude are beyond measure.

And for
ASHLEY HIRANO, HOPI HALL, ANDREW and
EMILY FROUG
the next generations will surely do a better job of it than we did.

Contents

Illustrations

Acknowledgments

"I get by with a lot of help from my friends." The Beatles will surely forgive the amplification. So many family members and friends have helped me during this arduous two-year journey down memory lane, I could not list them all. But several must be pointed out, not necessarily in order of importance:

Gretchen Thorson entered my life as a computer teacher years ago but continued as a close friend, confidant, and guide, without whom this manuscript would have been at least twenty years in the making.

And thanks to the greatest and wisest woman I've ever known — my wife, lover, best friend, advisor, tough but loving editor — Christine Michaels, my magnificent partner of more than twenty years, a godsend not only to this writer but to my entire family. We are all blessed having this great lady in our lives.

Lisa Froug-Hirano, who demanded I write this book or, more accurately, nagged and nagged the daylights out of me over the years until it was finished. My youngest daughter has always been a far greater fan of Hollywood than I ever was or ever will be.

To Stuart Kaminsky, world-class writer and good friend, without whom this book might very well have languished in my files. Stuart opened doors I didn't know were there. I am deeply grateful.

Tricia Brock, a charming young editor in Madison, Wisconsin, who had the courage of her convictions and bet on this book. Thank you. Tricia, where would these stories be without you? And to Gwen Walker who took over when Tricia departed. A marvelous pinch hitter.

And thanks to Cici Neber, who patiently waded through initial drafts of my early chapters, urging me to continue on, even seeking and finding an agent for me.

Thanks to my good friend and prolific writer Peter King, author of the witty, urbane *Gourmet Detective* series, whose enthusiasm for early drafts of this book buoyed my hopes for success.

Acknowledgments

James Fox and Gwen Feldman, founders and CEOs of Silman-James Press, started me on the road to authorship and encouraged me along through five books. My retirement career as an author would never have happened without these two wonderful publishers and friends who taught me everything I know about writing books.

The late Paul Bergin, an early enthusiast, insisted I include photos in the book, a thought I confess had not occurred to me. Special thanks to my longtime friends Connie Newman, Marge Bowers, Norman Corwin, and Madelyn Pugh Davis for lending me their personal photos for this book.

And thanks to Richard Glidewell, man of many talents: emeritus philosophy professor, writer, financial adviser, photographer, technological wizard, master of all crafts, who volunteered to take the photo of me for this book. If it's a lousy picture, blame Richard, not me. I'm actually fifty years younger than I look, or so I like to tell myself.

In memory of the late, great E. Jack Neuman, who put me on the path to an unexpected and surprisingly long career. Thank you Jack, wherever you are.

Hugs and kisses for Anne Nelson, the Grand Dame of CBS, who has helped me all along the way, with sound advice, good sense, and good cheer. Love you, Annie. Live forever!

And a special thanks to Jack's widow, Marian Collier Neuman, for lending me photos as well as her expertise and research.

My deepest gratitude to former Dean Gil Cates and present Dean Robert Rosen who brilliantly brought the UCLA School of Theatre Arts, Film, and Television into the twenty-first century. I learned far more about film sneaking into Bob's insightful lectures than I learned in my forty years in Hollywood.

And to countless others who shared their wisdom and cheered me on.

How I Escaped from *Gilligan's Island*

Introduction

The single most arresting aspect of Hollywood is its unpredictability. It is a business built on the rock-solid foundation of a floating crap game, which is appropriate since the motion picture and television businesses (identical in many ways) *are* floating crap games. The players come and go, they win or lose and hope the next roll of the dice will change their luck. And change it will. Overnight stardom is commonplace for people who have worked a dozen years to get to that one night.

In Hollywood you can be a hero one day and a bum the next, without so much as a phone call. I left for a one-week vacation in Mexico as a richly rewarded, lauded hero and returned to Hollywood to learn that during my absence I had become a pariah. The new management couldn't get me out of CBS Television City fast enough.

Surprise is the most persistent and potent drug in Hollywood. Just knowing that by getting up one morning (or going to bed one night) your fortunes can change dramatically will leave even the most reasonable person's nerves jangling like live wires. It's true that

3

Hollywood is a state of mind, not a city, town, or even a place on the map, but it is planet Earth's epicenter of drama.

We good burghers of these bizarre studio villages eat, sleep, and drink drama, which we sell at a tidy profit. Is it any wonder so many of us behave like inmates in an asylum?

If someone had told me as a kid growing up in Little Rock, Arkansas, that I would one day be working at each of the major studios in Hollywood, California, I would have laughed in his face. Like almost every kid of my generation, I grew up with the movies, about which I was nuts, and network radio, about which I was even nuttier. I loved showbiz as an audience loves it, not with any concept of winning the Screen Producers Guild Award or winning an Emmy Award the same year and being nominated for another a few years later. Such gilded trinkets were never on the distant fringe of my imagination. Nor did I exhibit even a hint of talent that might suggest gilded baubles were in my future. What I did have was an enormous appetite for enjoyment of the many entertainments in my life.

When I was four my mother took me to see my first movie, the original, silent *Ben Hur.* Because I was small and people were seated in front of us, my mother had me stand on the arms of the theater seat. She loved to tell the tale (over and over again) of me cheering and shouting for Ben to win the chariot race. Soon the entire audience moved to sit close to me, she recalled. "They loved your enjoyment as much as they enjoyed the movie, maybe even more. You were the best audience anybody ever had," she would brag shamelessly.

As luck would have it (I call it pot luck because in Hollywood none of us ever knows whether the luck we get is actually going to turn out to be good or bad in the long run) some of my sure-fire winners turned out to be flops *(Sam Benedict)* and some seeming flops were rousing successes *(Gilligan's Island).* You climb aboard one of these vehicles (more like bucking broncos) not really knowing whether you're about to win a trophy or be thrown on your ass. Having produced ten network television series in my lifetime as well as three movies made for television, I've experienced plenty of both. My life in "the business" (as we in "the business" call it!) was frequently a matter of luck. I got lucky many times, and unlucky just as often. My most important luck happened far away from Hollywood. It was the day my Navy crew was shooting sharks.

It was the precise moment when my life in Hollywood began, even though I was on the other side of the world, across the international date line. It was the day I changed from being an audience to an audience maker.

In late August of 1945, in the great lagoon of Eniwetok atoll in the Marshall Island chain in the remote reaches of the Pacific, a vast armada of war ships swung lazily at anchor pending orders to return to their home bases in the United States. Eniwetok was one of the staging areas for the no-longer-needed invasion of Japan. The Japanese had surrendered two weeks earlier; World War II was over.

Just outside the lagoon a lone subchaser patrolled slowly back and forth as if guarding the huge naval base. Aboard the *PC 800*, a 170-foot, 300-ton, steel-hulled ship resembling a miniature destroyer, I was the newly arrived commanding officer. My orders, when I took command the week after the war ended, were to search for downed aircraft. With the war over, there were of course no combat planes flying.

I had been taken by longboat out the narrow channel entrance where we intercepted the *800* about a thousand yards off shore. As I climbed up the ladder to report on board the skipper was there to greet me, his face one big smile. He almost hugged me with joy. My arrival meant his war was over, he could go home.

We did a hurry-up ship's inspection, a five-minute change of command ceremony, and he leaped into the longboat and was gone. I found myself with five officers and sixty men whose sole mind-set was going home. With no external enemy to fight, they were trying to cope with the enemy within: boredom. All of America and the rest of the world were seemingly at home celebrating victory, except us. The crew felt abandoned, in a kind of time warp. We were all anxiously awaiting orders as we lazily made just enough headway to hold our course. Fortunately, the seas were calm. The weather was hot and sunny, but the ship's movement gave us a slight breeze making the heat bearable. We were a young ship with young officers and crew. At age twenty-three I already had two years of subchaser duty in the backwaters of the Pacific under my belt. Older crew members had been the first to receive orders home. Among this young ship's company I was a seasoned pro.

The waters off Eniwetok Atoll were so crystal clear that looking down over the rail we could see countless schools of sharks circling all the way down to the smooth sandy ocean floor. These sleek prehistoric animals seemed attracted to our ship. I stood at the port side rail fascinated as I watched. But I was pondering what I was going to do with my life. I was just short of enough points in the Navy's discharge plan; it was only a matter of a couple of months at most when I would be ordered back to the States. I hadn't a clue what I was going to do as a civilian. I had graduated from the University of Missouri's School of Journalism with a BJ degree, but working on a newspaper held no interest for me, nor did advertising.

Smitty, our young bo'sun's mate approached me, "Request permission to shoot sharks, skipper," he said.

"Permission granted," I replied. The crew had to do something to fill the hours.

In a matter of minutes our entire port side afterdeck was lined with armed sailors eagerly scanning the shark-infested waters, choosing moving targets. Randomly, they opened fire: rifles, .45s, even submachine guns. The war against the sharks was on. The roar was deafening.

It was clear from the start the sharks were winning. For all the firepower we brought to bear, the bullets hit the water and were instantly flattened, rendering them harmless. The sharks were unfazed. Their numbers seemed to increase, as others were fascinated by the hubbub. But on deck the crew was frustrated.

"I've got it!" our cook shouted with the boisterous enthusiasm of a kid about to jump into his backyard swimming pool. Cookie rushed down the after hatch into our mess hall and almost immediately emerged triumphantly raising a big hunk of stew meat. Cheers went up from the crew. Quickly our bo'sun's mate grabbed a heavy line, a huge hook, and rigged a fishing line big enough to grab the *Queen Mary*.

The crew gathered around, full of excitement. Smitty hurried to the port side aft swinging his hooked line back and forth like a cowhand trying to rope a steer. The crew, frantically reloading, hurried to position themselves along the rail for the next phase of the attack. Cookie leaned over the railing, swinging his bait in a wide arc, then with one mighty effort let it fly. As soon as the stew meat splashed into the water a great gray shark leaped for it. It was the poor animal's last leap. Our entire store of small arms opened fire. The innocent victim took hits directly to his head, piercing cleanly between his eyes. He rolled over and, as the crew cheered, the dead shark's body slowly drifted down to the sandy sea floor.

Other sharks escorted the victim down to his final resting place, seemingly puzzled but not aggressive. None attacked him. They followed him until his curiously arched body flopped like a rubber toy on the sea floor. Then, swirling in an undersea whirlpool of their own making, they rose toward the surface.

On deck the crew began good-naturedly squabbling over who had fired the fatal shot. Then, bored with the game, one by one most of them began to stow their weapons. Only a few stragglers remained hoping to score again. They fired some random, half-hearted shots.

"Knock it off, men," I called to the stragglers, "you've proved your point."

"Aye, aye, skipper," they replied and drifted off to stow their weapons.

As skipper I was not required to stand watch; I was on duty 24/7. I went below to my cabin and pulled my little black Royal portable typewriter from under my bunk, slipped in two sheets of blank paper divided by a sheet of carbon paper, and typed:

"Anybody who looks at dead bodies long enough is bound to get tired of it, sooner or later." That sentence had nagged at me during the entire war against the sharks. I didn't know why, but I could not shake it out of my mind. Then I wrote another sentence and then another. My fingers kept adding new sentences that took on a life of their own and, finally, new paragraphs, then new pages. I was totally immersed in my tale, telling myself a story I did not know, having no idea where it was going to take me. On cruise control, I was writing as fast as my fingers could strike the keys. I was taking dictation from an invisible yet demanding boss: my imagination. Characters I had never met were speaking through my fingers and leaping onto the page, saying things that usually surprised me. It was one of the most exciting and powerful experiences I was ever to know in my life, and yet it was as effortless and exhilarating as breathing. As the hours miraculously turned into days and sentences became pages, I began to realize that I was a *writer*. This was what I was going to do with my life. I had not actually discovered my future life's work, it had discovered me. Somewhere in the clacking of pounding type-writer keys, the thought entered my mind that perhaps no one else would enjoy the story I was telling myself. Simultaneously came the realization that it didn't matter in the least. I was writing this story for me. Every sentence, every twist and turn the story took came as a delightful surprise to me. When the story told me it had been fully told and I wrote "The End," I discovered almost two hundred typed pages stacked beside my typewriter. I titled it "Enough Money."

That first single sentence was the moment my career in Holly-wood began. In the days that followed I discovered I'd written a mystery novella. I haven't the slightest doubt that my encounter with shooting sharks launched my career as a writer. I could hardly have imagined that I would spend the next forty years of my life in Hollywood as a writer-producer, encountering sharks of the two-legged variety, several of them shooting back at me.

I sent the manuscript to my former college roommate, E. (for Ernst) Jack Neuman, then working in Hollywood as a successful writer of radio dramas. Jack responded that he thought my story was terrific. He would get me an agent and felt certain the story would be published. He urged me to take my discharge in Los Angeles and consider a career as a writer, which idea, freshly minted in my mind, still seemed like a giant pole vault with no landing cushion. What if I had no other story to write?

Within weeks after my arrival in Los Angeles and an honorable discharge from the Navy, Jack fulfilled his promise and contacted an agent who liked the story. He quickly sold it for three hundred dollars to *New Detective* magazine, which featured my name on the cover of their May 1947 issue. Suddenly I was a *professional* writer! Neuman urged me to collaborate with him writing radio scripts. We soon sold several to the CBS Pacific Radio Network for ninety dollars, which gave each of us forty-five dollars a script. Meanwhile, I was also collecting twenty-five dollars a week for fifty-two weeks under the GI Bill of Rights. Within a few weeks, however, Jack took off on his own. He was in demand and easily doubled his income writing top-ten dramas like *Lux Radio Theater,* a half-hour series hosted by famed film director Cecil B. DeMille and featuring major movie stars every week in adaptations of hit movies. How Jack boiled down a two-hour movie to twenty-nine minutes never ceased to amaze me. No doubt that's why they paid him six hundred dollars a script, big money in 1946.

I continued to scratch out a living writing on my own just enough radio dramas for CBS's Pacific Radio Network, where I knew I had found a home and an unexpected career.

Gradually this morphed into producing and directing as the clock on network radio was rapidly winding down. My nine years writing, producing, and directing radio dramas for CBS were, in many ways, the most rewarding years of my life. But network radio was sinking rapidly under a tidal wave of television. Though I had no great desire to work in the new medium, the next logical step was television.

Producing ten television series was a succession of wild rides on the Hollywood rodeo circuit where I had more than my share of bucking broncos who threw me for several bone-crunching falls. It is no coincidence that one of the most upscale shopping streets in the world is named Rodeo Drive in Beverly Hills, California. The highs and the lows of those bizarre rides not infrequently knocked the breath out of me (and whatever else in me that was loose). I was quite literally lucky to have survived. Join me for an inside look at the other side of the tube where the pace is frantic, and fortunes are made and lost in the blink of an eye. There was always as much comedy and drama going on on the sets of the Hollywood studios as there was in your living room . . . except we had no commercial interruptions and no mute button.

It was during those years I learned a writer's best friend is his luck.

Welcome to Hollywood

Late one afternoon in April of 1946, the aging DC-3 touched down on the runway of Burbank Airport in the San Fernando Valley and taxied toward the terminal. Exiting the plane, I saw white wisps of gently drifting gold-tinged clouds brushed by the fading sunlight. The deepening blue sky was crystal clear. In the distance the Santa Monica mountains guarding Los Angeles seemed aflame in the last glows of sunset. There were no other planes on the runway, and the airport seemed nearly deserted. As the day faded, a gentle silence was settling over the vast desert valley. Inhaling the orange-blossom scented air, seeing the swaying palms, I was sure this was paradise. As much as I had loved the Hawaiian Islands during my year and a half aboard a subchaser operating out of Pearl Harbor and atolls far beyond, this place was going to be even more inviting and seductive—a paradise without the war. I was thrilled by the unpredictability of adventures beyond my imagining that lay ahead. To a kid from Little Rock, Hollywood was Oz.

Walking down the metal stairs, overnight bag in hand, I was resplendent in my Navy uniform, proudly wearing my appropriately tarnished Lieutenant (junior grade) gold-braided sleeves. (It was called "salty" to have green-stained gold braid on your uniform, especially your hat; it showed you were a seafaring sailor, not a desk jockey). E. Jack Neuman had promised to meet me at the terminal. Instead I was handed a telegram that read "UP WITH SICK SCRIPT. BUZZ ME. MR. BLUE. JACK." This was a play on Amos 'n' Andy's famous instructions to their secretary, "Buzz me, Miss Blue."

I had not seen my college roommate since we said farewell at the Columbia, Missouri, train station in June of 1942 when he hopped aboard a train to join the United States Marine Corps. Jack had enlisted shortly after Pearl Harbor, whereas a few weeks earlier I had enlisted in the Navy's V-7 program, which allowed college juniors and seniors to sign up and get a deferment until they graduated. We would then head for Columbia University's Naval Officer's Training Program in New York City the day following graduation. In their haste to accommodate the Navy, the university had forgone graduation ceremonies, dismissing us in early April, several weeks before the end of the semester.

But Jack had wanted to see action immediately with no waiting for the niceties of a diploma. Off he went, gung ho, to war.

Things didn't quite work out that way. After a few months in basic training, a subsequent medical exam disclosed scar tissue on his lungs. He was given an immediate medical discharge. Shortly after his release he came down with tuberculosis and ended up spending the rest of the war in VA hospitals. We exchanged letters throughout the war years, culminating with his urging me to take my discharge in Los Angeles, move in with him and his mom, and begin collaborating on radio scripts.

A stranger in a strange land, I took a bus to Hollywood, then a cab to Jack's address on Taft Avenue just off Hollywood Boulevard.

The long narrow street was guarded by forty-foot-high pencil-thin palms lining both sides of the street like anorexic sentinels. High above the very end of Taft Avenue, anchored into the side of the Santa Monica mountains, were enormous white letters, H O L L Y W O O D, lit by the fading sunlight; they seemed almost aflame in the fading light and much farther away than they actually were.

Jack lived in an old, three-story, faded white stucco apartment building next to the parking lot of Ralph's market on the corner of Taft Avenue and Hollywood Boulevard. It was the low-rent end of Hollywood. I walked up the three flights of stairs until I found his apartment at the end of the long narrow hallway. It looked like a building Sam Spade or Philip Marlowe might have lived in; it was of their era.

A thin, graying woman in a chenille robe opened the door with a cigarette dangling from her mouth. "Come on in, Billy," she greeted me. "We've been waiting for you. First, give me a hug. I'm Jack's mom. My name's Agnes, but Jack calls me Aggie, so you might as well, too."

I hugged this smiling, skinny, likable woman. "Jack's asleep," she continued, "the doctors told him he has to rest at least four hours a day, but he's recovering nicely. Still he insisted I wake him up. He'll be so happy to see you."

The tiny one-bedroom apartment was going to be my home for an indefinite stay. The Neumans would be charging me eighty dollars a month, room and board, until I found a place of my own. The Navy had shipped my footlocker to Jack's address, but there was no telling when it might show up. Meanwhile, I had only the uniform I was wearing, a couple of extra shirts, skivvies, socks, and a shaving kit.

As I entered the bedroom, Jack looked up groggily, much thinner than I had remembered him, "Willie, how you been?" he said, in a weak voice, as I tossed my bag on the other twin bed. "Aggie's going to sleep on the Murphy bed in the living room," he said, "but that's fitting for a good Irish girl. Honestly, we're both so glad to have you home." We exchanged a handshake, and he fell back to the pillow, exhausted.

Jack drifted off to sleep as I sat for a moment seeing what the ravages of TB had done to him. I had spotted an old Underwood office typewriter on a card table in the small living room. This, apparently, was going to be our office. Nonetheless, the prospect excited me.

Jack didn't own a car, so the next morning bright and early I took a cab to the Armory where I was honorably discharged and handed a terminal-leave paycheck for six hundred dollars. This was my entire net worth.

That night, Jack urged me to go out and see the town. "I wish I could join you, pal, but I just don't have the energy."

"I don't know anybody, I don't have a car, and I don't know where to go," I protested.

"Easy," Jack said, "just walk to the corner. That's Hollywood Boulevard; stick out your thumb, hitch a ride to the Beverly Hills Hotel. Anybody will stop to pick up a returning serviceman. Hell, you might even meet some interesting people, have a few drinks, have some fun. For chrisakes, Willie, you deserve to celebrate, you're home from the war!"

Doing as Jack suggested, I stuck out my thumb on the corner of Hollywood and Taft and almost immediately a black Ford two-door sedan pulled to a stop in front of me.

"Where to, sailor?" shouted a guy leaning toward me as he rolled down his window.

"I'd like to go to the Beverly Hills Hotel," I told him, "if that's not too much out of your way?"

"Not at all," he replied, "I'm going right by there. Hop in."

I climbed in finding myself sitting next to a nice-looking man of about forty in sport coat and tie, his dark wavy hair slicked back, wearing a pencil-thin mustache. The car looked almost new, which I mentioned to him.

"It's a '42," he responded, "the last year they made them. But I hear Ford's coming out with a '46, and I'm going to get one."

We rode in silence. I was surprised by how far it was from Hollywood to Beverly Hills.

"Here it is!" he said cheerfully, stopping at a dark corner at the base of a long, narrow, uphill, winding driveway. "It's up that driveway," he pointed.

As I started to get out of the car, suddenly he grabbed my thigh with a firm grip, leaning his face in toward me, "but why don't you come with me? We'll have our own party and play the Hollywood way."

"No, thanks," I said hopping out and slamming the door behind me. He zoomed off into the night. I was, indeed, a stranger in a strange land.

The lobby of this magnificent hotel was awash in bright lights and alive with throngs of people in a celebratory mood. They were streaming out of the bar, dozens of servicemen among them, probably new returnees, like me. The atmosphere was of an ongoing party.

"Billy! Billy Froug!" I heard my name called out, "Billy Froug from Little Rock!" said a very pretty redheaded girl rushing toward me. I had no idea who she was, but I recognized her escort, the actor Sidney Miller. Though he was now totally bald, his face was familiar from the various *Dead End* series of urban kids movies in which he usually played one of a gang of juvenile delinquents.

Seeing the look of bewilderment on my face she decided to help me out, "I'm Mimi Minton, Little Rock Senior High! Don't you remember, we danced together many times? You were voted the best dancer in our class." She gave me an extraordinarily warm welcoming hug, whispering urgently in my ear, "Meet me later."

Turning to her date, she said, "Sid I want you to meet my high school boyfriend Billy Froug, and be a darling, Sid, I left my jacket in the bar. Will you get it for me, please?"

"Of course," replied Miller, heading for the bar.

"Listen," she said in a rush of words, "I live on Holloway Drive just off Sunset, The Golden Arms, apartment 333, third floor, you can't miss it. Meet me there in about two hours, no, make it an hour and a half."

After seeing them leave the hotel, I began to vaguely recall this pretty young woman's face and even her red hair, except it was redder than it had been in high school. But beyond her soft southern accent, I hadn't a clue. I drifted into the bar and had a drink but kept looking at my watch. Civilian life was far exceeding my wildest expectations, and I wasn't even out of uniform yet.

Just before midnight, the cab let me off in front of a four-story apartment complex. Above the entrance was a large sign: The Golden Arms. I hurried up to apartment 333 and knocked.

Mimi was apparently waiting on the other side of the door. It opened instantly, revealing a milk-skinned redhead with a voluptuous young body displayed to perfection under a flimsy nightgown.

"What took you so long?" she hungrily demanded, a wonderful urgency in her voice.

"I got here just when you told me. It's a quarter 'til twelve."

"Never mind," she said, impatiently, "let's have at it. Get out of that heavy wool uniform," she urged me, "although you look gorgeous in it. This is Hollywood. Nobody ever wears wool clothes here."

"But I just flew in from San Francisco," I replied, desperately hopping around on one leg as I ripped off my trousers, undressing as fast as my hands could rip off my shirt without losing its buttons. "It's freezing up there."

"To hell with that, sweetheart, it's plenty hot in here," she said, cheerfully tossing off her nightie and leaping stark naked into bed. "Time for another dance. Sound good to you?"

"Couldn't sound better," I replied, crawling eagerly into bed beside her, my enthusiasm equaling hers. I don't actually recall dancing with Mimi Minton during our time at Little Rock high school, but I vividly remember this "dance," my first night in Hollywood. "I've been wanting to do this with you for a very long time," she whispered in my ear. Our passionate enthusiasm for each other during our coupling was without care or restraint. What a way to return to my life as a civilian! While we were ravishing one another as only a sailor home from three years at sea can, the phone next to the bed rang.

"Excuse me," she said, "I've got to get rid of this pest. He phones me every night at midnight." Picking up the phone she shouted full voice, "You creep! Your mother takes it under her armpit!" She slammed the phone down so hard it rattled.

At three o'clock in the morning I found myself standing at the curbside in front of the Golden Arms apartment. There were no cabs in sight, seemingly for miles. However, walking a short block up to Sunset Boulevard, an area of Los Angeles I later learned was called "the Strip," I caught a cab almost immediately.

Jack awakened as I fell into the bed across from him.

"Did you meet anybody interesting, Willie?" he asked, sleepily.

"You bet," I replied.

I couldn't imagine that the evening was merely a hint of the bizarre adventures that awaited me in Hollywood. I had no idea they would continue to surprise and bedazzle me for forty tempestuous years.

2

Hello, I Must Be Going

Don't stay out late,
Don't go to shows,
I'm home about eight,
Just me and my radio
Ain't Misbehavin',
I'm savin' all my love for you . . .

Fats Waller's megahit of the 1930s not only spawned a hit
Broadway musical review that toured the nation, it also
expressed lyrically our national obsession with the new
medium of radio. Invented in the twenties, radio and the later development of network programs heard nationwide on either NBC
or CBS (they had no significant competition) in the thirties unified
the nation. Listening to Jack Benny on Sunday nights on NBC was
practically a religious experience. Millions of Americans wouldn't
think of missing that network's blockbuster lineup of Sunday night
comics and variety shows: Eddie Cantor, Edgar Bergen with his pre-
cocious puppet Charlie McCarthy, Fred Allen, Fanny Brice ("Baby
Snooks")—all powerhouse show-business veterans, many of whom
had honed their skills in vaudeville—plus Bing Crosby, the nation's
first and most popular "crooner," in a class by himself. (An entire
generation of men tried to sing like Bing in their showers.) Before
there was Sinatra or Elvis, there was Bing, the voice of a generation,
arguably the most popular singer in American history.

The Saturday morning radio serials *Jack Armstrong, the All American Boy!* or *The Lone Ranger!* (the announcer would shout these show's titles as if announcing the Second Coming) were an integral part of the lives of millions of American boys of the thirties. Countless thousands of youngsters eagerly sent off cereal-box tops for rings, badges, toy guns, magic potions, or whatever else the show was hawking. Only on network radio were dramas, comedies, variety shows, classical music, quiz shows, news, commentary, and the like available to every home in America, all of whom had one or more radio sets, many with a radio in every room, with kitchens a favorite spot for a receiver. Almost overnight radio became an integral part of our lives, turning up in automobiles, in workplaces, as travel companions, even in our showers. Portability made the radio ubiquitous in American life. "I heard it on the radio" replaced "I read it in the paper" as a way to introduce tidbits of information. The golden age of network radio was the thirties, a decade of enormously popular entertainment programs that equaled, if not exceeded, the popularity of our most popular current network television programming, primarily because of its low cost and portability and also because radio had little competition. There were fewer choices in those days.

Today we have DVDs, VCRs, Walkmans, Discmans, plus games of every stripe and dimension, computers, phones, portable TVs, and a countless array of technological gadgetry, creating every sort of entertainment device inventors can conceive. More are being invented almost daily. Perhaps because of the many gadgets available, there is no longer the strong sense of personal connection people had then. But in those distant days if you wanted to connect with the world beyond, you had only your radio, and it was personal: "just me and my radio" as Fats Waller astutely summed up the experience.

So powerful was the popularity of network radio programs in the thirties that movie theaters had begun to offer "bank nights," giving away prizes to entice the public into leaving their radios for a few hours to go out to the movies. When *Amos 'n' Andy* was broadcast, some movie houses piped the program into their theater, assuring patrons they wouldn't miss an episode.

"Me and my radio" became the unifying theme of American

entertainment and popular culture for the decade and a half between World War I and World War II. After nationwide network radio was created in 1928 by the National Broadcasting Company, the sales of sets were beyond anyone's estimation. Receivers were being progressively downsized, then miniaturized, and they began selling like peanuts at a baseball game. Radio programs were the talk of the country. TV soaps today have never reached radio soaps' enormous popularity. Quiz shows quickly became national guessing games. "That's the sixty-four-dollar question," as heard on Goodson-Todman's hot new radio quiz show *Twenty One,* was a cliché of humorous puzzlement for decades before it was replaced by television's *$64,000 Question,* then, upping the ante, *Who Wants to Be a Millionaire?*

The nation's comic-in-chief, Jack Benny, gradually developed into a beloved, recognizable character; stingy, self-centered, manipulated by well-meaning friends, helpless in the company of a cast of earnest men and women who were very funny second-bananas. Benny became the master of reaction comedy, giving the laugh lines to his secondary actors or guest stars. Often he was called to the door only to discover either famous next door neighbors like British star Ronald Coleman and his wife, or Jimmy Stewart and his wife. Yet we became used to the oddball workman come to fix his phone or to mow his lawn.

Benny answers his doorbell:

Gardener (played by the master of comedic voices, Mel Blanc, who was also the voice of Bugs Bunny of "What's up, doc" fame): Hello, Mr. Benny, I'm your new gardener.

Benny: I see. And by the way, what's your name?

Gardener: Cy

Benny: Cy?

Gardener: Sí.

Benny: Which is it? Sí or Cy?

Gardener: Cy . . . sí.

Benny: Cy?

Gardener: Sí.

Benny: NOW CUT THAT OUT!

The nation's perennial number-one radio and TV comic of the '30s, '40s, and '50s, Jack Benny fiddles around just before leaving NBC for CBS because their parking was free, according to Benny's imaginative super press agent, Irving Fein. (courtesy of Irving Fein)

Long after he entered his fifth decade, Jack Benny continued to insist that he was thirty-nine years old. America was in on the joke. In radio, year in and year out, he was rated number one in the country. Benny was the rare comic who treasured his writers, keeping essentially the same writing staff throughout his long career: Sam Perrin, George Balzer, Hal Goldman, Al Gordon, Milt Josefsberg, and John Tackaberry. Benny himself sat in on writers' meetings, helping shape his fictional character. Few comedians were able to hold a staff together over so many years. I knew some of these guys and rarely, if ever, did I hear any complaints about their boss; remarkable in itself. Unfortunately, much of Benny's radio comedy came from sound effects and the listeners' imaginations. When his show moved over to television, though it was highly successful, it never reached the plateau it had in radio.

Benny and his writers created an endearing character whose stinginess became legendary. He had a heavily locked vault deep beneath his home, which he entered to the accompaniment of sound effects of a great creaking vault-door, in order to visit his money. It was so comically absurd it always generated a huge audience laugh. There was also a very funny old bank guard, who might have been left over from the cast of *The Count of Monte Cristo.*

In reality, Jack Benny was warm, generous, charitable, quite the opposite of the radio character he and his writers created. One signature of *The Jack Benny Show* was that the secondary characters were always hilarious. He wisely gave the jokes to his supporting cast. His tortured off-key violin practicing "Love in Bloom" was always funny. He seemed not to notice how terribly he played. It became his theme song. Just say "Jack Benny" to any fan of old-time radio and you are guaranteed to get a big smile or even a laugh in response.

The great radio comics did not need a laugh track; studio audiences were more than enough to cue laughter across the nation. They went for belly laughs and got them.

During one of Benny's most memorable radio programs, a stickup man accosts him. "Your money or your life," says the threatening mugger.

The famously penurious Benny takes a moment to think it over. Which is more important to him? His money or his life? This gets a huge laugh. But Jack Benny, known for his impeccable timing, turned to the studio audience and gave them his famous take: a look of bewilderment . . . which should I choose?

In CBS's big-audience Studio B, the response was building to the biggest, longest, laugh in the history of broadcasting. I happened to be in the Hollywood studio audience that night for the West Coast rebroadcast of the show. The roar of laughter was deafening. And then, after the initial explosion, Benny, bewildered, hesitates; another huge laugh from the audience. Then a longer pause. Then the nonpareil master of timing topped it with, "I'm thinking, I'm thinking . . ."

Now the audience response was a volcanic roar of laughter, three or four hundred people helpless with laughter, giving themselves to the master comic. The eruption built upon itself. It was also the ultimate showstopper. The actors stood frozen before their microphones, dumbfounded, unsure of what to do. Their lines couldn't be heard over the roar. A couple of the actors tossed their scripts into the air, letting the pages fall all around them, which got even more laughs. Benny, himself, was having a hard time not cracking up. No comedian was so quick to relish a good joke, even his own. There was no resuming the program. This was without doubt the longest laugh in the history of broadcasting. It lasted a full five minutes. Members of the audience had begun to exchange looks of communal enjoyment in the shared moment and gradually the laughter would start all over again. It was a moment of pure uninhibited pleasure that nobody wanted to end. Tears of joy were trickling down many a cheek.

The audience at home did not need to see Benny's take to get the joke. All over America people were laughing affectionately at Jack Benny, the ultimate miser. It had actually taken many years to build to this sequence. Not a joke in it; just the nationwide understanding of Jack Benny's carefully created miserly character.

"Your money or your life." It remains one of the grand moments in the history of network radio.

I presently belong to a group of writers who meet for a weekly lunch and rounds of liar's poker. As the bids go around the table, players who hesitate to bid or challenge routinely say when urged to get on with the game, "I'm thinking . . . I'm thinking . . ." It never fails to get a laugh.

More than sixty years later we are still paying tribute to network radio's king of comedy, Jack Benny, and, in a very real way, to network radio itself and it's ability to create a nationally shared moment.

Benny moved his sitcom to CBS television in 1950 where it remained a hit for twenty years. The running gag at CBS Radio Hollywood was that Jack Benny had left NBC because he didn't like the cost of his parking space.

The parking-space story was the invention of Benny's master publicist, Irving Fein, who wanted to keep Benny in the news while his deal to move to CBS was being negotiated by superagent Lew Wasserman. Fein spread the story that Benny was moving to CBS where the parking was free, whereas NBC charged twenty-five cents. Using Benny's fictional stinginess was an inspired publicity ploy.

It was said that David Sarnoff, founder, primary owner, and president of RCA, parent of NBC, paid scant attention to his stars' vicissitudes. The actors were to come to work, park in their assigned spaces, do their jobs, go home, collect their handsome paychecks, and not complain. Sarnoff's indifference to the temperaments of his stars may very well have contributed to Benny's and the other NBC stars leaving for CBS, but they actually changed networks for several million dollars and a guarantee of a prime-time CBS Television series. Added to this was CBS owner and president William S. Paley's personal attention and charm. He liked schmoozing with his stars. He understood in advance that, in television, as well as radio, it was the stars who mattered most. He phoned each of them personally to let them know they were most welcome at CBS and to tell them they could phone him any time, day or night (even at his home) and get a warm reception, if they should have a problem with the Columbia Broadcasting System. Many of them accepted his offer. Paley's was a hands-on approach.

Sarnoff had little use for this nonsense. After all, he was the young man who telegraphed the world that the *Titanic* was sinking, and he was the pioneer largely responsible for establishing network radio in the first place. He was a technological wizard and a certifiable captain of industry. Why should he pander to temperamental, overpaid voices? Besides, he had his first love, the Radio Corporation of America, to run. He hired an ad agency man to take care of such minor matters as radio actors at NBC.

By the late fifties NBC's entire Sunday night lineup of big-name stars had fled NBC as passengers from a sinking ship, while actually being brought over to CBS Radio with millions of Paley dollars. Paley was throwing money around like confetti. In 1948, CBS employees were informed that there would be no annual Christmas bonus that year. We all understood that our bonuses were actually paid in huge lump sums to Jack Benny, Burns and Allen, Edgar Bergen, Bing Crosby, and others. In spite of our annoyance, we admired Paley's ploy. We knew our boss was as crazy as a fox. What the industry and Sarnoff began to realize was that William S. Paley was not spending millions for radio stars; radio was old news, on the way out. He was building his CBS Television network, and he knew these people would be the foundation for it. Paley was among the few tycoons who saw the future. Even though that era's crop of superstars are now long gone, NBC has been playing a game of catch-up with CBS ever since. Paley's move was a stroke of programming genius unparalleled in the history of broadcasting.

Paley was a new kind of tycoon in America. Paley and Sarnoff, the two titans of American broadcasting, couldn't have been more opposite. Sarnoff was a hard driving, unpolished, egocentric man, with a European blue-collar background. Paley, on the other hand, was to the manor born. He was a scion of new money. Paley's family owned a cigar business. Young Paley had bought radio advertising to promote his family business. The campaign was so successful he decided to build his own network of radio stations, steadily expanding, signing up new stations, until he had created the Columbia Broadcasting System. Paley was a man of exquisite taste, a major contributor to the arts serving on museum boards, a social climber, a brilliant, handsome, persuasive, low-key salesman with a vision. Sarnoff had been commissioned as a general during World War II. Long after the war ended he insisted on being addressed by his military title. Paley was fashionable, polished, aloof, and elitist, traveling as far up society's social ladder as a Jew at that time was allowed. His World War II military rank was a mere colonel. After his return to civilian life he preferred to be called Mr. Paley by the employees of his company, including his top-level executives. He was almost a deity figure. Very few of us who worked for him ever violated that form of address. Sarnoff created a company that was conservative, formal, even stodgy, where the rules of behavior were set in cement. Paley, at least in the beginning, was somewhat of a liberal, a shade more freewheeling and even, at times, daring. In 1933 Paley launched CBS News, sensing the advantage of instant reporting the new medium had over print journalism. He began by hiring highly successful young newspaper men, one of whom was Edward Roscoe Murrow. Murrow, in turn, assembled the greatest news team in the history of mass communication. Although it was not a profit-making division, Paley not only backed it to the hilt but maintained a hands-off policy and demanded that his commercial programming do the same. The CBS News Division was autonomous. Paley held it sacrosanct, a decision he probably came to regret in later years with the arrival of Senator Joseph McCarthy. Soon CBS left stodgy NBC News in their dust. Conservative, old school H. V. Kaltenborn, NBC's star newsman, was hardly a match for Murrow and his young, enterprising newcomers. (Kaltenborn was later ridiculed for announcing, before the vote was counted, that Dewey had defeated Truman in the presidential election of 1948.) If you wanted in-depth, knowledgeable reporting, you sought out CBS. Under Murrow's leadership, CBS soon became the most honored and revered source of broadcast news in America. When Joe McCarthy appeared, Paley discovered too late that the price for these outstanding journalists was higher than he was prepared to pay.

For the decade and a half preceding World War II, network radio had united and helped heal America during the Great Depression. And then the nation went to war. When peace came, servicemen returned home to discover that while they were away, somebody had invented television.

By the mid-1940s, network radio was rapidly becoming irrelevant. But for us die-hard radio fans it was like watching the slow, lingering, inevitable death of a very close friend. Those of us who went to work in network radio were not unlike the buggy manufacturers and blacksmiths who understood that the horseless carriage was going to take over the world of transportation, yet were powerless to stop it. We had grown up with radio and had been happily hooked since childhood. *Radio was ours.*

By the end of the 1940s we could feel the hot breath of television blasting down our necks. But there was something deeper inside us that could neither succumb to the enemy nor rush to join its forces. We simply loved what we were doing and refused to do what we knew we eventually would have to do: leave radio to seek other work. Who leaves the womb without a struggle?

For those of us who grew up in network radio, it was no easy matter to walk away from the medium that had been an integral aspect of our youth. Every evening when my father came home from work, he immediately turned on the big Atwater-Kent radio in the corner of the living room. The radio remained on until we went to bed. My father was a news junky. He wanted to know what was happening all over the globe, and only network radio could tell him. CBS was our network of choice. This was where we could find Edward R. Murrow and his brilliant team of foreign correspondents: Howard K. Smith in London, David Schoenbrun in Paris, William L. Shirer in Berlin, Winston Burdett in Rome.

Listening to Gershwin's annual summer concert in Central Park with Oscar Levant playing Gershwin's *Rhapsody in Blue* was practically a religious ritual to me. I was as close to heaven as I ever hoped to get. My favorite, though, was Norman Corwin. Such was the talent and popularity of this writer that CBS gave him his own series, *13 by Corwin,* and later *More by Corwin.* His radio plays, sometimes written entirely in verse, were a tonic for American households starved for something other than news of the Depression or the preparations for war. His "On a Note of Triumph," celebrating the Allied victory over Germany, was broadcast live simultaneously by all three networks. For me "Triumph," written, produced, and directed by Corwin, remains the greatest single radio broadcast in the history of the medium. Other kids had Babe Ruth and Lou Gehrig as their heroes, but I had Ruth, Gehrig, *and* Norman Corwin and the magic that emerged from the Atwater-Kent radio, which was the centerpiece of our home. For a lonely only child, radio was a window to the world outside the narrow confines of Little Rock, Arkansas. Without realizing it, I was studying to become a radio writer.

During World War II our Armed Forces Radio Network kept America's servicemen supplied with superb entertainment, featuring the nation's greatest stars in every format conceivable, yet each program had its own distinctive appeal. Hollywood's major stars sang, told jokes, performed in sketches, answered requests, gave of themselves fully. On our ship we regularly received fifteen-inch disc transcriptions of these broadcasts, which we played over our loud speakers mounted on the mast when docked in port or even at sea when on patrol in calm waters. (*The Marriage of Dick Tracy*, an "opera" starring Bing Crosby, Frank Sinatra, Judy Garland, Dinah Shore, Mickey Rooney, Jimmy Durante, plus a cast of the greatest comics in American entertainment history, was so witty and original we played the recording again and again.) Radio was with the armed forces wherever they were stationed.

After my discharge from the Navy in 1946, my radio-writing career hadn't gotten off to a rousing start after the quick sale of "Enough Money." A top agent, Harold Hecht, phoned to tell me he hoped to sell it to Paramount if I would agree to let him represent me. I did, enthusiastically. But one arrow in your bow is woefully inadequate when hunting for work in Hollywood.

E. Jack Neuman had decided to go out into the marketplace on his own after a few weeks of working together and selling three or four half-hour radio scripts. We soon realized that splitting a ninety dollar script fee made for an inadequate income for both of us. His mother, a hard-working bookkeeper, quickly grew tired of sleeping on the living room Murphy bed and asked me to find a place of my own. Searching the town in my recently acquired well-worn '42 Oldsmobile convertible with two other homeless returning vets, Pete Curtis and George Cahan, was producing no results. We were unable to find anything in our price range. Los Angeles was unprepared for the enormous influx of returning servicemen who wanted a taste of paradise. Many L.A. landlords ignored rent control laws, charging whatever the market would bear.

Norman Corwin. The nonpareil poet laureate of network radio, Corwin was the master whose radio plays (sometimes written in verse) made idolaters of us all. (courtesy of Norman Corwin)

Jim Burkholder, a fellow freelance writer trying to get started in the movie industry after a couple of years in the marines in the Pacific, had joined our unsuccessful search for an affordable apartment. Burkholder was indignant about the lack of housing for returning servicemen. He had fought on the beaches of Iwo Jima, received a minor wound and a Purple Heart, but had come home bitter and angry. One day, following another afternoon without success, he suggested I join him that evening at a friend's home in Coldwater Canyon where there would be a meeting to protest the expected end of rent control.

At eight o'clock I parked on the street in front of a large, rambling, hillside colonial-style ranch house and went up the steep brick stairs to the front door. Whoever lived here had no worry about rent controls.

I was admitted by a butler in a crisp white jacket. The foyer was tastefully furnished in early American antiques. Currier and Ives prints were neatly hung on the walls. In the living room about fifteen or twenty people were casually seated in a semicircle on a deep-piled carpet before the fireplace, which was alive with a crackling fire. Standing at the mantel was a tailored, well-manicured man in his forties, addressing the assembled group of mostly young people. His hand held an unlit pipe, which he used as a prop to punctuate his gestures.

"Please join us," he graciously said to me, indicating the semicircle of people on the carpet. I squeezed in next to an extraordinarily attractive young brunette in a more than amply filled-out black turtleneck sweater, her dark hair pulled back into a ponytail. Burkholder, already seated across the room, gave me a welcoming wave, signaling with a knowing smile his approval of my choice of seating. This pretty young woman was a rent control protester I wanted to get to know. The mild-mannered lecturer, looking every inch the English gentlemen, complete with leather patches on the elbows of his British-tailored tweed jacket, continued his ambling, low-key talk, using his unlit pipe for punctuation, about the disaster that ending rent control would mean for the thousands of returning servicemen and women. Los Angeles was woefully unprepared to meet these housing demands. The speaker's casual, bland manner was designed for easy listening, but I had the beautiful, voluptuous brunette next to me on my mind. My sexual fantasies were fully charged but not by politics.

Once in a while I would catch such phrases as "for the good of the party" at the end of a sentence, without being fully aware of who the "party" was. Most of the comments were generic, anybody with liberal leanings could have made the same remarks with impunity. But there was an undertone of condescension and intellectual elitism beneath his comments, a hint of class warfare, of us-versus-them, though soft spoken. I didn't like his tone and began to wonder if I had wandered into a bizarre kind of communist "cell." We were well-dressed, clean-cut, shorthaired, well-barbered young people. There was nothing conspiratorial or subversive said by anyone in the room. His remarks provoked no comments or reactions. He was not reaching his intended audience, and there were no questions from the floor. As the speaker warmed to his subject of rent control, I gradually realized that this fellow was quietly promoting the Communist Party, even though the words were rarely mentioned. Years later during the Hollywood witch hunts, when the speaker turned out to be one of the original Hollywood "unfriendly" ten, I found it hard to believe anybody would follow this self-important writer-director anywhere, including into the Communist Party. His home was hardly the place you would expect to find a group whose alleged goal was, supposedly, the overthrow of the United States government. Nor was there anything sinister in trying to save rent controls in Los Angeles County.

Next on his agenda was a new book, which extolled the importance of American–Soviet Union friendship. Our speaker wanted the group to form a committee to promote sales. The pretty girl next to me volunteered to head the committee and, introducing herself as Judith, asked me to join her. Facing her now, I was even more impressed with her beauty and was sorely tempted to follow her anywhere, but not for ideological reasons. After second thoughts, I made a suggestion we have dinner one night and discuss rent control.

She gave me a withering look, "You're politically naive," she said curtly, turning her back to me. During the evening it soon became apparent that neither she nor the Communist Party was in my future.

As we left the meeting, Burkholder and I walked to our cars.

"Now that you've seen the Communist Party, Beverly Hills style," he said, with as much disgust as with sarcasm, "what did you think?"

"What I heard tonight was about as subversive as a sack of popcorn," I told him. "I was bored out of my mind."

Jim Burkholder and I parted company soon after that evening, because as he later said somewhat patronizingly, "You just don't get it." He was right. I am the son of Depression-era, Roosevelt Southern Democrats and the legacy of that liberal icon has planted an indelible imprint in my heart and mind. FDR was just left enough for me.

One evening during this period a friend of my parents phoned to ask me to have dinner with their friends Mr. and Mrs. Leo Oppenheim and their daughter, Betty, visiting from Oklahoma City. Helene Bernstein, ever the matchmaker, told me Betty had just returned from two years overseas. She had driven a clubmobile for the Red Cross on the Burma Road during World War II in the China-Burma-India Theater of War. Following that volunteer work she had become a file clerk for the OSS in Shanghai. This was obviously a unique young woman.

"You two have both been away so long, I think it's time you started thinking about getting married and settling down. Betty is a great girl, really," Helene Bernstein gushed. "You two have a lot in common. She's your age, quite pretty, petite, highly intelligent, and charming. You really ought to meet her. Be at Richlor's Restaurant on LaCienega at eight o'clock Thursday night. We'll all be there expecting you." I arrived to meet a young woman who fit Bernstein's description precisely.

Betty Oppenheim and I were married nineteen days later in Oklahoma City at the home of her parents. (We had actually known each other less than two days.) Like many returning veterans following World War II, we were all too eager to get on with our civilian lives and start having a family. Her parents were aggressively pushing for a quick wedding, which took me many years to fully comprehend. Her father told me her dowry was rent for a year in an apartment, then a home, and a new car if we needed one. Why were he and his wife pushing so hard for our quick marriage? Succumbing to considerable pressure from her parents, and probably fueled by my fear of finding nowhere to live, I agreed to the hasty wedding date. Their solution was to rush her into a marriage. I was the answer to their prayers.

After living in a hotel for some weeks, we found a tiny apartment in the San Fernando Valley. We tried to settle into what eventually became a thirteen-year rocky marriage, before which neither of us had had an opportunity to even get to know each other.

With the end of my twenty-five-dollar-a-week GI Bill checks, and with my ambitions for a family, I needed a steady job. I went looking for work at CBS Radio, the network of my youth, where E. Jack and I had sold a couple of our cowritten scripts.

In 1949 I was hired by Lloyd Brownfield, head of CBS Press Information, Hollywood, as a senior publicist for $83.50 a week. That was a living wage at the time. My assignment was to write for the daily mailer, which was sent out to all CBS Radio affiliates. The mailer was intended to pique their interest in the network's programs and especially their stars.

One of CBS's newest stars was a tall, pretty, young, red-headed woman named Lucille Ball. She had appeared in a number of B pictures and, according to the powers that be in New York, had a gift for comedy. Now she was being given her own radio sitcom, *My Favorite Husband.*

Brownfield gave me my first assignment: interview Ball and do a feature story on her for the mailer. I walked across CBS's Columbia Square courtyard and entered our big audience Studio A. The large auditorium was dark except for the lit stage where the cast was seated on folding chairs, studying scripts. They were on a rehearsal break. My good fortune, I thought, as I walked toward the stage where Ball was seated.

As I approached she glanced toward me, curiously.

"Miss Ball," I said, "I'm Bill Froug with CBS Publicity, and I'd appreciate it if I could have a couple of minutes of your time to do an interview."

She turned in her chair so she was facing me head on. She fixed me with cold eyes and a knotted frown.

"Kid," she said, "go shit in your hat."

When I reported the incident to my boss, he broke out into loud guffaws of laughter.

"That's Lucy, all right," Brownie said. "Dig up a studio bio of her, rewrite it, and send it out. And, by the way," he added, "welcome to the real Hollywood."

Early on I was not among the many millions who loved Lucy.

Having established that publicity was not for me, I began moonlighting, writing more radio dramas on my own, selling scripts to a series called *Rocky Jordan* about a cynical tough guy named Rocky who owned the Cafe Tambourine in Cairo. Any similarity to the 1942 movie about a cynical tough guy named Rick who owned the Cafe Americain in *Casablanca* was as deliberate as George W. Allen, KNX's program director, could legally get away with. (In radio you didn't need an Ingrid Bergman.)

Soon after I was offered a job by the Columbia Pacific Radio Network to become a full-time staff writer at $82.50 a week. I wrote half-hour radio dramas every week for a series called *Jeff Regan, Investigator*. Coincidentally, I was replacing the original series writer, E. Jack Neuman, who had left CPN to enter the more lucrative freelance market, where he was in demand. *Jeff Regan* was played by Jack Webb, a young actor just down from San Francisco where he had starred in another private-eye series produced there.

AFTRA, the American Federation of Television and Radio Artists, recognizing that their membership was working in a dwindling marketplace, had kept the minimum scale low on the grounds that low-wage employment was better than no employment at all. However, as their membership moved into television and motion picture work, many actors also moved into SAG, the Screen Actors Guild, which now represents almost all actors in those fields.

Shortly before writing my first script for *Rocky Jordan*, George Allen called me into his office. A big-bellied, pompous, pipe-smoking bureaucrat, Allen told me, "I'm firing Jack Webb. The sonofabitch is demanding fifty dollars a show! What makes Webb thinks he's worth fifty dollars? Anyway, your new Jeff Regan will be Frank Graham, and he's happy to get union scale, thirty-five dollars. Webb says he's developing some new cockamamie cop series he calls *Dragnet*. I say good riddance." (Webb took *Dragnet* to NBC where it ran for more than twelve years, beginning on radio and moving on to become week-in and week-out the highest rated TV series in the country. It made Webb a millionaire several times over, while also making him the most famous radio and TV detective of the following two decades.)

There were eight of us cranking out programs for the Columbia Pacific Radio Network, headquartered with CBS's fifty-thousand-watt, owned-and-operated radio station KNX in Columbia Square on Sunset Boulevard and Gower, in the heart of Hollywood. CPN's sole reason for existence was the time difference between New York and the West Coast. Transcribing a show for rebroadcasting at a later time zone was forbidden by the FCC. National sponsors wouldn't pay prime-time rates for a program scheduled to reach only the West Coast audience at five o'clock on Sunday afternoons. Therefore, prime-time programs such as *The Jack Benny Show* had to be performed live twice, once for New York and again for Los Angeles, the major markets advertisers wanted to reach.

I was assigned an office next door to staff writers Madelyn Pugh and Bob Carroll Jr., who were writing Lucille Ball's new sitcom, *My Favorite Husband.* I told them about my bizarre encounter with Ball when I had requested an interview with her. Their response was laughter.

"It was probably Lucy's idea of a joke," Pugh said.

"You see," Carroll added, "Lucille Ball has no sense of humor. She's a brilliant comedienne, but she doesn't really understand what's funny and what isn't."

"We sometimes have to explain our jokes to her, but she performs them perfectly," Pugh added. "We'll introduce you," she went on. "I'm sure you'll find she's very nice."

I declined. Pugh and Carroll, along with producer-writer Jess Oppenheimer, went on to write or cowrite the entire first four years of *I Love Lucy* (with Bob Weiskopf and Bob Schiller as added writing contributors in the fifth and sixth years). *I Love Lucy* remains the most popular half-hour sitcom in the history of television, apparently destined to rerun until planet Earth expires.

As the postwar cost of living kept rising, we CPN staff writers were finding it more and more difficult to live and support our families on our $82.50 weekly salary. We approached George Allen about a raise but he refused to even discuss it. Network radio was, as

Madelyn Pugh Davis and Bob Carroll Jr., fellow $82.50-a-week CBS Radio writers who quickly moved on and up to the big time, co-writing and co-creating almost a decade of *I Love Lucy* TV shows, the #1 hit comedy in the nation. Madelyn and Bob were never to work for $82.50 a week again.

everyone knew, in decline. When our request for a ten-dollar-a-week raise met the same fate, we gathered at Brittingham's for lunch and decided to try for a one-dollar-a-week increase. Even this modest increase met with stony silence. Allen refused to talk to us. The idea of a strike briefly crossed our minds, though we had little faith in the idea or enthusiasm for it. We decided to take our case to our union, the Radio Writers Guild. We had nothing to lose.

One night four or five of us climbed up the stairs to the second floor of our seedy union headquarters on Cherokee Avenue, a slightly-more-than-disreputable area that crossed the western end of Hollywood Boulevard. A tall, thin, balding man in horn-rim glasses came out to meet us in the waiting room. He introduced himself as Harry Victor Langer, a member of the RWG board. None of us had ever dealt with him, but he had the look of an old-time, blue-collar union man. And we needed a union; for the time being that was good enough.

After listening to our problem he paused thoughtfully, lit another cigarette, and made his carefully couched response:

"Obviously, you people are expecting the guild to support a strike, if you decide to vote for such a foolish idea. However, aside from urging you not to take that vote, I can only tell you that you will get no help from us. For one dollar a week, my advice is suck it up. These are difficult times, be grateful you've got jobs."

He snubbed out his cigarette and turned to face us, his face suddenly a portrait of the benevolent patriarch.

"Look, I like you people, and I admire your guts. We need more working stiffs with your courage, but now is not the time. Besides, the party will not allow you to generate the kind of headlines your strike would create. Serious things are happening in Washington these days. The party says we must lay low. My advice to you is to go home, sleep on it, and forget it."

As we silently filed out into the night away from the noise and glitter of Hollywood Boulevard, we said very little, probably embarrassed by our naïveté as well as annoyed by Langer's comments.

We dropped our demands for a raise, each of us recognizing that the noose was tightening for people working in network radio anyway. Langer had actually done us a favor, reminding us it was time to move on. He turned out to have been a one-term board member of RWG who vanished from the Hollywood scene as mysteriously as he appeared.

Contrary to Senator McCarthy's assertions, the Communist Party never enjoyed any kind of stature or acceptance in Hollywood. The few scattered members we were to encounter in our careers were by and large benign, dissatisfied liberals who felt they had nowhere else to go to express their political passions. They had no passion for revolution, nor had they had any influence whatsoever on any aspect of the entertainment industry or its product. The senator was never able to prove that any of them did. Long before McCarthy began his witch hunt, communists in Hollywood were as rare as three-toed sloths and just as well organized. In the final analysis, it seems their only function was to assure the election of right-wing, militant politicians who needed a cause they could use to arouse the naive populace. The myth of the communists' conspiracy provided a platform for fear.

3

Going, Going, Gone

On April 9, 1949, a tragic event took place in San Marino, California, that had a surprising impact on the entertainment industry in Hollywood. A three-year-old child named Kathy Fiscus fell down an abandoned well. In answer to her parents calls for help, volunteer rescuers began arriving along with big lights, digging rigs, rescue paraphernalia, and workers by the score. Within hours big trucks bearing new remote television broadcasting equipment rolled in from Los Angeles independent station KTLA, among others, accompanied by a young television reporter named Stan Chambers. Clearly we were going to be treated to a media circus unlike anything the nation had ever witnessed. Chambers promptly informed viewers that KTLA would be carrying the Kathy Fiscus rescue story around the clock, until the bitter or happy end. The camera was tightly focused on every agonizing moment, while Chambers began calling it play by play, not unlike a sports event, while solemnly, breathlessly, conveying the urgency of it all. It was a tour-de-force performance.

Within a few hours TV sets began selling like popcorn. Antennas sprang up overnight on rooftops all over town. The Hollywood trade press headlined the phenomenon. There were about two million television sets in Los Angeles County when the marathon television coverage of the rescue attempts to save little Kathy Fiscus began. In a span of twenty-four hours the increase in sales was too rapid to accurately measure. In 1950, 9 percent of American homes had television sets; by 1959 the percentage had risen to 72 percent. The incoming TV tidal wave was actually a tsunami, crashing over us in part by real-time televised events from all over the country, similar to the Kathy Fiscus tragedy. In many a mogul's home the realization was reinforced; television was offering something movies could not duplicate: actual in-your-face, life-and-death drama. It was a *happening*. People riveted to their television sets were not rushing out to their neighborhood theaters to see a show when the show they were watching at home held far more drama and suspense than anything the fiction kings of Hollywood could conjure up. Theater box offices all over the country were beginning to feel the impact of the new medium. The enemy was closing in more rapidly than anyone in Hollywood had forecast.

The moguls could deal with New York live TV dramas, as much as they had not welcomed it. New York live TV plays were appealing to the intelligentsia, an audience the Hollywood studios generally found too miniscule to be worth catering to. Yet there had been some cold comfort since the New York people had frequently delivered highbrow dramas with serious subject matter. Movies were created by and for working-class folks. Intellectuals' tastes had always been of little consequence to Hollywood, anyway. But the rescue of a three-year-old child! This was a dastardly attack from a hitherto undreamed of opponent.

Many studio heads had publicly stated that TV was a novelty that would eventually wear off, as all novelties eventually did, a passing fad, nothing to panic about. They loathed the new upstart and wanted no part of it, but something had to be done and soon.

Not only was the boob tube taking over the world of entertainment but along with it a power the equal of the moguls. The television networks now ruled entertainment. The formerly high-and-mighty studio owners now had to kowtow to johnny-come-lately, inexperienced network television executives who knew nothing about producing visual entertainment for the masses, and worse yet, sponsors who knew nothing about anything except selling soap.

Hollywood's rank and file who did the grunt work (grips, camera crews, set decorators, editors, writers, producers, director, actors, etc.) could read the same handwriting on the wall and for them it spelled "jobs." They understood that the skills that had made them professionals in the motion picture world would just as well translate to the small screen. Making movies is still making movies, no matter how long the finished film runs or how large the screen exhibiting it.

The Kathy Fiscus rescue attempt was yet another immediate reminder that our time as radio writers was running out. Unlike the moguls, we had no studio soundstages to protect and no overhead, other than our families. We had typewriters and could travel from job to job without breaking a sweat. There would always be a market for our stories. Since the first cavemen painted pictures of their hunts on cave walls, people had gathered to hear their tales, in caves or around campfires. What difference did the locale make? A good story is still a good story. Stories are soul food for the human species. We can not deal with life's difficulties without them. For verification, check out the world's religions.

We staff writers for the CBS's Pacific Radio Network's sometimes lunched at Brittingham's Restaurant just across the courtyard at Columbia Square. It was always crowded, noisy, and the food was poor, but it was a two-minute walk from our offices on the second floor of the west wing of Columbia Square. On April 10, 1949, a significant new topic of conversation was added to our lunch: Kathy Fiscus and television's coverage of the rescue attempt. Local radio covered it only sparingly. Many of us did not own TV's, but now we were considering the possibility of buying the beast. In its early days, TV was for housewives, the wealthy, the unemployed, shut-ins, and the lame and halt. Only a few of us owned a set and some of us swore they would never buy one or at least delay buying the damned thing until it became a necessity. Kathy Fiscus was another matter altogether.

My wife and I reluctantly joined the TV-buying mania. We bought our first TV, a thirteen-inch table model GE and fixed ourselves like celery stalks in front of the tube, rooting for the rescuers to bring Kathy Fiscus out of the well alive. Alas, it was not to be. On April 11, when Kathy's tiny body was finally brought to the surface, she was dead.

In the evenings when I came home from work, we began exploring this tiny window to a black and white world. We struck gold! The aptly labeled Golden Age of Television (as it was not yet called) was broadcasting live one-hour- or ninety-minute-dramas from New York almost every night of the week. Night after night on programs with names like *Philco Television Playhouse, Kraft Television Theatre, Robert Montgomery Presents, Playhouse 90,* and the *United States Steel Hour,* original plays written for television appeared in our home. Each series was an anthology with different characters. There were different stories every week, stories about ordinary lives. This was an era of adult drama (when adult meant mature) unlike anything we had known or seen before.

New and previously unknown playwrights appeared nightly out of the New York skies: Paddy Chayefsky, Robert Alan Arthur, Rod Serling, Horton Foote, Ernest Kinoy, Reginald Rose, and others—a cornucopia of previously undiscovered talent consistently writing at depths not seen before or since. Giants strode across our little TV screen every night. Here were stories and subject matter that Hollywood historically found too mundane for its interest. Real-life dramas, with unglamorous everyday people, sans glitz, struggling with difficult everyday problems (think Paddy Chayefsky's *Marty* and J. P. Miller's *Days of Wine and Roses,* Rod Serling's *Requiem for a Heavyweight,* Reginald Rose's *Twelve Angry Men,* among many others), brilliantly written and directed with sensitivity, taste, and style. All have become uniquely American classics. These live TV scripts became the basis for successful movies written by the same writers, who collected Oscars as well as critical raves. As of this writing, *Twelve Angry Men* is playing on Broadway, years after the movie version and several more TV versions. New York live television had shown Hollywood the way to do it. American audiences were seeing real life versus reel life as entertainment. For millions it was a heady, new experience. Over time, however, it became clear that neither the networks nor the Hollywood studios had any interest in the lessons taught by New York live television. They had their own agendas, and it was entertainment, entertainment, entertainment. They had no interest in what they deemed "highbrow" fare.

There were new directors, too: Sidney Lumet, John Frankenheimer, Paul Bogart, Franklin Schafffner, and others. And there were exciting new young actors, unknown to Hollywood, who appeared from nowhere: Paul Newman, Joanne Woodward, Eva Marie Saint, and Rod Steiger were but a few of these non-Hollywood talents. These were, by and large, theater people. Few of them had ever been inside a motion picture studio soundstage.

But the icing on the cake was a Sunday afternoon ninety-minute program on CBS called *Omnibus*. First broadcast in 1952, it was immediately heralded by the critics as an outstanding example of what television at it finest could produce. The program was hosted by a young, urbane Englishman, new to American audiences, by the name of Alistair Cooke. Every Sunday here was a smorgasbord of plays, poetry, music, comedy, outstanding original documentaries, live and filmed performances, interviews, highlights of great Broadway theater—segment after segment of nonpareil entertainment plus stimulating cultural and intellectual fare. In other words, something splendid for everybody. It was as if the entire lexicon of the arts was suddenly appearing before our eyes. *Omnibus* was hands down the greatest television series in the history of the medium.

In October 1953 CBS canceled *Omnibus* and replaced it with an entire Sunday afternoon of NFL football. It was a seminal moment in our culture, and at that moment in our history America changed for better or worse, take your pick.

Coincidentally, the oldest market principles took over and prime-time television packed up and moved to Hollywood. It was, in large measure, a question of supply and demand. The unprecedented explosion of the public's appetite for the new medium brought advertisers stampeding to get their messages across to the populace. New York did not have the physical capabilities in place to meet television production demands. Hollywood, the old movie studios specifically, were hurting from the loss of box office revenues. They had enormous empty soundstages and hundreds, if not thousands, of skilled moviemaking crews. The studios needed tenants, the crews needed jobs. The move was inevitable.

Add to these market considerations another of equal importance and you put the nail in the coffin for New York's nightly television production. The great lineup of nighttime TV dramas could be recorded only on low-quality kinescope tapes, not fit for reuse or syndication or the countless residual marketplaces. Programs on film, on the other hand, had an almost limitless life span and could be rerun endlessly, making a profit for the producers for countless years to come. It was no contest. New York's loss was Hollywood's gain.

My wife and I had become addicts of New York live television before the mass migration began. Around the offices of our CPN writing staff, we found ourselves discussing the previous night's plays, impressed by the quality of the work they were doing, night after night. Much as we may have wanted to, we could no longer ignore the new kid on the block. The horseless carriage was here to stay, and each of us had to figure a way to climb on board.

We were working writers. In addition to Madelyn Pugh and Bob Carroll Jr. we included Bud Swanton, who later became editor and head writer of the long running *Perry Mason* TV series, and Kathleen Hite and John Dunkle, who were regular contributors to CBS's western classic *Gunsmoke*. One of our little group, Bob Ryf (a frequent *Rocky Jordan* writer, with a PhD in education), became president of Claremont College. Larry Roman later wrote two hit Broadway comedies, *Under the Yum Yum Tree* and *P.S. I Love You*. Roman also had several of his screenplays produced, one of which starred John Wayne. Writer for writer, our training in writing weekly half-hour radio mysteries, comedies, and adventure potboilers served as a launching pad for at least a half-dozen writers who went on to become members of television's most reliable writing workforce. Paradoxically, writing for a sound-only medium seemed to have honed our talent for writing for visual media, television, feature motion pictures, or Broadway. Dramatists need no specific venue. Our work can play on street corners, in cafes, anywhere people gather, with equal success. Technology merely added another venue.

Working independently of each other, Adrian Gendot, Joel Malone, Larry Roman, Bud Swanton, or Bob Ryf were assigned to rotate writing weekly half-hour private-eye melodramas *Jeff Regan, Investigator* as well as *A Man Named Jordan* (later renamed *Rocky Jordan*). Mady Pugh and Bob Carroll Jr. also wrote *A Memo from Molly* (our West Coast sitcom), and freelancers wrote our mystery series *The Whistler,* both of which were our most popular shows. They were broadcast to the West Coast only on Sunday evenings. To keep myself interested, I began to inject satirical humor into the *Jeff Regan* series. It was during this stint that I soon became bored to death writing formulaic, simplistic good guy–bad guy melodramas. It was too easy. That decision gradually became my career mantra: no more formulaic, cops-and-robbers shoot 'em up stuff. This was not a moral decision. It was only a matter of trying to keep myself interested in my work. However, my first child, Susan, had been born, and already a second, Nancy, was on her way. Financially as well as emotionally, I was tied to my job.

CPN existed solely for those less commercially viable West Coast time slots. In other words, we were writing solely for the smaller audience. We were known inside CBS Radio somewhat derisively as "those people down on the second floor." The third floor was occupied by the upper-echelon folks who directed, produced, and oversaw the Hollywood-originated network programs such as *Suspense, Escape, The Hallmark Hall of Fame, Gunsmoke, Johnny Dollar, Broadway Is My Beat, Dr. Christian, The Fifteenth Precinct, Sam Spade,* and *Richard Diamond for Hire,* starring Dick Powell. All our soap operas originated in New York.

As we entered the fifties, the topic that seized us all was Senator Joseph McCarthy of Wisconsin and his House Un-American Activities Committee. McCarthy was making headlines daily with charges of communists working in the State Department. The senator's technique was to wave a sheet of paper during a press conference, proclaiming it contained an ever-increasing list of names, the exact number of communists in the State Department. He wouldn't reveal the names, and his totals varied from day to day. The nation's press promoted him (or should we say "created him") with front-page headlines as though what he was saying was the newly minted gospel truth. As we later learned, it was indeed a publicity gimmick. McCarthy had no names to reveal. Meanwhile, his House Un-American Activities Committee began supposedly "investigating" communists in the entertainment industry, holding highly publicized hearings, and calling headline-making witnesses. McCarthy was, in fact, a reckless alcoholic, primarily dedicated to making those headlines and indulging in political showboating while boasting that he alone was saving America from the communist. (Today the present administration substitutes "The terrorists are coming! The terrorists are coming!" Fear always seems to work.) For all the committee's investigating, it never found a single instance where anyone inserted any communist propaganda in any American movie or radio program. However, the committee managed to create national hysteria that destroyed the careers of many talented, innocent people and, in the process, ripped the Hollywood community into warring factions. When HUAC came calling, Hollywood panicked. The studio moguls turned out to be gutless wonders, eager to prove their Americanism. Fear does strange things to people. There were purges of people whose only "crime" was to have attended a Russian War Relief rally during World War II when Russia was our ally. Some committed the even greater sin of donating used clothing to the starving victims of the siege of Leningrad.

Once in a while, as the CPN staff writers gathered for lunch at Brittingham's, the subject of discussion was McCarthy and the blacklist his witch hunt created in Hollywood. In those dangerous times, even our booth could have been bugged and our voices were lowered to just above a whisper. Full-page ads regularly appeared in the Hollywood trade papers (*Daily Variety,* the *Hollywood Reporter*) essentially proclaiming "we are more patriotic than you guys. We are true Americans, and you aren't." It was the Super Patriots (those who backed the committee) versus those who felt HUAC was unconstitutional, the Right versus the Liberals, as it pretty much remains today. (In those days, the Right had not yet claimed that God was a Republican.) Ward Bond, a character actor who was part of director John Ford's stock company (sometimes known as "the Irish mafia"), appointed himself the arbiter of patriotism. Another member of the

Irish mafia, a John Ford actor named Victor McLaglen, went out and bought his own army of motorcyclists. He was going to be ready when those commies attacked Hollywood! On the upside, a prominent Hollywood attorney with an impeccable reputation quietly let it be known that for a one-time fee of ten thousand dollars he could arrange to have "comsymps" (commie sympathizers) cleared so they could go back to work. The town had gone mad with fear, led by MGM's Louis B. Mayer, who was fiercely patriotic, and hurriedly followed by Harry Cohn of Columbia Pictures and Jack Warner of Warner Brothers. The studio moguls' mantra became, in effect, "My flag is bigger than yours," and each scrambled to prove they were more American than anybody else in the country.

But our biggest buzz was CBS's decision to initiate a Loyalty Oath requiring all employees to sign or accept the unspoken risk of being fired. CBS never actually told its employees they faced dismissal for refusal, but the implication was unavoidable. We even heard that one of our secretaries had abruptly left the company rather than submit to the craziness.

It was obvious to us that CBS feared McCarthy more than other broadcast networks because he had labeled us "the Red network." Of course it was a ridiculous accusation, but this was an era when people were guilty by reason of accusation and proof was not needed. The only court that mattered to the senator was the court of public opinion. Even a hint of left-leaning sympathies could send network advertisers running in panic to other venues. Hollywood was gripped with fear, fiercely divided between the pro-HUAC and anti-HUAC partisans. Studios were conducting purges of anyone even suspected of not hewing to their pro-HUAC party line. People labeled pinkos or comsypms were being fired and blacklisted without a hearing, cause, or explanation, and, having been thus tainted, were unable to get work with any studio in town. Those years of the blacklist were unquestionably the most disgraceful in Hollywood's history.

After *Jeff Regan* had run its course, I was promoted to director of the Columbia Pacific Network writing staff (a meaningless title) and soon after to network program supervisor in 1952. Moving up to the third floor was a big deal back then. It was the home of the Hollywood programming department for CBS Radio, Hollywood, where our network shows emanated. My new boss, Guy della Cioppa, vice president of programs for CBS Radio, Hollywood, was a youthful, handsome, flamboyant, delightfully theatrical man with wavy dark hair and Italian features whom we all called Del or Guido. He wore tailored Italian suits and dashed about the third-floor offices in a grand, if effeminate, style. He confided to several of us tales of his largely imaginary romances with his secretary, and later with actress Sarah Churchill, the daughter of the Prime Minister of Great Britain, to whom he sent gifts and flowers. (When questioned by another actor in a show in which she was playing a role, Sarah Churchill angrily brushed aside the notion that she had had any sort of romantic liaison with the peripatetic della Cioppa.) He sometimes called his junior executives into his office one by one to tell of his agonizing mistreatments and rejections. Sometimes slumped over his desk, running his fingers through his thick wavy hair, he was the operatic figure of a rejected lover. We were all eager and sympathetic listeners. Guido was a charming gentleman, utterly without guile. He was married and had a daughter, but his wife seemed to pay little mind to della Cioppa's operatic love affairs, perhaps because she understood their fantastical nature.

Summoning me to his office, lamenting the wrongs his secretary Lorrie had done him while assuring me how arduously he had pursued her, it was easy to be led into empathizing with his pain. Yet according to her, she had never given her boss the time of day. We all understood that Guido was a decent and kind man who was simply in love with love. One morning Del invited me into his office to show me a large, dark fresh stain on his carpet.

"Lorrie walked into my office this morning with an open bottle of ink, which she angrily poured on my carpet!" he lamented. "What on earth did I do to deserve this?"

The incident of Lorrie pouring a bottle of ink on Guido's carpet gave all at least a week of gossip. What, indeed, had della Cioppa done to warrant this?

For her part, Lorrie remained steadfastly silent, leaving our third-floor staff with more time to wonder.

"He knows," she finally told me one morning, "ask him."

Nothing in CBS's morning soap operas equaled the daily drama of Guy della Cioppa and his flamboyant, imaginary love affairs. We all loved him. He brought flair and drama to the sad demise of our beloved network. The truth was we had little else to do, except for Anne Nelson who had business affairs to run. It is shameless to admit that those of us who worked for him enjoyed his romantic fantasies, while poor della Cioppa was wracked with misery. Still, we offered him our friendship and support along with sympathetic ears. We were a happy, sad little family on CBS Radio's half-empty third floor. We all knew our days in this friendly ambience were rapidly dwindling in number. One by one some of our better writers and directors were drifting off into television or features. Offices were emptying. We were becoming something of an upscale ghost town.

One day I met a young writer coming out of our editor John Meston's office. Walter Brown Newman had delivered his pilot script for a new Western series Meston and director Norman Macdonnell were working on called *Gunsmoke*. After receiving an initial script from David Friedkin and Mort Fine, which was quite good but not on target for their vision, Meston and Macdonnell commissioned Newman to write a new one. These two men were determined to create a new kind of adult Western, one in which the characters and stories were not stereotypical but were as true to the actual old West as they could make it. For example, the marshal would not have one favorite horse he rode, nor would he be a flawless hero in a white hat. Broad as their parameters were, they were looking for a writer who could render their vision in twenty-nine pages for an audition disc. It was not going to be easy to convince the New York management to embark on a new series of programs while our good ship *Network Radio* was sinking.

Walter Brown Newman had done just that. Enthusiastically received by management on both coasts, Meston and Macdonnell received a go-ahead to make a sample show. (In radio days these were called auditions, not pilots.)

As the network supervisor assigned to the show, it was clear from the start that neither Meston nor Macdonnell wanted to have anything to do with the new kid on the block, not that there was anything I was required to do, other than read the material and make whatever suggestions I might have. As it happened, I had none. Newman had done a brilliant job.

Reading Newman's script I understood why it had won unanimous approval and a go-ahead for production. It was possibly the best radio script I had ever read.

Newman had created characters who leapt off the page—always the signature of an outstanding writer. They were all there: Matt Dillon, Chester, Doc, Kitty, Hightower, the newspaper editor. Not only had he created living, breathing characters, the story was adult, even compelling. It was not your typical shoot 'em up Western. It had its own style and flavor and above all a sense that what you were reading was the real thing, the West as it was lived. Clearly, Newman was a writer who had thoroughly researched his material.

From that single twenty-nine-page script the entire seventeen-year season of the *Gunsmoke* television series was built. Meston and Macdonnell carried it from a successful run in radio into television, with Macdonnell eventually producing the TV show with many of the scripts written by Meston or adapted from the radio scripts.

I made it a point to try to get to know Walter Brown Newman. It wasn't easy. He was a painfully shy man, private, reluctant to share his feelings with others. He was a transplanted New Yorker who had been an Army Air Force navigator and instructor in World War II.

Newman stubbornly insisted that he owned neither a television set nor a radio, and he wasn't about to buy one either. He did not subscribe to a newspaper. "I figure if something important happens, somebody will tell me," he asserted. He devoted himself to his wife, Connie, and their children. For leisure time he read the classics. A devout birdwatcher, he would hop into his old Plymouth with a pair of binoculars and disappear for hours. Perhaps that partly explained why it was so difficult to get pages out of him, as producers were forever complaining after he became a much sought-after screenwriter. Newman prided himself on being an amateur magician, but one trick he could not teach himself was to deliver a screenplay in a timely manner. Walter Newman was a producer's worst nightmare and best delight. In one instance I know of firsthand, he fussed over page one of an original screenplay he was writing, titled *Christmas*

Walter Newman, hot-tempered, world-class screenwriter who demanded his credit be removed from *The Great Escape* and *The Magnificent Seven* because the director allowed star Steve McQueen to switch his dialogue. (courtesy of Connie Newman)

Eve, for an entire year, typing and retyping the same page, changing a word here, a word there, even if only to correct punctuation. He was a perfectionist gone quietly off the chart. He could laugh about it to himself, but that changed nothing; he still drove producers nuts, until they read his material.

Newman wore faded, used army/navy store jackets and steel-rimmed glasses long before wearing war surplus clothing became fashionable. He had a small office above Manny's tailor shop in a blue-collar stretch of Santa Monica Boulevard, furnished with an old used desk and an overstuffed chair with the stuffing falling out. Newman was a sucker for young beginning writers. They could drop in any time and talk for hours about the craft and art of screenwriting. Yet when I interviewed him for my first book, *The Screenwriter Looks at the Screenwriter,* he complained that I had forced him to give away some of his secrets. Indeed I had, but as we became life-long friends I realized that he had forgiven me.

He had written other radio plays for CBS. Some had been produced and directed by Macdonnell, others by actor-director Elliot Lewis. Reading them I was struck by the richness and warmth of the fully developed characters. Newman's oeuvre was the human comedy: every character struggling to survive the vicissitudes of life, each in his own unique way. Every situation he explored managed to have almost equal elements of harsh reality and tenderness. Here was a writer who loved the common man and understood his foibles; he particularly delighted in con men who, in his scripts, often managed to con themselves as much as anyone else. Yet none of Newman's characters were ever saccharine or cloying. Indeed, many of them had more than a touch of larceny, but they were funny. Clearly the author empathized with the desperate souls he created. Newman's dialogue was the stuff of genius.

It turned out that Newman, while writing radio scripts, was doing more than a little moonlighting on the side. He also wrote the screenplay for *The Man with the Golden Arm,* which won Academy Award nominations for Frank Sinatra and composer Elmer Bernstein. He also wrote the screenplays for *The Great Escape* and *The Magnificent Seven,* loosely based on Kurosawa's classic Japanese film *The Seven Samurai* (Newman's adaptation, most of it original material, spawned several sequels). Newman, the quiet, reserved gentleman, had, it seemed, a hair-trigger temper. After seeing the final cuts of *Escape* and *Seven,* in spite of the director's pleading, Newman demanded his own name be removed from the pictures. Director John Sturgis had given the lines of one character to another. Newman found that intolerable. Collaborating with Billy Wilder, Newman wrote *Ace in the Hole,* which Wilder once said was his best picture. Newman and Frank Pierson received joint screenplay credit for the 1965 hit *Cat Ballou,* which won them an Academy Award nomination and Lee Marvin an Oscar.

Among our many troubles at CBS, Hollywood, was the growing awareness that our Sunday evening *Hallmark Radio Hall of Fame,* one of the last remaining sponsored series, was rapidly sinking into last place in the Nielsen ratings. It was only a matter of weeks before the show would be canceled. The long-running series had gone to seed in recent years, becoming obsessed with eighteenth- and nineteenth-century historical dramas. It was hopelessly old fashioned, both in subject matter and presentation. The radio actors even sounded like they were wearing wigs.

When the ad agency representing Hallmark complained about the show's lowly ratings, it was suggested that the show needed updating; more modern stories about popular heroes who lived in and were famous in the twentieth century. Della Cioppa asked me to update, produce, and direct the revamped series. We changed to modern stories from the point of view of the famous people who lived them. In a few weeks we lifted the series from the bottom-rated radio drama to the top-rated, using contemporary stories narrated by people like Joe DiMaggio (a quiet, reticent man and a pleasure to work with) who narrated a brief drama about his relationship with Yankee manager Miller Huggins. Later, Ira Gershwin narrated the story of his brother George's untimely death.

Ira Gershwin invited me to his Beverly Hills home where we taped our interview in his sunny dining room. He turned out to be everybody's image of a warm, good-natured, charming, Jewish uncle. In the midst of our conversation he casually commented, "You are sitting in the chair George was sitting in when he suffered his fatal brain hemorrhage." The drama about Ira and his brother's relationship, with Ira narrating via tape (by now CBS had relaxed its restrictions on presenting taped material), was one of the highlights of that season.

General William F. Dean told the story of his battle field capture and three-year imprisonment by the North Koreans during our "police action" in Korea in the early 1950s. It turned out the army had prevented him from telling the true story of the North Koreans planting one of their most dedicated Communist Party members in the cell with him, which Dean immediately understood. The two men talked for months on end. Dean came out of these conversations believing that his cell mate had made an excellent case for communism, though he still disagreed with it. After Dean's release, while being debriefed, he was warned by his army superiors not to express his political opinions. Thus, he had not spoken out before his retirement. James Poe, later an Oscar-winning screenwriter, wove an excellent half-hour radio drama about Dean's prison experiences, with the general himself narrating via tape.

Then Major (now General) Chuck Yeager narrated what it was like breaking the sound barrier. (Our soundmen had a field day!) And the inimitable Helen Hayes starred in eight of our dramas, two of which were excerpted from her Broadway shows. Of all the stars I have worked with in my career, no one ever came close to having the work ethic and the class of Helen Hayes.

Lifting *Hallmark* to the number-one spot in radio drama was not exactly an earth-shaking achievement; there were only three or four dramas left on all three network radio schedules. Network radio was sinking even faster than we expected under the rapidly rising tidal wave of television.

A most unexpected and delightfully off-the-wall kind of recognition came my way one Sunday evening when I returned home from our broadcast and idly went to work on the *New York Times* Sunday crossword puzzle. I ran into a horizontal clue that read "Producer-Director of CBS Radio's *Hallmark Hall of Fame*." I counted five blank spaces but was momentarily stumped. I pondered this oddity for a moment, then wrote in the letters F-R-O-U-G. It fit. Pity the poor puzzle aficionados; it must have driven them up the wall.

The *Hallmark Radio Hall of Fame* was broadcast Sunday evenings

Writer E. Jack Neuman *(left)* and legendary actress Helen Hayes *(center)* discussing Neuman's script for CBS Radio's *Hallmark Hall of Fame,* with the series producer-director Bill Froug *(right)* looking on. Hayes was a Republican even a liberal could love. (from the author's collection)

before a live audience of six hundred and was hosted by the sweet-natured curmudgeon Lionel Barrymore. The actor and I got along famously. Barrymore, a member of the royal family of the theater, was a great raconteur. During rehearsals Lionel would regale us with his wonderful tales. He particularly liked to tell stories about his late younger brother, matinee idol John Barrymore. John was widely considered among the greatest actors of his generation, and Lionel adored him. One of my favorites was about "Jack" (as Lionel always called him) going into a Western Union office to send a scathing telegram to his agent in New York. The clerk watched Barrymore angrily scribbling his message on the counter.

"I can't send that," the horrified clerk told the actor. "The law does not permit Western Union to transmit obscenities."

Bill Froug, producer-director of CBS Radio's *Hallmark Hall of Fame,* with host Lionel Barrymore. Author, painter, composer, member of the "Royal Family" of the theater, Barrymore posed as irascible curmudgeon but was in fact sweet natured and kindhearted. (from the author's collection)

"Jack wasn't happy with that response," growled Lionel. (Lionel always growled when he told a story.) "So he went outside and paced the sidewalk, his rage against his agent only increasing. Finally he had the answer. He hurried back inside, took out a blank Western Union pad, and angrily scribbled a new wire. When he was finished he thrust it in the face of the hapless clerk. 'Send this, my good man,' he ordered, 'there's not an obscene word in it.'"

"The Western Union clerk read the wire, blanched and replied, 'Yes, sir, Mr. Barrymore, I'll send it.'

"Jack's telegram read: UNABLE TO JOIN YOU AND MR. HOCK FOR GOLF TOMORROW. SUGGEST YOU GOLF HOCK YOURSELF. signed John Barrymore." Lionel laughed so hard while telling his stories, I sometimes feared he would fall out of his wheelchair. A composer, gifted painter, actor, and sometime director, he was a remarkably multitalented as well as warmhearted and delightful man. Severe arthritis in both hips had confined him to a wheelchair.

As we rehearsed for our annual Christmas broadcast of Dickens's *A Christmas Carol,* Lionel, who delighted in playing Scrooge, muttered into his mike, "Typecasting."

"Quiet on the set! We're rehearsing." I said into the control booth mike. My amplified voice boomed out over huge audience Studio B.

"Will you listen to that kid ordering me around?" Lionel growled to the cast, "Just who the hell does he think he is?" The actors at their microphones were nonplussed. After a dramatic pause, Lionel added, "I like that fucking kid! He's okay. Now, come on, you people quiet down and let's rehearse."

The modern approach worked. Hallmark kept the series going for an additional two years. However, thirteen weeks after Lionel's death in 1954, Hallmark canceled the series. It marked the end of sponsored big-star network dramas. We understood that Lionel's death was coincidentally the death knell of network radio. Former MGM contract player, character actor Edward Arnold (*Diamond Jim, It's a Wonderful Life,* and others) filled in as host until the season ended. Arnold was as surly, opinionated, and self-important as the parts he usually played. I came to understand his success, he *was* the epitome of typecasting.

With unsponsored time slots to fill CBS, Hollywood, programmed inexpensive half-hour radio dramas under umbrella titles like *Escape, Romance,* and what have you. The key to the network in its last-ditch struggle to survive was containing program costs. Della Cioppa asked me to produce and direct *Sunday Playhouse* in the old Hallmark time slot and then *Romance,* which was an umbrella title under which I could direct, produce, or write anything I felt like doing. It was a heady experience to be handed thirty minutes of network air time every week with no guidelines, no instructions, and no restraints other than those routinely provided by our broadcast standards department. In those days obscenities and objectionable subject matter were not only unacceptable but unthinkable. It would not have occurred to any of us to include obscenities in our shows. Bizarre as it may seem in retrospect, we had no desire to debase our medium, nor did we need trash language to write our plays. It was a vastly different culture in the mid-twentieth century. Network censors, seemingly borrowing their regulations from the motion picture code, took as their primary function the protection of the nation from sex or anything remotely suggestive of it. Violence on radio was never a problem since it consisted solely of sound effects, gunfire, horses' hooves, the occasional sound of a blunt object, car crash, or even the rare scream or gurgle of someone being attacked or strangled.

Taking over *Romance* was like receiving a notebook with blank pages and being told "write anything in it you like, whatever it is, we'll pay you for it." It was exhilarating. I decided to seek out scripts that were out of the ordinary. A former prison inmate wrote a half-hour drama about his first month behind bars. He called it *Fish;* it was a chilling look at life behind bars. I experimented writing a few two-character comedy-dramas, some worked, others didn't. One, *Pawhuska,* loosely based on my Aunt Laura's life as a shopkeeper in the Oklahoma Territory, worked out so well that I adapted and later sold it to *Jane Wyman's Fireside Theater,* a new TV series.

Meanwhile, Walter Newman's radio scripts, produced a year or so earlier, were beginning to be bought for television. Each and every one is a timeless classic: *Spring Over Brooklyn, The Big Hello,* and *The Hooligan,* his adaptation of a two-character Chekhov short story, which Newman placed in the old West. It was a delight to produce and direct these gems on radio with a new cast. Anne Nelson, our business affairs director, told me my budget for *Romance* was nine hundred dollars per show and if I could do it for less so much the better. We did Westerns, sci-fi, fantasy (several Ray Bradbury stories), comedy, and the like. Novelist Robert Nathan came to the studio and narrated a dramatization of his most recent novel *(Sir Henry)*. Christopher Isherwood narrated a new radio play he and Aldous Huxley had cowritten *(Hands)* about a faith healer. They liked the show so much they gave me a second script of theirs to direct *(God Is Dog Spelled Backward)*. I found it senseless and declined. The minimal money these highly talented writers received was of little consequence to them. Like all of us, *they loved radio.* As television's subject matter shrank, ours expanded. We received a letter from a fan club of professors and their wives at the University of California in Santa Barbara. They said they'd put aside Saturday evenings at eight to listen to *Romance* and discuss it afterward over coffee and dessert. It reminded us that there were still a few pockets of listeners around the country. The latest Nielsen ratings put our audience at about three or four million regulars listeners, and shrinking—an unacceptably low number in the heyday of network radio when big sponsored shows might accrue forty million or more listeners. But to those of us in our semi-isolated show business world, they were a godsend. I was close to heaven and knew it, albeit on a shrinking island of entertainment as we slowly were inundated under television's rising seas. We were in denial, resisting the terrible reality that soon we would have to find another place to work.

Howard Barnes, vice president of network programs in New York, summoned me to New York for high-level meetings to discuss program ideas that might attract the attention of the media press, if not an audience of multimillions. I suggested we bring back *The Columbia Workshop,* the legendary radio program that had launched the career of Norman Corwin, and proposed we start with Aldous Huxley's *Brave New World* as two half-hour shows. Barnes was enthusiastic but preferred to update the title, calling it *The CBS Radio Workshop.* Anne Nelson figured we could deliver the show for a total budget of about nine hundred dollars per half-hour and then suggested Huxley might be willing to narrate it, if we would prerecord his narration. In short order Nelson reported back that we had a deal and, best of all, Huxley was enthusiastic and willing to prerecord his narration.

I wrote the two half-hour scripts over two weekends, sticking close to Huxley's classic. We sent him copies and I received an invitation to lunch. Huxley lived in a small, old, stucco Spanish-style house in West Hollywood on King's Road. He cordially welcomed me at the door. His wife, Laura, served us tea sandwiches and soup in their small, sunny, breakfast room. Having read and admired all of his novels, and knowing of his remarkable history, I could hardly believe my good fortune. I was having lunch with Aldous Huxley.

"I projected the brave new world as occurring six hundred years after Henry Ford built the first assembly line, as you know," he said over soup. "I'm sorry to say, my timing was far off the mark. Today my negative utopia seems only fifty years ahead of us, if that much."

"Maybe it's happening now," I suggested, "the rampant promiscuity, the society demanding we all behave 'even as little children.'"

"The idea of mending things is becoming increasingly foreign," he added. "I thought of my slogan 'Ending Instead of Mending' as a sort of dark word play."

"*Brave New World* would make a marvelous musical," I suggested to Huxley, somewhat tentatively.

"Of course, I agree with you," he said, smiling. "It's an excellent way to present the material. Unfortunately, I no longer own the rights. I've sold them to the Crown Prince of Siam."

Our lunch was made even more delightful by his genuine enthusiasm for my adaptation. He even apologized for the minor revisions he had made in the narration I'd written for him. I probed to see if he had reservations about my adaptation. He had none.

Broadcast live (except for Huxley's prerecorded narration), the two half-hour shows received critical acclaim. Bernard Herrmann composed and conducted a unique and highly original score for *Brave New World.* Hearing it years later, one can clearly recognize the precursor of his *Twilight Zone* theme. Herrmann, famously temperamental and equally brilliant, had scored many of Alfred Hitchcock's best films. These two half-hours are still occasionally rebroadcast on public radio stations. Recently *Brave New World* was listed among the fifty greatest radio broadcasts of the twentieth century. Nothing in my career has ever come close to the feelings I had upon reading that extraordinary recognition. My Emmy Award doesn't equal it.

Eminent author-philosopher Aldous Huxley, reviewing Froug's adaptation of CBS Radio's *Brave New World,* listed as one of the fifty greatest radio broadcasts of the twentieth century. (from the author's collection)

In the spring of 1956 Guy della Cioppa accepted a menial executive job at CBS Television City and left his office amid fond farewells. The staff gave him a farewell luncheon at the Hollywood Brown Derby. The third floor was now truly a ghost town. I was summoned to New York by Howard Barnes yet again. I knew it was likely we would discuss my being appointed to take della Cioppa's job.

When I arrived Barnes confirmed my suspicions but he added an unexpected qualifier. He wanted the approval of his boss, CBS Radio's executive vice president Lester Gottlieb.

We met that night in an upscale New York restaurant bar. Gottlieb was waiting for our arrival. He was a sharply featured, somewhat fidgety man who seemed impatient to get the business at hand over and done with, every inch a New Yorker. After a quick but cordial greeting, he fixed me with a look and abruptly said, "I'm thinking of something," waiting expectantly for my response. When I responded with a blank look, he added, as if I should have read his mind, "We're playing twenty questions," he insisted.

Rather than being intimidated, I accepted his challenge and began the usual first round with the "animal, vegetable or mineral" question. Fourteen or fifteen questions later I had narrowed it down and said, "Thomas Payne."

"That's it!" he replied, surprised, smiling broadly. Turning to Barnes, he announced, "You've got yourself a good man, Howard. I approve."

Returning to Hollywood, I moved into della Cioppa's spacious, beautifully furnished third-floor corner office and surveyed my new domain with a mixture of pride and "what'll I do now?" My new title—Vice President of Network Programs, CBS Radio, Hollywood—was impressive but quite obviously I was presiding over the fading fragments of a formerly prestigious program operation. Among my first callers was a tall, handsome, impeccably groomed man in a well-tailored, sharkskin suit. He introduced himself as John Neil Reagan. As it turned out, he was Ronald Reagan's younger brother. Neil was head of the Hollywood office of a major advertising agency.

"This is very important," Reagan said standing rather formally across the desk from me. As he took a folded piece of paper out of

Farewell party for CBS Radio vice president Guy della Cioppa, seated with business affairs director Anne Nelson *(left)* and newly minted vice president William Froug *(right)*. Della Cioppa was off to CBS Television and ignominy. (courtesy of Anne Nelson)

his inside jacket pocket, his voice took on the tone of a commanding officer delivering orders to a member of his staff, "You're going to need to write these names down."

Dark suspicions were beginning to creep into my mind, as I dutifully took up a pen. However, being brand new at the executive game I decided to avoid assumptions.

"Proctor and Gamble does not want any of the following people employed in any capacity on any programs it sponsors," Reagan said as he began slowly reading off names. I was taken aback as the significance of this little ceremony hit me. Here it was in my face, an actual blacklist. I was face to face with the messenger himself, blacklist in hand. It was a surreal moment.

I had been a vociferous protester of the blacklist and was one of only three CBS employees to write a protest letter to William S. Paley, founder and CEO of CBS, arguing that members of the Communist

Party were instructed to sign loyalty oaths, so of what value was the gesture? I pointed out I had served three years on active duty as an officer in the United States Navy. The Navy did not question my loyalty, why should CBS?

I remained silent, though I found the reading of the names repugnant. My first week on the job hardly seemed the time to get into an argument with the ad agency for one of CBS's few remaining and perhaps most important sponsors, so I kept my opinions to myself. Listening to Reagan reading names, I realized Proctor and Gamble primarily sponsored soap operas, and the soaps were all produced in New York. CBS Hollywood had only a few people involved in his bailiwick. But, as the reading went on I recognized he was after many more than soap actors. I heard the names of a couple of my friends working for us on the West Coast. When he paused for a breath I asked why he was blacklisting so many people.

"My agency is not blacklisting anyone," Reagan blithely assured me, with a straight face. "We are merely protecting our client's best interests. They are paying for the programs, they are entitled to decide whom to hire or not hire. It's that simple."

Thus I learned that nobody really blacklisted anybody. Sponsors who bought programs merely made certain no person tainted by questionable past associations was allowed to besmirch their programs. This same ceremony was going on at movie studios and in network executive offices all over Hollywood. HUAC focused on the entertainment industry where they were guaranteed the biggest headlines. Plumbers, carpenters, day laborers, studio grips, and sound men were safe from blacklisting. No headlines there. The rapidly spreading virus moved from network to network, studio to studio, carried by men like Neil Reagan, no doubt loyal Americans all. Terrified networks as well as movie studios eagerly jumped on the bandwagon. Lists became codified, unquestioned, passed from ad agency to ad agency, studio to studio. Many loyal Americans of the liberal persuasion were now deemed security risks to their country.

Radio's experience with the blacklist was unique inasmuch as, unlike the studios, it involved sponsors. It had all come about in a bizarre fashion.

One Laurence A. Johnson, who owned a chain of supermarkets in Syracuse, New York, had become obsessed with the "Red scare" created by HUAC. Johnson let the press know that he would not stock any product on his shelves from any company that hired a communist or, as it was called at the time, a comsymp or alternately "sympcom." After Johnson trumpeted his boycott of suspect corporations, the story ignited and became a national wildfire, consuming Madison Avenue's ad agencies in its path. Major ad agencies began receiving panicky phone calls from their biggest clients demanding reassurances that none of the shows they sponsored employed any of these dangerous radicals. The purging was embraced by advertising agencies who acted as messenger boys for frightened food and produce manufacturers.

Johnson became so emboldened by the national spotlight that he began issuing a monthly newsletter titled *Counter Attack,* a companion piece to *Red Channels,* the bible of the blacklisters, to spread the word on the rapidly growing subversives in our midst. (Anyone listed in *Red Channels* was rendered unemployable. No trial, no hearing, no evidence presented, no right to face one's accuser was available to these new untouchables.) He sent letters to broadcasters suggesting that if they wanted to avoid the embarrassment and potential revenue loss that would follow hiring anyone even suspected of being a comsymp, they had better make certain every executive in their company received a monthly copy of *Counter Attack.* CBS requested that every one of it's top executives prominently display a copy of *Red Channels* on his desk. It showed all visitors that CBS was a company of certified patriots. No communists work here! Johnson's blackmail, *Counter Attack,* arrived in my mail promptly on the first of the month. As the madness gradually tapered off, Johnson was sued for libel by an entertainer named John Henry Faulk. Faulk won a judgment of $3.5 million. Laurence A. Johnson had the good sense to die of a heart attack before he faced the tragic consequences of his campaign for a 100 percent communist-free America.

After Reagan left my office, I dutifully followed my corporate instructions to phone our law department and read them the names. Though I have no direct knowledge of this, I suspect whichever lawyer answered the phone wrote down the names and put them away in a file. Throughout my year's tenure as vice president I never consulted anybody about casting or hiring decisions, nor did I check either *Red Channels* or *Counter Attack* before or after hiring anyone. My copies of these publications remained in my drawer, ignored. I knew that one of our outstanding writer-producer-directors was listed in *Red Channels,* and even though no other network would hire William N. Robson, we did again and again, with a special glee, for show after show. He received on-air credit for his services as writer and producer-director. Robson's "crime" was that he attended a rally for Russian relief during World War II when Russians were our Allies in the war against the Nazis. There were no repercussions from Laurence A. Johnson or Joe McCarthy, which only told us how inconsequential network radio had become.

After the madness had subsided, Edward R. Murrow hired Bill Robson as a writer-producer-director for *The Voice of America.* The republic still stands. McCarthy is long since dead, but his legacy of fear and paranoia lingered on many years after him.

The general manager of KNX, Merle Jones, phoned to congratulate me on being named an officer of the company and to invite me to join him for an industry meeting at the Hollywood Roosevelt Hotel the following week. He suggested we share a cab.

Jones was a fit, trim, white-haired, distinguished, conservative, middle-aged gentleman, reserved and low-keyed. Just the sort of man I thought was perfect casting for a corporate executive. We had little to say to one another during our cab ride. As we were pulling up in front of the hotel he turned to me, lowering his voice and said, "We've got to get rid of that Chet Huntley fellow, he's a pinko." At the time Huntley was KNX's top-rated newsman, highly regarded by the community and his fellow reporters.

"I thought he was a registered Republican," I replied.

"I don't care what he says he is, he sounds like a pinko to me," Jones replied, as we exited the car.

As it turned out, Chet Huntley went to NBC where he teamed with David Brinkley to form the most popular news duo in the history of television. Apparently neither the public nor NBC was able to detect his pinkness. Some of his fellow reporters later told me Huntley was basically apolitical, as I've discovered most reporters are.

Paley was especially eager to prove himself and his network were 100 percent loyal Americans. Being a Jew with a company labeled "the Red network" by McCarthy must have been a double whammy for Paley. Most of us on the West Coast regarded HUAC as an unconstitutional lynch mob. But CBS Radio was small potatoes to the House Un-American Activities Committee. They stated that they were after big game: movie stars, writers, directors, Hollywood studios, and movies in general. There was no political capital to be made from fading network radio. However, Paley had his burgeoning CBS Television Division to worry about.

Many years later when I read President Reagan's denial that there was ever a blacklist in Hollywood, I found it incredible that he had had so little communication with his younger brother. Perhaps they were not on speaking terms.

CBS had decreed that no officer of the company could receive on-air billing, even though they were free to perform on-air functions. Being unbilled executive producer of the *CBS Radio Workshop* was keeping some of my creative juices flowing. We booked the best hyphenates left in radio to write-produce-direct episodes of the series, the blacklist be damned.

Stan Freberg suggested he do a half-hour comedy built around his nonpareil talent for satire. We tried out his idea on one of our *CBS Radio Workshops.* It was a delight. Out of Stan's idea came his CD series *The Stan Freberg Show,* which is essentially recordings of those broadcasts. We did a drama on ESP based on research at Duke University, a Japanese Noh drama, a play in verse about a New Orleans jazz musician, *Jimmy Blue Eyes.* We adapted those lesser-selling novels we could afford, anything that seemed challenging.

Summing up my feelings about the magic of radio, I had written the opening lines actor William Conrad read on that initial broadcast: "CBS presents the *CBS Radio Workshop,* dedicated to man's imagination. The theater of the mind." It was amusing to hear a radio personality recently mention radio as "the theater of the mind" and credit the metaphor to Oscar Wilde, who was dead decades before the invention of radio.

I've never met anyone who worked in network radio who didn't love it. Television and even the movies have rarely come close to achieving what we could with merely the human voice, sound effects, music cues, and our imaginations. Listeners provided their own casts and locales, and they were better than anything Hollywood could equal.

Although my future seemed inevitable, I had no burning desire to enter Hollywood television. What I was beginning to see on our thirteen-inch screen at home was predominately mindless crap. The moguls whose studios were producing most of these new series filmed in Hollywood loved movies, but they despised television, primarily because it was eroding their box office receipts. It appeared their feelings toward the upstart medium were reflected in their shoddy programs. Since television had relocated from New York to Hollywood, it had abruptly plummeted from "golden age" to "vast wasteland." It didn't seem to be a coincidence.

My nine years at CBS Radio had been the best circumstances any creative person could want. Ironically, sitting comfortably in my posh corner office on the third floor of CBS's Hollywood headquarters, I was within spitting distance of the birthplace of Hollywood, the exact spot where *The Squaw Man,* the first feature movie in the history of Hollywood, had been filmed in 1914. Yet, as far as the motion picture industry was concerned, people still working in network radio were on a minor, inconsequential planet. With sponsors vanishing by the minute, we were now free to do pretty much what we wanted to do. We were paid little, even for that time. Even so, actors eagerly returned to perform in these programs, as did more than a few stars who got their start in radio. We could take on an endless variety of stories, every week something new, every week a new challenge. By and large, none of us were typecast. Our actors could play comedies and dramas with equal ease. Players like William Conrad, John McIntyre and his wife, Jeanette Nolan, Cathy and Elliot Lewis, Parley Baer, Jeff Chandler (Ira Grossell at the beginning of his radio career), Virginia Gregg, Sandy Berns (who later played a neighbor on the *Bewitched* series), Jack Klugman, Jerry Housner, Larry Dobkin (who became a highly respected TV director), Richard Crenna (Walter on *Our Miss Brooks,* in both the radio and TV versions),

Raymond Burr (who became Perry Mason with ease and unparalleled success for many years), Ed Begley, John Dehner, and scores of other talented actors arrived in our CBS Radio studios, full of enthusiasm and eager to perform at the microphone. Often they earned about thirty-five dollars for a full afternoon's work.

Jack Kruchen, while continuing to perform on radio, became a featured song and dance man in MGM's *The Unsinkable Molly Brown.* We all knew Jack Kruchen as an excellent radio actor—but as an actor who could sing and dance? Never. Those of us who had known and worked with Kruchen were dumbfounded by his superb performance in a musical, but we were not surprised at all when he won an Oscar nomination for best supporting actor in *The Apartment.* Richard Crenna, one of our CBS Radio favorites, soon developed a big career in motion pictures and television, moving with ease into major roles in hit feature series like the Rambo pictures, *Body Heat,* and others. Ed Begley starred on Broadway in *Inherit the Wind,* written by radio writing team Jerome Lawrence and Robert E. Lee, who also wrote the Broadway hit *Mame.* Radio actor John Dehner starred in his own CBS-TV series, *Big Hawaii,* and played major roles in many features, such as *The Left Handed Gun.* Radio actors Frank Lovejoy and Charles McGraw were cast in or held starring roles in World War II action melodramas. All of these talented people continued to insist that, even after big paying movie and TV jobs came their way, radio was their favorite medium in which to work.

One day my friend George Rosenberg, one time agent for Bing Crosby, Ethel Merman, and other stars of great magnitude, stuck his head in my office door and yelled, "Froug, when are you going to get out of silent pictures!" Rosie was a great kidder with a famous sense of humor but, beneath his needling joke was truth. "Radio was yesterday, kid!"

Rosie was an outgoing, charming, highly intelligent man. I liked him even though he never let up on me. "Get the hell out," he said the next time he dropped by, with a sense of mock urgency in his voice "you want me to get you a job? Hell, I can get you a job. Doing what I don't know."

Another day he stuck his head in my doorway to shout, "You know where the blacksmiths are now? They're working at Santa

Anita or Hollywood Park. You gotta go where the action is, Palsy. They'll be bulldozing your office any day now."

One day while trying to develop the art of doing nothing, my secretary told me I was wanted in Studio One. I hurried out of my office.

Entering Studio One I discovered Freeman Gosden and Charles Correll (a.k.a. Amos 'n' Andy) seated at a rehearsal table, their scripts open before them. I was struck by their upscale wardrobe. Both looked as if they'd just come from the barbershop, professionally shaved, carefully trimmed. They were, in fact, southern white men. If you didn't know they were millionaires several times over, one encounter would have told you. Gosden glanced up, his look was neither friendly nor welcoming. They nodded and muttered a half-hearted greeting. Gosden and Correll had been reduced to roles as disc jockeys. It was like imagining the royal family in a porn movie. They certainly didn't need the work, but they could not let go of their alter egos. No doubt Amos and Andy were as real to them as were their own families. It was said that frequently they would slip in and out of the characters they had played for over thirty years, to the astonishment and delight of whomever they were addressing. It always guaranteed a laugh. I had never met these living legends and was more than a bit awed at the prospect. I'd worked with dozens of movie stars in my young career, but Gosden and Correll were in a constellation all their own. In the early days of radio no comedy team seized the nation like *Amos 'n' Andy,* on the air at dinnertime one night a week.

Such was their popularity that movie theaters interrupted screenings and turned on radios in order for their audiences to hear the latest shenanigans of Amos 'n' Andy. The characters owned the Fresh Air Taxi Company and were members of "The Mystic Knights of the Sea," a lodge run by a con man called "The Kingfish," who managed to create trouble at every turn. Gosden and Correll played the entire cast of characters. Their bumbling attempts to keep trouble away riveted a nation struggling to emerge from a devastating depression. In a word, they were hilarious. As a kid growing up in Little Rock, I could bike down my neighborhood sidewalks any summer evening and hear the voices of Amos 'n' Andy coming out of the open windows without missing a line of dialogue. Although they worked from scripts, the entire program seemed improvised. Their roots were clearly in minstrelsy, and they were beloved all across America by blacks and whites alike. Approaching the table where they were going over their script, Gosden looked up giving me an openly hostile stare.

"As I drove into the studio today I noticed a white Corvette in the parking lot with a Stevenson sticker on the rear bumper." His deep voice and rich southern accent startled me. Was I hearing Amos or was it Andy? He continued, "The car was parked in the space marked Vice President. Is that your car, Mr. Froug?" I told him it was.

"Well, personally I don't give a damn who you vote for," he said, suppressing his considerable anger, "but I don't think it's appropriate for a vice president of the Columbia Broadcasting System, which is regulated by the FCC, to display partisanship. Unless you remove that bumper sticker, I will consider discussing this with Bill Paley, who you may know is a personal friend of ours."

"Sir," I said, "do whatever you think is best." Gosden was not pleased with facing a young upstart. He decided to play his trump card. "You know, my wife and I frequently fly to Washington for a weekend of bridge with the president and Mamie. Ike and I usually play a round of golf together, if the weather is good. I consider the general to be a personal friend of mine."

"No, sir, I didn't know you and the president were friends," I replied, as politely as possible, then added, "I'm not going to take off my bumper sticker, sir. Do whatever you feel you have to do."

I beat a hasty retreat. Exiting the studio's double doors I clearly heard Gosden, grumble to his silent partner, "I'm sick to death paying out good money to that goddamned NAACP."

Amos 'n' Andy was now also a TV sitcom, the characters being played by black actors, but recently there had been complaints lodged by the black community over the stereotypical nature of the characters. It was a measure of the huge cultural changes taking place in the United States that a program—once the most popular series in radio history and considered a national treasure when it turned visual following World War II—had become a subject of outrage, offensive to the children of the generation who had adored it.

Walking back to my office, I had an inner smile imagining the level of Gosden's outrage had he known I secretly allowed a young sailor named Rod McKuen and several amateurs to record a singing commercial for Adlai Stevenson in the same studio a few nights previously. Gosden's wrath would have been off the chart, especially if he'd known my wife and I were among the amateurs singing: "Let's All Vote for Adlai! Let's All Vote for Adlai!" Not surprisingly, Ike obliterated poor Adlai; the election was not even close.

It was increasingly clear to me that I was posing uncomfortably as an executive. I wasn't cut out for the job. CBS had made radio a separate division of their broadcasting empire with the creation of CBS Television. They needn't have wasted the ink on new stationary; the truth was that the two divisions rarely had reason to speak to one another. The people at CBS Television regarded those of us "left behind" (in radio) as if we all had leprosy and were to be avoided at all costs. Making that lateral move from CBS Radio to CBS Television was fraught with humiliation and rejection as witnessed by my former boss, della Cioppa, now reduced to being a glorified gofer for Red Skelton.

It was an interesting paradox that the same CBS-TV executives who looked down on us radioites with such contempt had put our CBS Radio series *Gunsmoke* on their television network schedule. This series became the number-one-rated TV drama on CBS for many years, written primarily by radio writer John Meston and produced by Norman Macdonnell, the producer-director of the radio *Gunsmoke*. Several of our former CPN staff regularly contributed teleplays to the series, Kathleen Hite and John Dunkle among them.

In fact, most of CBS-TV's schedule was filled with CBS Radio programs that, overnight, went visual. From Jack Benny and Burns and Allen to Lucille Ball, almost every hit show in the television division's schedule originated in radio, and most of these shows were being written by former radio writers.

One day a well-dressed, smiling young man entered my office and introduced himself. We shook hands.

"Hi, my name's Ray Sackheim," he said. "I dropped by to ask if you'd be interested in going to work producing television. I have an offer for you, and I'd like to be your agent."

"Let's hear it," I replied as we settled in to talk.

"My brother, Billy Sackheim, is executive producer in charge of television at Screen Gems, and he's planning on hiring a producer with a writing background to work with him. He already has two producers on staff, but he's interested in you for the third slot. The money is seven hundred dollars a week, and I can only get you a thirteen-week contract. I'd appreciate an early response."

I liked the way he got right to the point. Screen Gems, the television subsidiary of Columbia Pictures, did not have a reputation as a class operation. So far they'd been turning out some low-budget potboiler series, and the trade papers had reported they'd recently failed to sell any of the many series pilots they'd made. I'd never heard of Billy Sackheim. Thirteen weeks was not much time to prove myself in any job, much less in a medium brand new to me, where you told stories with pictures, not just voices, sound effects, and music. I had never been on a soundstage nor inside a Hollywood studio. I didn't know one end of a camera from the other and had no idea that movies were made by shooting the same scene several times from different angles. I only knew it was time to get out of the funeral business.

"You've got a deal," I said to Billy Sackheim's brother.

4

Volcano Man

In June of 1957 I reported to Billy Sackheim at Screen Gems. Their offices were located in an old three-story walk-up apartment building facing the service entrance to Columbia Pictures studios, just off Sunset Boulevard in the heart of Hollywood, two short blocks from my former CBS Radio office. Yet, in Hollywood's thinking, it was the distance to Mars.

Entering his office I discovered Sackheim wearing a golf shirt and an alpaca cardigan sweater, practicing his golf swing with an imaginary club.

Sackheim was a handsome man of medium build, bald, with a fringe of closely trimmed red hair circling his bare dome. He had sharp features and keen piercing eyes. He warmly welcomed me with a cheerful smile and hardy handshake.

"Welcome on board," he said. "I'm sure we're going to do some good work together. I'm very happy you decided to join us." Sackheim's generosity of spirit and camaraderie suggested he was right.

I probably had been hired because Sackheim had heard of my work at CBS Radio, though he never mentioned it. Or perhaps he had read the trade paper's glowing reviews of *Brave New World*. Whatever his reason I was not about to question him. It was exciting to come to work for a major motion picture studio, albeit in its television division.

He laid out my marching orders clearly and directly. Screen Gems had been given an order from CBS Television, Hollywood, to produce a couple of hour-and-a-half movies for *Playhouse 90,* a series usually broadcast live. Sackheim wanted me to produce two of them. CBS-TV was unable to keep up the pace of producing a ninety-minute live show every week, so they farmed out ninety-minute films for occasions when they couldn't meet their airdates or merely needed to give their live operation a breather. The major motion picture studios, reluctantly converting to television production, were faced with problems of another stripe. Whereas during their pre–World War II heyday, all the Hollywood studios combined had turned out a mere six hundred feature movies annually, now television was demanding ten times that much production. Cranking out enough film to fill the enormous demands of the small screen was an order of a mind-boggling magnitude. While the major studios had the production facilities and trained production personnel available, where were they going to get the supervisors (producers) to oversee the huge new enterprise? There were not enough established producers in all of Hollywood to begin to fulfill the demands of this omnivorous glass tube, and the few who were trained had no experience working against television's demanding schedules which made no time for polo on Sunday afternoons. But the studios recognized that their first need was good stories. They turned to writers. Studio heads, as much as they detested writers ("schmucks with Underwoods," as Jack Warner had famously declared), had always known that scripts were the foundation upon which all motion pictures were built. Studios looked upon directors as essentially "traffic cops" (as Billy Wilder once called them) who went to work after the screenplay was in place—or sometimes while it was being written. Their primary job was to protect the budget. Writers understood the importance of the written word and, if they could not themselves deliver the goods, they would know which writers to hire to do it for them and, just as importantly, how to get the material in the best possible shape (i.e., rewrite it) to go before the cameras. Studios decided to hire writers and turn them into writer-producers, or "hyphenates" as the trade press and the industry took to calling these new writer-producers. They always billed the *writer* half of the hyphenate first.

Thus was born the Hollywood hyphenate. (For the auteurist critics, it is interesting to note that studios did not turn to directors or actors to become television hyphenates—writers only need apply.) They understood that directors tell stories that are first written by writers. They needed a person whose job was to get a script approved (by the ad agency and the network), then hire a director, a cast, and finally get the show on the soundstage filmed, edited, and delivered every week to the network—the overseer in charge of it all. It was a demanding, high-pressure job, but it offered writers steady work, a contract at good wages, an important title, and a chance to be a supervisor, if not the final boss. The bosses were the sponsor, the network, and the executives of the production company, in that order. Studio execs soon came to understand that in the world of television they had a tiger by the tail, with little control over the outcome. Once one of their series was sold to a network, studio execs became eunuchs at the orgy, limited to keeping a sharp eye on the budget. CBS, NBC, ABC, and their advertisers owned Hollywood television.

Screen Gems had an order from joint sponsors Alcoa Aluminum and Goodyear Tires for a season of half-hour film dramas called *Alcoa-Goodyear Theatre*. Sackheim wanted me to produce at least six of these. He advised me that the two other producers already on staff, James Fonda and Winston O'Keefe, were also looking for properties for the series. We would work independently of each other. His plan was to challenge each of us to come up with scripts good enough to film. "A little friendly competition is a good thing, you know," was the way he put it with a smile. Sackheim felt I should have the edge because of my background as a writer; neither Fonda nor O'Keefe were writers. Sackheim, himself a hyphenate, was executive producer of all television shows coming out of Screen Gems, thus giving him story, script, and cast approval before we were green-lighted to go into production.

I liked Sackheim's precise, direct manner of laying out my assignment. Somehow I had a sense of great latitude rather than restriction. Chatting with him in that first meeting, I recognized a man who knew what he wanted and was determined to get it.

Sackheim showed me to my new office just down the hall from his; it obviously had been the living room of someone's apartment not many years earlier. The office still had showers and bathrooms at the end of the long rectangular room. There was a comfortable sofa, a long narrow coffee table, and two deeply cushioned chairs, in addition to office furniture. It took a while to get comfortable working out of somebody's former living room.

"Whenever you have an idea or a script you want to do, come see me first," he said as he exited.

I had thirteen weeks to learn how to be a television producer. I hadn't a clue as to what a television producer actually did. Nor had I any story ideas for either of the series assigned to me. I was starting at ground zero, in a brand-new and mysterious world. I was surprised how comfortable it all felt. Settling into my new office I began to make frequent trips across the street to the soundstages and editing rooms at Columbia Pictures' studios to watch feature films and television series being filmed. I quickly discovered there was no difference whatsoever between shooting a feature film and a television film. TV simply went about it at a much faster pace.

I had an entirely new language to learn: "day out of days" meant laying out a shooting schedule; "six-thirty for seven" was the usual actor's call, 6:30 A.M. for makeup, 7 A.M. report to the set; "the answer print" was the final edited, dubbed, ready-to-deliver-to-the-network film. I was surprised to learn that filming on the set was routinely shot on a ten-hour day and quite often on twelve-hour days or longer. There had been instances of filming around the clock. I was, however, not prepared for the boredom of watching a movie being shot. It was my biggest surprise. I knew I would never be able to endure the tedium of directing a film, which usually required standing on your feet for the better part of ten or even twelve hours every day, while the crew reset the lighting for a different camera angle, a process that sometimes took hours. The stars had their dressing rooms in trailers on stage where they retreated for peace and quiet between takes, while

the director hung around the stage chatting with various key personnel, generally the cameraman, the assistant director (the top sergeant
on every set), or the script supervisor, the only person on the soundstage who knew exactly what was going on at all times. It was clear
from the start that when I needed information (how long are we running? how's the director working out? how's his pace?), only the script
supervisor could and would give direct, objective answers. I learned
to lean on these remarkably talented and knowledgeable women,
most of whom had had many years of experience in the business.

I began to hang out in the editing rooms bugging the editors for
information about what they did and how they did it. It soon became obvious that telling a story is still telling a story, whether in a
radio drama, on television, or in a theater. Only the technology for
telling it is different. I was surprised how quickly I became comfortable in the film world. Agents began to submit scripts and call to sell
me their clients—writers, directors, actors, or whomever they represented. I became familiar with the Players Directory in which almost
every actor in Hollywood (and many in New York) appeared with a
photo, agent's name, and phone number. Updated semiannually, by
the time a new Players Directory came out, a producer's copy was as
well thumbed as a missionary's Bible. The directory was our casting
Holy Writ. Whereas, I had had nothing to do a few weeks before in
my final months at CBS Radio, now I was getting phone calls and
visitors all day long. Without Sally, my valiant secretary, my office
life would have been a madhouse. Most of the material I received
was unusable. My thirteen-week clock was ticking and, at least so
far, it seemed I was striking out. Out of the blue, Sackheim brought
me a copy of a short story, "The Guy in Ward Four," written by Leo
C. Rosten and published in the *Atlantic Monthly*.

"Paul Monash's agent submitted it to me." Sackheim said. "Read
it and see if it interests you. Monash wants to do it; Monash is a very
good writer."

Sackheim's act of generosity was an exhilarating moment. He was
nursing me along, letting me know he wanted me to succeed without putting any pressure on me.

The story was about a psychoanalyst treating a crew member of
a World War II bomber who is suffering from what we now call

post-traumatic stress disorder. His patient is the only member of the crew who crawled out of the plane after a crash landing, seconds before it exploded, killing the rest of the crew. The doctor is the focus of the story. He begins to realize that he is merely helping his patient recover enough to be sent back on another mission. The psychiatrist himself is sinking into a depression and questioning whether what he is doing is medically ethical. "First do no harm," begins the Hippocratic oath. Is he violating his oath by treating these young men to become fit enough to get killed? I loved the story and hurried down to tell Sackheim I wanted to do it. He was practicing his golf swing.

"Who do you see playing the psychiatrist?" he asked me.

"Richard Kiley," I replied.

"Good idea. Have you met with Monash yet?" he asked.

"Not yet," I answered.

"First tell business affairs to make a deal for the TV rights to the story, then ask them to make a deal for Monash to adapt it. Phone his agent and set up a meeting with him. Make sure Monash sees the film the same way you do. If he does, find out how soon he can deliver a first draft. When it comes in, work with him until you are satisfied with the script. When you are done show it to me then, not before. Start figuring out who you want to direct it. Paul is a fine writer but you may have to push him. Check the availability of Kiley. I think you've got a winner here. Don't disappoint me. Go to it."

Thus I discovered what a television producer does: the exact same thing a radio producer did or a movie producer does. After the deals were firmed, Monash and I met, talked story, and quickly found we were in agreement as to how the finished episode of *Alcoa-Goodyear Theatre* ought to look. The first draft was nearly perfect, which turned out to be as rare as the Hope diamond. Monash did an easy polish; Sackheim was happy. He suggested we hire Arthur Hiller to direct his first U.S. film, even though it was only a half-hour film. A Canadian recently arrived in Hollywood, Hiller did a splendid job. Kiley delivered a superb performance and was a joy to work with. The episode played very well, and everyone at Screen Gems was pleased with it.

Rosten's story was later made into a feature motion picture titled *Captain Newman, M.D.* starring Gregory Peck, Tony Curtis, and

Angie Dickinson. Too bad they didn't hire Paul Monash to write the screenplay; it would have been a much better movie.

In any event, my first time at bat I had a hit, thanks to Sackheim. We booked Arthur Hiller for two more episodes, and he delivered fine work every time. He was a graduate of NBC's *Matinee Theater,* an ambitious live daily one-hour drama series that became the spawning ground of many new writers and directors flooding into the nascent field of television. Like Arthur Hiller, several of the latest arrivals in American television were Canadians. Toronto, in particular, seemed to be an especially productive breeding ground for new talent.

Hiller went on to a big-time movie career, directing such blockbusters as *Network, The Americanization of Emily, Silver Streak, The Out-of-Towners,* and others. Arthur was later to crown his career as president of the Directors Guild of America and president of the Academy of Motion Picture Arts and Sciences. Hiller is that rare and hugely successful gentleman who has remained humble all his life.

One day an agent sent in a freelance teleplay, which, while not well written, seemed worth developing. It had an idea behind it. Before putting in any serious time on it, I gave it to Sackheim to see if he agreed. The next day I was summoned to his office. As I walked in, Sackheim was seated behind his desk with the script in hand. Seeing me he leaped out of his chair yelling, "How dare you give me a piece of shit like this! This is worthless crap, and you know it!" He threw the script against the wall, pages went flying in all directions,

"I just wanted to see if you thought it was workable material," I explained, defensively, somewhat stunned by his reaction.

"Didn't I tell you not to bring me anything until you were satisfied with it? God damn it, when I say something I mean it!" he shouted at the top of his voice. "Doesn't anybody around here take me seriously?" He glanced quickly around the room. There was nobody but him and me. His tone suddenly softened.

"Maybe the guy can write," he concluded, "but this is a terrible example to show to anybody. Don't waste my time on crap like this."

"Don't get desperate," he advised me, suddenly paternal. "You're going to get some real crap coming in. Ignore it. We've got enough to do without trying to save some half-assed writer's hide. Do you understand me?"

"I do," I said, heading for the door. "I'm very sorry to have wasted your time."

"It's okay," he replied, apologetically, "don't mind me, I just need to let off steam every now and then. You're doing fine, just don't feel like you have to press. By the way, I've told them to pick up your option for another thirteen weeks."

This was my first experience with the volcanic Billy Sackheim. I learned again and again that the man, like a volcano, was usually placid and agreeable on the surface, but his capacity to erupt violently always lurked just beneath the affable facade. Other producers reported that Sackheim, when deeply offended by a poor teleplay, would not only fling the script at the wall but, in especially egregious cases, follow by banging his own head against the wall, shouting obscenities. From that day forward I stuck to telling him script ideas first before considering doing any work on them, which was precisely what he had told me to do the first day I reported for work.

My next-door office neighbor was an impeccably dressed middle-aged gentleman named Gene Rodney, the producer of the popular *Father Knows Best* series. Gene and I began walking to lunch together through the Columbia lot and out onto Gower (known in Hollywood as Gower Gulch, because that's where the cowboy extras working on Columbia pictures used to hang out). Just off the corner of Gower and Sunset was a hamburger joint named Sam's Square Grill. Sam's place was usually packed at midday. Lunching with the good-natured Gene was a treat; as we ate he always told me the storyline of the *Father Knows Best* episode he was preparing for production. By the time he got to the end of the tale he sometimes had tears in his eyes. "And Jim decides his boy has such a good report card, that in spite of the dangers it represents, he buys him a bicycle for his birthday!" and down flowed the tears. Who could not love a producer who cries for his characters? Corny though it may have been, the consistently popular *Father Knows Best,* written by freelancers but most often by Paul West (Gene's favorite), was a benchmark series in the history of television. Like its title character (played by noted movie star Robert Young), Gene Rodney was always a soft-spoken, sweet-natured, courtly gentleman. Lunch with Gene was an hour of tranquility out of the stress of my beginning days in television. Thanks to Sam's Square Grill hamburgers and my friend Gene Rodney's story-telling ability, I never needed to watch his series.

One day a young agent brought me a script mimeographed on legal-size yellow paper. "It's a BBC teleplay," he said, "but once you start reading it you won't be able to put it down." He was right. That night, reading Kenneth Hughes's "Sammy" was a riveting experience. It was thirty-some pages of monologue. A small-time London hustler in his seedy apartment is on the phone trying desperately to raise a few hundred pounds before the loan sharks he is in debt to arrive and beat the crap out of him. There was an urgency in the character, as he first tries to raise money selling cheap cashmere sweaters, then phony pearls or knock-off watches without luck: "It's just like a Rolex, I swear you can't tell the difference." We realize he has previously stiffed most of his customers with worthless (perhaps stolen) merchandise, and in the process has destroyed his credibility.

Sammy's desperation intensifies. He switches to begging his cronies to loan him money, and when that fails, he finally pleads with his brother, then his mother. But he has used and abused all of his friends and his family. Clearly Sammy is nearing the end of his wheeling and dealing life. Though "Sammy" was written in cockney-flavored dialogue and was clearly British, the humanity of the character came through. His nationality was meaningless; his feelings and actions were universal.

The writer did not provide the dialogue of the people Sammy was hearing on the other end of the phone, only his responses to it. The drama is played entirely off Sammy's increasingly desperate, pathetic pleading. Sammy is a figure of both pity and empathy. It was impossible not to connect with his plight. The considerable task of the actor would be to give his entire performance to a prop phone. A thirty-minute monologue would demand extraordinary acting talent. I could see the film as I read the script. The character leaped to life off the pages. As I read, I felt the only actor who could play this part and hold an audience for a half-hour monologue would be Mickey Rooney. I was tremendously excited by it.

Racing into Billy Sackheim's office the next morning, script in hand, I announced, "It's a half-hour monologue. Mickey Rooney is the only actor in town who can play it, who has the energy and dynamic persona to play it. It's a natural for *Alcoa-Goodyear Theatre* and it will win us an Emmy!"

"A thirty-minute monologue?" he responded dubiously as I handed him the teleplay, "it'd better be good. I'll read it tonight."

Clearly Sackheim was beginning to build confidence in me, but with only a thirteen-week deal (albeit the second thirteen) and six of them already behind me, I was skating on thin ice.

The next day Sackheim called me in. "You're absolutely right. Mickey Rooney is perfect casting. If you can get him, schedule it for production. And, you're also right, we could win an Emmy."

We messengered the script to Rooney's agent. He called the next day saying Rooney wanted to play the part and would work for our top-of-the-show money. We had a deal.

We hired a New York writer Sackheim recommended, Al Brenner, to change the colloquial cockney slang to a New York equivalent and make a few trims. Otherwise, the script remained identical to Kenneth Hughes's original. However, we decided to change Sammy to Eddie because there were anti-Semitic references in the English script. We wanted them out.

With a one-set, one-actor production we felt that we could safely experiment with a new director. How difficult could it to be? We chose a new man, Jack Smight, just in from New York live television, who had no previous film experience. How could he go wrong?

As it turned out Mickey Rooney could have directed himself. Once on the set, Smight merely had to say "Action" and Rooney was off and running. Standing there near the camera I could only stare with amazement as this superb actor picked up the prop phone and instantly became Eddie, making his desperate pitch to his customers, his brother, and finally his mother; a lonely, isolated man pleading for his life. With no actor to play against, it was a virtuoso performance. Rooney's face broke out in sweat, his eyes searching the tiny apartment as if seeking divine intervention. Mickey Rooney's performance defined talent. He was even better than I had imagined.

When Smight called "Cut" in order to change camera angles, Rooney would immediately run outside and start playing catch with one of his buddies he'd brought along, apparently to limber up between takes.

When the new camera setup was ready and the assistant director called Rooney back to the set, he'd merely ask the script supervisor where he had been sitting or standing at the break. Once Smight quietly said "Action," Rooney instantly transformed himself from the ballplayer outside the soundstage into Eddie. He picked up the lines exactly where he had left off. His face suddenly became soaked in sweat; his plight was so real we could all feel it. He needed no fake tears or sweat. It was all Rooney. Rooney worked that character to perfection, adding touches not in the script, such as often glancing at the clock on the mantel, to underscore his character's desperation. I stood next to the camera transfixed. As Eddie's deadline approached, tears of defeat began streaming down Rooney's face. Everyone he called had turned him down. The loan shark's hoods were on their way to nail him. Our last shot was of Eddie answering the pounding on his door then backing away in terror. On screen we saw only the shadows of two big men, obviously the hoods moving ominously toward Eddie. We needed no shot of these characters beating the crap out of Eddie; our imaginations filled in the brutality. (This ending would be unacceptable in today's television, which demands we see the beating and the bloodletting.) When we finished shooting after a little more than two days, the entire crew gave Mickey Rooney a richly deserved standing ovation.

"Thanks, guys," Rooney said, making a beeline for the exit.

The film actor's art is perhaps the most amazing of all. As I was to observe so often in my long career, nothing was more astonishing than to stand by a camera talking to an actor wearing makeup who, when called, would abruptly cut off casual conversation, weave past the camera crew, walk a few steps in front of the huge Mitchell camera, and instantly become a character totally unlike themselves. After the director says "Cut," these artists can immediately return to themselves, pick up the conversation exactly where they left off without missing a beat. No matter the scores of times it's happened,

I am still astonished by the talent of a professional film actor working at his or her craft and art on a motion picture soundstage.

As Sackheim, the editor, and I watched Mickey Rooney in the dailies, it was clear we were witnessing a tour-de-force performance.

"There's a problem," the editor said as we watched. "Our director didn't shoot any cutaways. We've got four minutes of film more than we need with nothing to cut to so I can trim it down."

"That stupid son of a bitch!" Sackheim shouted. "He couldn't direct traffic!" But he quickly changed tone, his manner suddenly reasonable and thoughtful. "It's an easy fix. We see Rooney often glancing toward the clock. We'll get a second unit to go into the set and shoot that mantel clock from every angle that'll match his glances." He turned to the editor.

"Take some footage with you to the set, and make certain our second unit camera matches his glances." Then he said to me, "Make certain they don't strike the set. That Smight is an idiot." It was the solution only a professional could have known, and it was, indeed, an easy fix.

Smight went on to direct *Midway, Harper, No Way to Treat a Lady,* and many other features. His first television film directing assignment launched his career.

When the print was edited we showed the rough cut to a few Screen Gems executives. They came out of the projection room with raves, "It's an Emmy for Rooney, no doubt about it," was the consensus. You could feel the excitement around the Screen Gems offices. We had something special.

About a month later, Sackheim summoned me to his office. "Listen," he said, more than somewhat awkwardly, "Screen Gems is nominating *Alcoa-Goodyear Theatre* for an Emmy. We are going to mount our advertising campaign around *Eddie.* We think we've got a shot at it, but we all feel certain Mickey Rooney is a shoo-in. By the way," he added, "when the Academy sent us the card for our nominations, there's a space where you fill in the producer's name. I just wanted you to know I put my name in. It doesn't really matter. You, Jim Fonda, and Win O'Keefe are each producers of your own episodes but I'm the exec of the entire series. *Capishe?*"

"Sure," I replied, "whatever you like," and I meant it.

The National Academy of Television Art and Sciences Award Ceremony for the 1958–59 season was held at the Earl Carroll Theater on Sunset Boulevard. The big room was packed. Betty and I were assigned seats behind Sackheim and his wife, Joanne. Screen Gems had taken out full-page ads in both Hollywood trade papers, *Daily Variety* and *The Hollywood Reporter,* for *Alcoa-Goodyear Theatre* featuring a large photo of Mickey Rooney in his role as Eddie. Their entire campaign was based upon Eddie, no other film in our series was mentioned. We thought we had a chance, but were almost certain Rooney would walk away with a statuette.

When the emcee announced "and the winner is *Alcoa-Goodyear Theatre,* accepting the award is the producer of the series, William Sackheim," Sackheim bolted out of his seat, almost ran up the aisle, and accepted the award. He said, "I want to thank James Fonda, Winston O'Keefe, and William Froug."

My wife said to me, "But he didn't produce *Eddie,* you did."

It turned out to be *Eddie's* night. Jack Smight won an Emmy as best director, and Al Brenner won one for adapting Kenneth Hughes's script. But Mickey Rooney did not take home an Emmy. Fred Astaire won the Emmy for best performance by an actor.

Entering the men's room after the ceremonies were over, I discovered Rooney at the sink staring at his image in the mirror. "Fuck 'em!" he yelled. "Fuck 'em all! Who needs the bastards!" He turned away from the sink and staggered drunkenly out the door, barely able to navigate. Who could blame him?

I thought it might be nice to own one of those gold-plated statuettes, especially since I'd earned it. The next day I phoned the Academy offices and asked them if I was entitled to an Emmy. They were more than a little embarrassed and apologetic. By that afternoon an Emmy Award was delivered to my door.

The next week I received a follow-up call from the Academy advising me that as a result of this incident (and others similar to it) they were going to revise their award procedures in the future to include statuettes for the producers as well as the executive producers of any award-winning series. Thus it has been since.

Following our Emmys, Sackheim presented me with an unusual

assignment. He and a friend of his, Dan Ullman, had written the story "Before I Die." Sackheim wanted me to get a writer and turn it into a *Playhouse 90* film. "Read this and tell me what you think, ASAP," he said as he handed it to me.

Taking the story back to my office, I read it at once only to discover a serious problem: it had a strong first act, a good second act, but no third act, no resolution to the story. When I returned to Sackheim's office with my comments, he erupted.

"For Christ's sake, I *know* it has no third act, why the fuck do you think I gave it to you? Danny and I couldn't make it work, now it's your job to come up with a third act! And leave me the fuck alone!"

But as was often the case with Sackheim, having exploded, he quickly settled down, suggesting writers who might be good for the project. Sackheim was, himself, a screenwriter with several movie credits. I was flattered he thought that I could solve a problem he and Ullman hadn't been able to fix. Sackheim suggested I work with a New York writer, Bernie Giler. "You two will get along great," he assured me.

Sackheim was right. Giler had a street-smart New York sense of humor. We dug in our heels and began talking story or, more precisely, talking the missing third act of a story. A kid is on Death Row, he has a burst appendix, a young doctor from the nearest emergency room is called in to save him. Before going under the anesthesia, delirious with fever, the kid babbles the story of his alibi and his innocence. The doctor has saved the life of a man he now believes is innocent but who is scheduled to be executed the following week. It preys on his mind. He decides to look into the kid's alibi and visits the socially prominent woman whom the condemned man says can prove his alibi. The kid claimed he had spent the night of the crime with her. But she had told the police that she has no recollection of this kid, and certainly not of picking him up in a bar. Our young doctor realizes that even if she did remember she couldn't admit it. She would disgrace her wealthy, socialite husband and possibly destroy her marriage.

What would make this woman confess to her one-night stand and save the kid's life, while destroying her own? This was the problem we had to solve. It was the key to developing a third act.

For a couple of days Giler and I tossed possible solutions to this question to each other, often coming up empty-handed. Finally, we figured out a way to use our doctor-sleuth's knowledge of the disease of alcoholism to threaten her with exposure in order to force her to confront her lies. The woman's husband will be told the full story anyway. Trapped, her confession followed. The lesson for writers always is when you are in trouble with a story, let your characters solve your problem for you. The lesson I was learning about American television is that pace and energy are the key ingredients in television writing, producing, and directing. Pace can and does cover a multitude of sins, and it's the sense of excitement and discovery that is so endemic to the American psyche. What we came up with was neither art nor artful, but it worked. The script, while formulaic, was well written. Sackheim was proud of us and gave us a green light for production.

Meanwhile, Billy's brother, Ray, notified me Screen Gems had picked up my option for a third thirteen weeks. While casting *Before I Die,* I ran into an unusual situation. We cast Richard Kiley as the doctor and Kim Hunter as the key witness. We had several hospital scenes in the script that called for nurse extras. During my meeting with our casting director, Ira Uhr, I brought up the subject of casting the nurses. I wanted to make certain we had professional-looking women, not bimbos.

"You don't cast the nurse extras," Ira said, cutting me off sharply. "Irving Briskin takes care of that. He has the script and that's his order."

"But why?" I replied. "They're not even speaking roles."

"So much the better," Uhr replied. "Mr. Briskin has them come to his office so he can personally interview them. You figure it out. Next subject."

While visiting the set during shooting, I was struck by the number of large-breasted, peroxided blondes we had as nurses. Some wore too much makeup. When I asked the makeup artist about this, she snapped her response, "That's the way Mr. Briskin likes them."

Irving Briskin was head of Screen Gems; his brother Sam was second in command to Harry Cohn, the often-reviled head of Columbia Pictures. I had met Irving Briskin only once. It was the day he welcomed me to Screen Gems. He was a tall, very large man with gross features, whose speech was garbled, as if he had a cigar in his mouth, even when he didn't. Briskin kept a spittoon close by his oversized office swivel chair. He dressed in a rumpled, drab fashion, almost pajama-style, which I assumed was meant to be Hollywood casual. He appeared a kind of gentle giant. I was soon to discover that every Screen Gems producer had twenty-five dollars a month automatically deducted from his paycheck. When I asked Sackheim about it he told me it was a donation to Irving's Hollywood temple. "If you object," Sackheim told me, "you can take it up with Irving, but I don't recommend it."

Irving Briskin's boss was one of Hollywood's infamous moguls, Harry Cohn. It was widely believed by Hollywood experts that of all the ruthless studio moguls, Cohn was the worst.

I never met the man, but one day I arrived in the Columbia Pictures small executive dining room in time to hear someone telling a Harry Cohn story, which had taken place in that very room. Clearly, I was about to hear authentic Hollywood lore, even if untrue.

It seemed Cohn had come in to lunch one day, taken his place at the head of the table reserved for him, and after sitting down, slid a ten-thousand-dollar bill from his wallet. He handed it to the person seated next to him with instructions that he feel the bill, then pass it around the table, while Cohn instructed each person to feel the bill. "Rub it between your fingers," Cohn is alleged to have told each person at the table.

When the bill came back to Cohn, he snapped it open loudly, making certain everyone had seen it. Before sliding it back into his wallet he spoke to the table, "Now you guys know what it's all about."

Stories about these larger-than-life Hollywood moguls were usually apocryphal, but it was still fun to hear them, especially when told in the setting in which they allegedly happened.

My favorite Harry Cohn story was told to me by a grip working on the lot who swore it was the truth. It seems Cohn was making one of his noon strolls around the studio lot, checking out his empire. Upon seeing Cohn it was customary for everyone to run for cover, swiftly vanishing into soundstages, offices, workshops, anywhere to avoid being spotted by him.

"And this is why we all run for cover," the grip told me. "One day a guy sat in the shade eating his lunch, his back to his approaching boss."

"Everybody runs when I come on the lot," Cohn said to the man, "so why didn't you?'

"The guy turned around and stared Cohn in the eye, 'Because I'm not afraid of you, that's why.'"

"Good for you," Cohn allegedly told him, then added, "you're fired."

Harry Cohn died in 1958; the studio was shut down for the day. A memorial service was conducted on the lot in Columbia's largest soundstage. It was packed to overflowing. Passing by on my way to one of our soundstages, I saw the mob scene as people scrambled to get in. Comedian Red Skelton was there and made his famous remark, "This proves if you give folks what they want you can always get a big turnout." He worked the crowd, repeating his line several times and getting a laugh with each delivery. By the next day almost everybody in Hollywood was repeating his line, until it became a part of Hollywood lore.

Later that season the Screen Producers Guild announced nominations for its awards. *Before I Die* received a nomination as Best Television Motion Picture for 1958, as did *Eddie*. *Eddie* won. I was presented with a beautiful, modern Saul Bass–designed trophy. Sackheim was there at the ceremony applauding. I was later told that Sackheim had been a member of the nominating committee.

The following day Sackheim's secretary phoned to tell me the boss wanted to see me right away. I hurried down to Sackheim's office where I found him slumped over his desk, his muscular hands massaging his bald scalp. I'd seen this posture before and knew it meant trouble.

"Come in, *boychik*, we've got ourselves a problem," he said as I entered, "please sit down."

I sat across the desk from him as he sat up to face me, "In case it has escaped your attention, *boychik*, Jack Lemmon is the number-one box-office star in America, and he has just won an Oscar as Best Supporting Actor for his role in *Mr. Roberts*."

"The word has reached me," I replied, "he's terrific."

"But what you may not know is Lemmon is presently renegotiating his contract with Columbia Pictures, and also he's engaged to be married to an actress named Felicia Farr who is allegedly one of the most beautiful women on the planet but not generally regarded as exactly a heavyweight in the acting department. Are you beginning to catch on?" I confessed I hadn't a clue.

"Columbia Pictures has decided it would be a perfect time for us to come up with a starring role for Felicia Farr, *capishe?*"

"So we're looking for an *Alcoa-Goodyear Theatre* for her to star in, right?"

"Wrong. Remember, we're talking Jack Lemmon, the number-one box-office star in America. We have orders to come up with a starring role for Felicia Farr in a *Playhouse 90* film."

Sackheim was beginning to talk like our television boss, Irving Briskin, with his slobbering speech style, dribbling the words, as if he couldn't quite get the things out of his mouth. It sounded like Hollywood gangster garble—Edward G. Robinson in a yellow alpaca sweater.

"Okay, I'll look for a story for Felicia Farr,"

"Wrong again," Sackheim replied, beginning to enjoy the moment. "You're going to get yourself a writer and hole up with him until you two come out with a complete, ready-to-shoot teleplay in, say, three weeks."

"Three weeks!"

"Two weeks, if possible," he responded. "Yesterday wouldn't be soon enough. When the studio gives orders, they don't kid around. Start right now, make this your top priority. I can even suggest a writer who is supposed to work fast, cheap, and not too bad."

"Who?'

"A kid named Gene Roddenberry, who has been writing some *Highway Patrols* over at Ziv. They're high on him. I suggest you give him a call, see how the two of you get along. If you don't think you can work well together, it's okay by me, but if not, get somebody else quick. Got it?"

As I was getting up to leave, Sackheim added, "Have you seen *Gilda?*"

I admitted I hadn't.

"Good," said Sackheim, "I was thinking maybe a story like *Gilda* might work. Rita Hayworth, beautiful woman of mystery, foreign setting, whose primary job is to look like you'd like to fuck her. Acting not required, that kind of thing."

"I'll get a print and run it," I replied.

"No!" said Sackheim, "the last thing we want is to get sued by whoever wrote *Gilda*. And make sure Gene Roddenberry hasn't seen it either. By the way, Columbia likes Cliff Robertson, and that character actor Thomas Mitchell. Go to it, I've got faith in you."

"Okay," I responded, "we'll do something like *Gilda,* only not *Gilda,* which neither of us has seen."

Roddenberry and I got along superbly because we both decided the only way to approach this job was to somehow enjoy the absurdity of what we were doing—and work hard. Roddenberry was a former cop who had been a speechwriter for the LAPD's former chief William H. Parker, whose name is on the police building in downtown Los Angeles. Roddenberry told me he had also been an airline pilot. He was a man with a big, easy laugh, great warmth, and a generosity of spirit. It would be impossible not to like him.

A big galoop of a man with a huge smile, Gene had a slightly hooked nose and a rich sense of humor. We spent two entire days talking story ideas within Sackheim's parameters. There is a certain camaraderie that develops between writer and producer working in collaboration on a story. With Roddenberry and me it was an almost immediate connection. He took to calling me "Arkansas" and I called him "Roddenberg," which was a mutual recognition of how much we were enjoying this insane challenge. Sackheim's dictum: *"Gilda* but not *Gilda"* was creating a formidable roadblock. At the end of the second day Sackheim suddenly popped into my office, "You guys got anything you like yet?"

We hadn't.

"Listen," he said, "there's an old steamboat out in Burbank on Columbia's back lot. Why don't you drive out there, look around, see if there's anything out there that might give you something?"

Roddenberry and I saw the sights of Columbia's back lot, which looked exactly like what they had all become: relics from the days of the powerful Hollywood studio system, now long gone, murdered by television. There apparently had been scant attention to maintenance. We settled on using the remnants of the old steamboat; a coat of paint and some movie magic by the set designer and decorator and—voilà!—a working steamboat would be ready to sail down the Mississippi with passengers and crew. That gave us Felicia Farr as the beautiful, mysterious lady who traveled the Mississippi, looking for easy marks. It also gave us the mark, an obligatorily handsome riverboat gambler, Cliff Robertson. Soul satisfying it wasn't, but in our haste, we would leave no cliché unturned. *Gilda* it probably wasn't, unless, of course, *Gilda* had a Mississippi steamboat in it.

We talked the rest of the day, building on equal parts of enthusiasm and desperation. When I told Sackheim what we'd come up with, he gave us an okay, and Roddenberry went home to write. He delivered a shooting script in a little over two weeks. It wasn't great, but it was indeed adequate. Sackheim took a quick read and green-lighted us for production.

Felicia Farr was as beautiful and as limited in her acting range as advertised. Jack Lemmon visited the set every day, mooning around like a sick puppy.

One day, shooting on our Columbia soundstage, I got a call from the set to hurry over. David Lowell Rich, our director, and Cliff Robertson, the star, had been physically separated before they came to blows. Robertson, a "method" actor, had refused to accept Rich's explanation of his motivation for angrily leaving Farr's stateroom. There was some jawboning, but the camera crew and the assistant director got the two calmed down and filming proceeded.

I took Robertson to dinner that night to help smooth troubled waters and discovered him to be a charming, intelligent fellow but with dark, unspecified suspicions of the people with whom he was working. However, he agreed to put whatever was troubling him aside and finish the job. We parted amicably and I left the dinner feeling good about the meeting. We went back to work without incident and finished the picture on schedule.

Sitting with Sackheim in the projection room watching the rough cut of *Natchez,* I can candidly report that the film was not the worst ninety minutes ever shown on television, but it was close.

When the production wrapped, a grateful Jack Lemmon invited

me to his home for a drink. I quickly discovered he was unquestion-ably one of the nicest, most gracious, down-to-earth movie stars I had ever met. Standing behind his bar he told me, "I can't wait to get old so I can play character parts."

He got his wish, delivering outstanding performances year after year; an Oscar for *Save the Tiger*, brilliant in *Some Like It Hot, The Apartment, The Days of Wine and Roses, The China Syndrome, The Odd Couple, The Fortune Cookie, Grumpy Old Men*, and many more. I doubt if there is another American actor who can equal his range. He died recently, leaving behind a legacy few actors could touch. For me, he was among a handful of the greatest film actors in the history of motion pictures.

Gene Roddenberry went on to create, write, and produce a little-noticed series he called *Star Trek*.

My first year in television had been a gut-wrenching rodeo ride with plenty of thrills and spills. Even by Hollywood standards Sack-heim is a figure of such striking originality, no screen or television writer who has ever crossed his path can forget the experience. He is of the school of men about whom it is said they don't get heart attacks, they give heart attacks. Sackheim was my first and probably best tele-vision mentor. He had the best story mind I'd ever encountered.

I was among the first beneficiaries of that group of television executives who realized that the best way to deliver the enormous amount of program material required for television would be to turn writers into producers. All television series today are produced by hyphenates. All producer credits you see on a TV series today are likely to be writers who negotiated for that title.

A few years later Sackheim and I each found ourselves elected to the board of directors of the Producers Guild of America. Our rela-tionship had been cordial if not close and personal. Later, the battle of the Producers Guild and the Teamsters Union would put a strain on our cordiality from which it would never recover.

Sackheim and I saw little of each other over the following years except at PGA board meetings or industry functions. In the spirit of let-bygones-be-bygones, I phoned Billy a few years ago to congratu-late him on the splendid directing job his son, Dan, had done on a *Law and Order* episode I'd just seen. When I finished giving him my message he erupted. "You stupid son of a bitch!" he yelled, "You got me out of a sickbed to tell me this!" It was reassuring to learn that even in his seventies, Sackheim had lost none of the fire in his belly.

Nonetheless, after I had gone to work at UCLA, he phoned to ask if I would teach his son screenwriting.

Recently one of my former UCLA students employed at Universal as a screenwriter phoned to tell me he was working with a mentor of exceptional story insights combined with explosive reactions and generosity. The mentor's name was Billy Sackheim. It's good to know a new generation of screenwriters was learning from the volcano.

It was becoming increasingly apparent that television programming was undergoing a seismic shift. Slowly but surely anthologies were vanishing from network prime-time schedules, replaced by variations of comic strips—one-dimensional characters in Western series (replaying the great mythology of the opening of the West) such as *Wagon Train, Have Gun, Will Travel, The Rifleman, Maverick, Gunsmoke, Tales of Wells Fargo,* and many others. Ratings for *Alcoa-Goodyear Theatre* and *Playhouse 90,* while never robust, were sliding. The public wanted good guys versus bad guys, black and white with only a little gray. No doubt ancient Greek audiences felt the same way. It didn't take a genius to see that major changes were taking place in network TV prime-time schedules. Nielsen ratings, the shrine at which all mass communication executives worship, were telling them the audience wanted heroes (and villains) whose adventures they could follow week after week. The public wanted a fascinating character (preferably with a distinctive gimmick) plus story hooks that would keep them coming back to find out how their hero would deal with that week's crisis. These genres were becoming known as franchises, as in private eyes, marshals, homicide cops, doctors, lawyers, firemen, rangers, what have you. Network chieftains were asking producers to first identify the franchise of their series leading characters. It didn't take a latter-day Paul Revere to warn us. Prestige series were going the way of all anthology television. As they had fled New York in favor of Hollywood, now they were vanishing altogether. Series television was what the network brass wanted. We had already been told that renewals of *Playhouse 90* and

Alcoa-Goodyear Theatre were highly unlikely; they would be replaced by one series or another.

Sometime toward the end of that first year at Screen Gems, a man named Harris Katleman arrived at my office. He introduced himself as the West Coast head of film production for the Goodson-Todman Company. He was a lean, handsome man in an offbeat kind of way, with twinkling eyes and a crooked smile—a portrait of Rodeo Drive by way of Las Vegas with Gucci attaché case, Gucci loafers, and even Gucci belt buckle. His Italian silk suit was perfectly tailored for his lean body. Yet there was something endearing about the slickness of this walking cliché. He was right out there, and he advertised it. Superficial though he seemed, I liked his forthright manner. As they liked to say in Hollywood, beneath the superficial bullshit was the real bullshit. The first product the great salesmen sells is himself. He had been an agent with the legendary MCA, a talent agency that was widely known as "the octopus" for its dominating presence in almost every aspect of show business. As he wove his seductive pitch, it became clear that he was probably a bit of both, agent and salesman. In any event it is always fun being wooed.

Katleman told me that Mark Goodson, head, cofounder and co-owner of Goodson-Todman Productions (the most successful producers of game shows in television and radio history), a man reputed to be worth $500 million from his game-show empire, had decided he wanted to expand his operation by creating a Hollywood film division. Katleman and Goodson had selected me to become their first producer. Goodson had acquired the rights to Raymond Chandler's Philip Marlowe private-eye character. He had signed Phil Carey to play Marlowe and had rented office space and production facilities at MGM. But first he needed a pilot in order to sell the series to a network. Goodson wanted me to produce the pilot and the series, if it sold. Katleman offered me a one-year contract at more money than I was presently making, assuring me a bright and profitable future as Goodson-Todman's film business increased. I would be in on "the ground floor," a participant in a limitless future with Goodson's wealth backing up the new enterprise. It was obvious Katleman was a skilled salesman, and I knew my present job was going to vanish soon. The future was staring me in the face and it wore a Vegas smile, which turned out to be uncannily appropriate.

I was now the proud father of three daughters and a son. Alas, my boundless joy of parenthood was heavily counterbalanced by the ugly reality that their mother and I had made a tragic error in rushing into marriage after a one-day acquaintanceship in the summer of 1946. From the beginning, our marriage had been an unstable, roller-coaster ride; the vehicle in which we had been careening was finally, tragically spinning off the track. All the shrinks in Westwood and Santa Barbara could not save it. My psychiatrist finally gave me the verdict after a session with my wife: "It is a dance of death in which you are a willing partner." The pain of the divorce was almost unbearable, but continuing the marriage would have been even more unbearable. In the end there was no choice.

Though the collapse of our thirteen-year marriage was predictable, it's ending was no less traumatic. In divorce nobody wins. Fortunately, my children (now adults and parents, themselves) and I continue to maintain a close, mutually loving relationship.

Harris Katleman's offer had come at a devastating moment in my personal life. Now, more than ever, circumstances demanded I strike out in new directions and maintain a strong income to support two households. I accepted the offer without hesitation. It seemed my future in this new business of producing television was going to be an opportunity for a possibly steady and substantial income. Mark Goodson would quickly prove how wrong my thinking was.

5

The King of Game Shows or "Shoot Her in the Stomach"

Mark Goodson, an intelligent, sophisticated, entrepreneur, mingled with the New York showbiz elite. The world of entertainment is a meritocracy. Nobody cares if you murdered your mother, if you can come up with a showbiz winner. Goodson did not murder his mother or his father. He was born of poor Russian immigrants in Sacramento, California, and his parents had been determined he pursue an important profession like doctor or lawyer. (His father, Abraham, formerly a masseur, owned a small health-food store in Berkeley.) But young Goodson, who was awarded scholarships to the University of California, Berkeley, was highly enamored of theater. He directed several campus plays, won a medal for extemporaneous debate, and worked part-time at a local fish market. He graduated from Cal in 1937 wearing a Phi Beta Kappa key. Soon he found his way into radio as a newscaster and station manager.

In 1941 Goodson moved to New York and got work as a freelance announcer. He and a young radio writer, Bill Todman, teamed up and packaged quiz shows with ever increasing successes. As often happens in the world of entertainment, out of nowhere they found themselves at the top of their domain, producing hit radio shows in daytime as well as nighttime slots, and a few years later revamping the same shows into television hits. In short order Goodson-Todman Productions was king of quiz shows, and Mark Goodson was the head of Goodson-Todman. (Todman's primary function was as salesman for the company.) Every show they agreed to produce magically turned into money, big money. The cost of producing these shows with a cast of amateurs (members of the audience) was buttons compared to the budgets of comedy, drama, or variety shows, and they often got better ratings. Their cost per thousand viewers-to-advertisers was manna from heaven, which made them the darlings of the networks. But they got little respect from the big name prime-time producers, the Hollywood studios, or the movie crowd in general. A quiz show is still, after all, a quiz show, no matter how high the ratings.

Goodson was proud of his shows, which were not only enormously popular but had made him a megamillionaire, on the way to becoming a billionaire. But quiz and game shows were nonetheless the clown act of television, the cotton candy, the place where exhibitionists with no discernible talent amused *boobus Americanus* by making fools of themselves. Like the clown who wants to play Hamlet, Mark Goodson aspired to a higher level, a grander stage. He wanted status.

Big-screen Hollywood is elitist territory; it was already feeling somewhat demeaned by the very existence of the small screen, with its low-budget inanities like wrestling and mindless talking heads. Quiz and game shows were on the wrong side of the tracks, to movieland factotums. Would anyone in the motion picture studio executive suites really believe that producing *What's My Line?, Beat The Clock, Family Feud,* or *Match Game* was a stepping-stone to producing big box-office movies? The red carpet was not out.

Goodson-Todman was a New York operation. Though Goodson was born and raised in California, he seemed to avoid the West Coast as much as possible. Possibly lack of respect was one reason. In Hollywood he was not well known. He hired West Coast professional people to watch his game shows daily and report back to him, as he did one veteran Hollywood TV producer, retiree David Levy. Levy was on a weekly retainer for a number of years. He and Goodson were in touch by phone almost daily, rarely meeting in person. Levy passed along his comments and whatever Hollywood insider gossip Goodson might find of interest.

I had met Mark Goodson briefly at an industry function. He was a more-than-somewhat pompous man of short stature, blond, good looking, well groomed, nattily dressed. Though gracious, in a noblesse oblige sort of way, he seemed to have something of a chip on his shoulder. He struck me as a man more than a bit too full of himself, used to giving rather than taking orders and having them obeyed promptly.

He had begun his working life studying and directing college dramas. No doubt he longed to continue on that upper-echelon path. But with no firm go-ahead on any movie projects he might have had in development, he was left with television, the place in the fifties where old movie stars and movie wannabes of every stripe and description wound up, like a kind of small-screen Death Valley. In those days television was a quasi graveyard where even zombies might come to back life. "Washed up? No longer getting the big movie roles? Try the small screen!" (Witness Loretta Young, Jane Wyman, Barbara Stanwyck, Robert Taylor, Ronald Reagan, Dick Powell, and others.)

Few in the movie business were able to accept that, ironically, that same TV graveyard was gradually giving birth to a new generation of creative talents, talents who would one day become the next film generation and would take over Hollywood, not only as writers, directors, producers, and actors but as studio executives. Indeed, the day was not far away when *all* of the Hollywood studio heads would be former television people.

When Goodson decided to invest his time and money in a television pilot based upon Raymond Chandler's famous private investigator, Philip Marlowe, it was only natural that he would prefer to take the project to the studios of MGM in Culver City, California, the former lion king of the motion-picture industry. MGM had discovered that, as a worst-case backup, they could lease their empty soundstages and offices to outside TV production companies. MGM, in its waning movie days, was still living off its reputation of having been the greatest motion picture studio in Hollywood's history.

The Culver City lot was the last of the major studios to finally give in to the reality that they could no longer ignore television. The movies had been hit hard at the box office in the fifties with the emergence of the new medium. The other major studios had gone into TV reluctantly, with little enthusiasm and a lot of contempt (they felt they were slumming, and aiding and abetting the enemy) but had nonetheless come to recognize that if you couldn't beat the enemy, you'd better join them. Early on, Columbia Pictures had formed a television subsidiary, Screen Gems. Twentieth Century Fox already had programs in prime time. Warner Brothers was producing several highly popular one-hour series, notably *77 Sunset Strip, Bourbon Street Beat,* and *Maverick.* MGM was reluctantly playing catch-up.

So formulaic were these Warner Brothers TV one-hour series that during a Writers Guild strike, with the studio running out of new scripts, they simply recycled the old scripts, merely changing the names of the characters. Thus *Sunset Strip* became *Bourbon Street Beat* and vice versa. If members of the audience noticed the recycling of used material, there were no public complaints. Not even the trade press wised up until it was old news.

Boris Sagal, late of the Yale School of Drama and one of the most in demand of television's new crop of young directors, had directed several of these scripts earlier. He didn't recognize that he'd done the same script a few months earlier on another series until he finished shooting it.

To protect themselves from Writers Guild wrath Warner Brothers credited these various recycled remakes to a new writer, "W. Hermanos" (Warner Brothers). When finally detected, it became an inside industry joke.

Reporting to shoot the pilot at MGM for *Philip Marlowe,* my office turned out to be on the main street of MGM's Culver City's Lot number 1. Metro had been the Tiffany's of motion picture studios in Hollywood's golden years. "More stars than there are in the Heavens" had been their PR slogan. In Hollywood terms, there was some truth to it. Certainly in its heyday before World War II, Metro, as it was called, had more superstars than any other movie studio. Their belated decision to join the enemy was without enthusiasm and accomplished with a significant degree of condescension, which they displayed whenever the opportunity presented itself.

When I parked my car on the MGM lot directly across the narrow street from the imposing Thalberg Building, MGM's administrative headquarters, I felt a new thrill. MGM was the home of many of my childhood movie memories. I was a teenager with Andy Hardy (Mickey Rooney and I are about the same age), swashbuckled with Gene Kelly (in high school I took fencing lessons at the local YMCA), had fallen in love with Myrna Loy (all of us kids' dream wife), wished that I were a big, macho, lady-killer like Clark Gable, admired the extraordinary talent of Spencer Tracy, wanted to be as handsome as Robert Taylor, was awed by the cold beauty of Greta Garbo, and dazzled by the young talent of Judy Garland. These were my idols.

Even though Goodson-Todman was only leasing space, I was going to be playing in the Yankee Stadium of Hollywood! I strolled under the street-wide span over the entrance proclaiming Metro-Goldwyn-Mayer, identified myself to gate guards Kenny Hollywood and Stanley Kowalski, then strolled down the main street, dodging sets being wheeled toward soundstages, passing extras in makeup, and thinking to myself, this is really it! This is the actual, alive and functioning Hollywood of my imagination. I was unprepared for the euphoria of it.

Settling into my new office, I immediately went to work. The first order of business for any film or television producer is to choose the right writer for the right project. I had had a few weeks to think about *Philip Marlowe* and who might best translate Raymond Chandler's famous detective into a television hero. I knew the man I wanted for the job and hired him that first day. James Moser was a top radio and television writer. Among his many other credits was his radio pilot and subsequent scripts for the highly popular *Dragnet,* first for radio and later as a television series. He was a key writer for the series. *Dragnet* remains the most popular cop series in the history of broadcasting, with the possible exceptions of the more recent *Hill Street Blues* and *NYPD Blue.*

Moser was a stickler for accuracy. It was said of the *Dragnet* radio series that if it actually took fifteen steps to walk from the homicide office of the Los Angeles Police Department to the captain's office, the sound man was ordered to make *only* the sound of fifteen pairs of footsteps, not one more or one less. Jack Webb, the creative force behind the series as well as its star, and Jim Moser were on the same page when it came to insistence on authenticity. Moser was known to be choosy, but I was eager to work with him.

Jim was an exceptionally lean, even gaunt man with an odd jutting jaw. He spoke in terse sentences, his speech reticent, his manner studious and serious. After our initial conversation discussing ideas for the series, he agreed to bring me an outline for a pilot script. I hoped for the crisp, hard-edged dialogue that was Moser's signature.

Next came my meeting with Phil Carey, the actor Mark Goodson had chosen to play Marlowe. After one glance at the Players Directory, I immediately recognized Carey as the tall, handsome, second lead in Errol Flynn and John Wayne movies. I felt we had a problem with him as our private eye. He was too blond, too handsome, too youthful, and possibly a bit bland. His face lacked life-worn character, it didn't look as if he'd lived in it. He was also somewhat wooden as an actor. There was no mystery in him, no hint of a hard life as a private eye. Most troubling was his boyishly open, handsome face, which suggested he had no secrets nor had known any pain. He was hardly what you would expect from the hard-boiled, world-weary, Philip Marlowe. But he was Mark Goodson's choice. It was a done deal.

Carey dropped by for a visit. A most friendly, charming man, he was taller and even better looking in person than I'd expected. I told him of my concerns. A more agreeable actor would be hard to find. His response was, "Do anything you want with me. Turn my hair black, wrinkle me up, I'm all yours."

Bill Tuttle, head of MGM's makeup department met us in a small makeup room in his department. A warm and generous man, Tuttle had done makeup for Clark Gable, Gene Kelly, Van Johnson, Mickey Rooney, Robert Taylor, Richard Burton, Fred Astaire, and the entire firmament of Metro's stars. Once we got Phil in the chair with all the lights on, Tuttle studied his face and felt as I did. We needed to age Carey, to weather him a bit in order to give his face a tougher appearance with a harder background. After trying out several ideas, mustache, scars, wrinkles about his eyes and his forehead, we finally settled on a small scar on his left cheekbone. Carey was happy with it, so we were in business.

Next on my agenda was finding the right director. When agents came calling at my office, I told them that I wanted a fresh new talent who knew how to handle a camera. I wanted a film man.

One agent claimed he had just the guy, a "brilliant" talent, a "genius" waiting for somebody to discover him. And, best of all, he had a film he said would prove him right.

Sitting in the projection room watching a low-low-budget independent film called *Stakeout on Dope Street,* it was apparent the agent was not speaking hyperbolically. Irvin Kershner was clearly the best director I'd seen in years. Brilliant, definitely; genius, maybe.

We made a deal that day for Kershner to direct the pilot for *Philip Marlowe.* The following day a tall, very lean, blond, balding young man ambled into my office and introduced himself as Irvin Kershner.

We knew immediately that our chemistry was in sync, and that we were going to work well together, but I doubt if either of us guessed that this meeting would lead to a long but eventually frustrating partnership.

Harris Katleman phoned to say Mark Goodson was skeptical about my hiring a new director but, since he was pleased with Moser, he would not disapprove. It was my first inkling of the extent to which Mark Goodson would involve himself in our pilot.

Moser's script was right on the money, Kersh and I began to scout locations and set a shooting schedule.

Katleman let me know that Goodson was satisfied with what I was doing. It seemed Katleman was in phone contact with Goodson hourly. For Katleman, approval from Goodson was akin to dispensation from the pope.

Kersh shot the pilot with all the style and originality I'd seen in *Dope Street.* Phil Carey was fine, but he had a softness in his manner and voice that no amount of makeup could cover. He still seemed far too much a kindhearted young man to be the hard-boiled Philip Marlowe. There was nothing potentially dangerous about this actor; in a word he was unexciting.

In any event, when completed and shown to ABC and potential sponsors, *Philip Marlowe* was sold immediately and scheduled for Tuesdays at 9:30 P.M. beginning in October, 1959. Katleman told me Goodson was boasting to his pals how easy it was to make a big score in Hollywood right off the bat. Even Katleman was sometimes amused by his boss. That pilot, Katleman said, was the hottest of the season; everyone was jealous of Goodson, so he said. Katleman's reverence for Mark Goodson escaped bordering on the absurd only because of his healthy sense of humor.

We began setting up meetings, calling writers whose work I admired and booking directors. Within a few weeks we had at least five writers hard at work on stories. Our initial show order was for thirteen episodes, but we kept a few assignments in reserve in case we found a writer we wanted to use a second or even a third time. Unfortunately, Jim Moser's agent said he was unavailable to write an episode. (There is at least three times the money for writing a pilot, and the writer of a pilot receives a residual for every episode shot for the life of the series, no matter who the subsequent writers are.)

As it happened Moser was writing and researching his *Ben Casey* series, which was to become the first medical series to achieve a remarkable ambiance of realism.

Kershner's agent told me, in the politest terms (he had other directors he wanted to sell), that since his client had scored big in an important television assignment he was no longer available for episodic television. (Like the writers of pilots, the pilot director would also receive residuals for the life of the series.) The agent's plan was to put Kershner into features or into his own television series, both of which he successfully did.

Kersh directed no more episodic series except the series he and Andy Fenady created and co-owned, *The Rebel*. Following that television excursion, Irvin Kershner went on to become a big-name feature film director with several important film credits: *The Luck of Ginger Coffey, The Flim-Flam Man, The Empire Strikes Back, Never Say Never Again,* and many more. He became a darling of film critics.

There was never any doubt in our minds that Kershner was headed for the big time in a big way.

When the first story for *Philip Marlowe* came in we sent it, as ordered, to Goodson for approval. It was Charles Beaumont's excellent published short story "The Loner," which Chuck adapted for our series. Within a day or two Goodson called to tell me he didn't like the story and hoped I would do better with the next one. In short order I discovered Goodson intended to micromanage every aspect of the production from the story outline to script to casting to editing. I'd heard about his style with his game shows. He was reported to continuously tinker with them until he got them precisely the way he wanted them, and then tinker some more.

After he received the second and third stories, the calls from Goodson had a tone of thinly veiled anger. He questioned names of characters, offered advice on casting, directors, even locations. There wasn't an aspect of any story for which he didn't demand an explanation. Often he was argumentative, letting me know he knew what television audiences wanted. After all, he had four or five game shows among the top-ten-rated TV series.

Finally, by the time the fourth story was sent to him, his calls were openly hostile. "In the first place," he said, "I don't like these mood pieces you're doing. I want more action. In your Hollywood murder story I think it's obvious that Marlowe, instead of hauling her off to jail, should shoot her in the stomach. She's a killer." Being on the defensive was becoming increasingly uncomfortable for me, so I reacted accordingly, suggesting he give me some space and a little faith. After all, I had produced the pilot without his help. How about a little latitude?

It was the second time Goodson had instructed me to have Marlowe shoot a woman in the stomach. I found his manner irritating and his ideas sometimes absurd and even incredible. He was now lecturing me on television drama. This job was turning out to be a nightmare.

Katleman came by with a look of deep concern on his face. "I'm sorry you and Mark aren't getting along," he said. "I agree with him. Your stories lack action."

"You mean they're unconventional?" I countered. "They are, and I plead guilty."

"Call them what you will, the stories are too introspective. Marlowe isn't taking enough action."

"By the way," I asked him, "what is Goodson's fixation with Marlowe shooting women in the stomach?"

"How should I know?" he responded. "There's a guy coming out from New York to talk to you about your storylines," he continued, "he's with the network, his name's John Calley. He wants to have lunch with you tomorrow. You can level with him, tell him your problems. All he wants to do is to help make the series a hit. "

I met John Calley for lunch in the MGM commissary the next day. He was a handsome, well-tailored young man who looked the picture of the young, sincerely dressed network executive. As soon as we ordered he got directly to the point.

"I understand you're having problems getting Mark Goodson to approve your stories. Goodson hasn't let me read them yet because he says he doesn't like them. I might be able to help you out."

I immediately and unwisely, as it turned out, began unloading my frustrations with Goodson's habit of nitpicking every story. "He might as well write them himself," I told Calley. "He's driving me nuts. Stories can always be revised," I reminded him, "but not to fit his crazy ideas."

"Why doesn't he like your stories?" Calley asked.

"He says they're short on action. I personally think the threat of violence often can have more dramatic tension than violence itself. He doesn't agree. Twice he's suggested Marlowe shoot the woman character in the stomach. Is he a latent homosexual? What's that about, shooting women in the stomach? I just can't figure him out. He's trying to produce this series by phone. And he's driving me crazy."

"I'll see what I can do to help," Calley responded, noncommittally, avoiding any discussion of either my stories or Mark Goodson. He was so friendly that I failed to make proper note of his evasiveness.

During our brief conversation he was vague about his job, merely assuring me he could be "helpful." His manner was empathic. I came away from the lunch encouraged, believing I had an understanding friend in court. He assured me he'd help solve this problem.

Around ten o'clock the next morning a solemn faced Harris Katleman walked into my office with an announcement, "You're fired. You have until noon to pack your office stuff and get off the lot."

"Why?" I asked, incredulous.

"Why in hell did you call Mark Goodson a fag?" he demanded.

"I didn't. I was just reacting to some of his ridiculous comments about our stories. What's going on?" I asked him. Like a clumsy dentist, I realized I had inadvertently struck a nerve with Mark Goodson.

"You had lunch with John Calley yesterday who just happens to be one of Mark Goodson's closest friends. He phoned Mark as soon as he left the lunch. He told Mark you called him a fag. By the way, Calley had read all of your stories and he hated them. Anyway, we're paying you off. We'll buy up your contract for the year. We're throwing out all the stories you have in work. You'll want to call the writers and tell them they'll get their story money, but they might as well forget about going to script."

I glanced at my watch, "I've got two hours to get off the lot. You call them." I told him, angrily.

"We're bringing in Gene Wang to replace you," he responded. "He'll be taking over your office this afternoon. Be sure you're gone."

"Who's Gene Wang?" I asked.

"He was the producer of *Perry Mason*. I've talked to him. He has a new approach and his own writers. I'm really very sorry about this, but Mark's mind is made up. No use calling him, he won't speak to you. Be off the lot by noon if you know what's good for you. Mark is serious."

I shed no tears when the *Philip Marlowe* series was canceled in its first and only season. John Calley later became president of Columbia Pictures. In Hollywood they call him "Black Jack."

Goodson was never able to expand his empire beyond game shows. His dream of creating a film production company vanished. But he kept his billion dollars and no doubt added many more millions before he was gone.

Goodson's dream of building a Hollywood-based film company didn't live up to his hopes or ambitions. Thanks to his introduction to Irv Kershner's work on *Philip Marlowe,* he made a deal with Kersh and his then partner Andrew J. Fenady for Goodson-Todman to be the production entity for their new series *The Rebel,* which ran for almost four seasons. However, its ending left him with no dramatic series, nor any significant recognition by the motion picture industry. In perhaps a final gesture for motion picture legitimacy, he donated The Mark Goodson Screening Room to the American Film Institute's film school in Los Angeles.

It was no coincidence that Goodson chose the Hillside Cemetery in Culver City as the site of his final resting place among the graves of such luminaries as Jack Benny, Al Jolson, Dinah Shore, and Eddie Cantor. In death, if not in life, he is obviously where he longed to belong.

Looking back these many year later, I do recall a couple of the stories were undoubtedly lacking in action and probably were too introspective. With hindsight, we all have twenty-twenty vision.

6

Paradise Found, Paradise Lost

Being fired by Mark Goodson at that exact moment in time was one of the luckiest timings in my career.

Twentieth Century Fox had sold a new one-hour series to ABC called *Adventures in Paradise*. It was about a young ex-Korean War veteran named Adam Troy who ran a freight and taxi service among the islands of the South Pacific aboard his sail boat *Tiki*. The noted novelist James Michener had created the series for Fox. Martin Manulis, a highly regarded producer of New York live television was executive producer. In Hollywood the best way to get a project launched (movie or TV series) is to have at least one important "element" attached to it: a big-name star, an important director, writer, or producer. Manulis sold his series partly on the strength of having a big-name writer attached to the project—James A. Michener, author of *Tales of the South Pacific* upon which the hit musical *South Pacific* was based. Michener's reputation as a best-selling author was just about to take off big-time. That he himself had nothing whatever to do with the writing, producing, editing, casting, directing, even consulting on the series was irrelevant. The Michener name tied in with *Tales of the South Pacific* was the key element in the sale. Manulis chose as "line" producer Richard Goldstone, a producer whose credentials were in feature motion pictures, not television. My agent advised me that Goldstone was looking for writers. He suggested to Goldstone that I was a perfect fit for the series.

While in the Navy, my ship had been ordered to atolls from Midway Island to Johnson Island below the equator to Eniwetok and Majuro across the international date line. I had fallen in love with the South Pacific, the circular coral reefs, the arching palms waving in the ever-present breezes in sunny skies over pale greenish blue waters and paradisiacal lagoons. No doubt this idyllic view of mine was born of the fact that my subchaser's duties primarily consisted of escort services hundred of miles from the bloody scenes of island invasions going on far to the west of us. We escorted wounded ships home from island invasion battles or assured safe passage for our own submarines on their way into enemy waters. We saw no action though we dropped a few depth charges in vain; enemy subs were probably long gone. Yet I had spent two and a half years at sea in the backwaters of the Pacific Theater of War without being in harm's way. I had served my country, done my duty. Clearly, *Adventures in Paradise* was the series for me.

My agent arranged a meeting with Goldstone, who turned out to be a friendly, open-faced, gracious gentleman. He had produced the first Cinerama movie. I told him of my background and pitched him a couple of story ideas. He immediately put me to work on an assignment. He liked the script when I turned it in and brought me back for another and another. Writing about sailing the coral island reefs was like writing about my home away from home for three years.

Goldstone and I got along famously. We had the same point of view for the new series: exploit the South Pacific, try to find stories that were indigenous to the area and could not happen anywhere else. Dick did not write, so he welcomed a hyphenate on board. (Critics complained that the series was unlike the real South Pacific, that Michener's imprint was missing. We would have most certainly welcomed him, but he was not available.) We, however, knew the South Pacific firsthand.

After producing a couple of my scripts, Goldstone confided that he found producing a weekly one-hour series overwhelming. He had unspecified health problems and asked if I would be interested in rotating with him, writing and producing my own teleplays whenever I had one ready. He hoped I would commit to producing and writing at least nine of my own scripts during the coming season, more if possible. He also welcomed me to produce the teleplays of other writers. I was free to write and/or produce any teleplays Goldstone and I liked. We were virtually on our own. It was a heady experience. The series already had a few regular contributing writers, thanks to the series story editor, Max Lamb.

I moved into an office adjoining Goldstone's on the second floor of the Old Writers Building on the Pico Boulevard side of Twentieth Century Fox's Westwood lot. The building had an English-cottage, idyllic look about it, surrounded by tall, lush pine trees, beautifully maintained flower gardens, and leafy tropical growth. The offices on the ground-level floor had flagstone patios leading into the gardens. Walking up the stairs one could get a feel for what old Hollywood must have been like; the walls and offices of the building were comfortably musty with history and they exuded a kind of antimodern random casualness. It was a place clearly designed with writers in mind.

One of our most remarkable writers was John Kneubuhle. John was the son of a shipwrecked American sailor who had been marooned on American Samoa and had married the island princess. It turned out that the princess had a real head for business. In no time at all the Kneubuhles owned island airlines, shipping interests, and a great deal of land. They became one of the wealthiest families in American Samoa. John was sent to Yale where he graduated with honors. He was a gentle but troubled soul who truly knew the territory. As a consequence, he wrote several of our best scripts.

Fox had offered me a one-year contract with an option for a second. The money was not spectacular but good enough, especially since I'd fallen in love with the series. Money had never been uppermost in my mind; working with people I liked and respected was always of primary importance to me.

The Fox lot was unlike any other in the world of motion picture studios. It was spacious with great areas of open lawns dotted with huge pine trees and sweeping concrete walkways, lushly landscaped. The great soundstages were clustered at the northeastern end of the vast studio acreage. The commissary was close by, where the food was excellent and inexpensive. We producers were allowed to eat in a small separate executive dining room, which was not made less pleasant when dining at the table next to Marilyn Monroe, Yves Montand, Lawrence Olivier, or whichever star was currently filming a feature. This was a truly insulated world of great natural, as well as theatrical, beauty. It was easy to let yourself get lost in this dream world and even regret returning home to reality.

We were allotted bicycles, and I used mine daily to take pages to mimeo, to visit sets, to go to lunch, or whenever I could find an excuse to simply ride and admire the lush sweeping lawns and the tree-filled scenery. No other Hollywood studio could equal Fox's natural splendor.

A very special treat was a drive to the back lot (the unpaved road was too rock-strewn for biking) to visit the *Adventures in Paradise* lagoon. Studio art directors had created a masterpiece of set design for feature films as well as for our series. I took to brown bagging my lunch on sunny days and driving to our primary location. I'd sit on our sandy beach looking out on our palm-lined, one-acre lagoon at the far end of which was a small aged shack and pier. It was almost impossible to tell any of it from the real thing, even for a man who had seen it and lived it. The set designers had shown once again what the magic of the movies was all about.

Sitting on our small sand beach I could relive the days when I sat under coconut palms on Majuro Atoll in the Marshall Island chain. Even then, eager as we all were to get home, we realized we were living in a dream world. Crew members on shore leave would pass time smashing the great, surprisingly heavy, fallen fruit against the rocks until they broke open, then digging the crisp milky-white meat out of the shells with pocket knives. The war had ended by then, and we were left in the blissful backwaters where our only job was killing time until we were ordered home. Lazing in the shade of coconut trees on a sunny day cooled by ocean breezes was a beautiful way to sit out the clock.

Our *Adventures in Paradise* lagoon was as realistic as Hollywood artisans could replicate it. Our good ship *Tiki* was snuggled up next to our pier, facing the two-story, ramshackle hotel. Of course, there was no actual shack, no hotel. The palm trees in the distance were all sitting in huge wooden containers disguised by hundreds of smaller potted plants. The lagoon had been an empty acre of Fox's back lot, bulldozed down a few feet, asphalted, then filled with city water for a feature film some years earlier. Fish had been added to keep the water algae free.

The hotel was merely an expertly weathered facade and the *Tiki*, though a superb replica, was not floating snugly at the dock. It was in fact supported by cement pillars on the asphalt bottom of our lagoon. Lunching there, eating a peanut-butter-and-jelly sandwich, it was hard to remember that this "ship" had nothing below the water line, no sails, only folded rolls of ordinary canvas. It was our double for the real *Tiki*, a large ketch docked in San Pedro Bay, which rarely went to sea with our cameras and star aboard. There was, in fact, a third *Tiki* on our soundstage, which was a scaled-down version of the real ship, with folded-down masts and solid wooden decks. The boat's interior staterooms were located on another area of the same stage. In addition we had great wind machines, water pumps, and hoses with huge nozzles with which to douse our stage ship to emulate heavy seas. Before there was computer-generated special effects, our skilled crews did it the old fashioned way, by hand.

The star of *Adventures in Paradise* was Gardner McKay, the skipper of the *Tiki*. He was widely publicized as one of the most handsome men in the world. It was not an unreasonable appraisal. Tall, lean, dark-eyed, with wavy black hair, he was most women's dream of what a movie star ought to look like. Actually, McKay seemed troubled by his lavishly publicized good looks, and he wasn't at all happy about being an actor. He disliked Hollywood and its trappings and wasn't comfortable with his life in the spotlight. He was, in reality, a writer by inclination and temperament. As a consequence, he tended to be moody, withdrawn, and even disinterested, but he did his job with a minimum of fuss.

One day he broke down on the set. He was taken to our little studio hospital, given a shot by our studio doctor, and returned to work

The author aboard the *Tiki,* docked in the back-lot lagoon of Twentieth Century Fox's *Adventures in Paradise*. The ship had concrete pilings below the waterline. (from the author's collection)

within a day or so. In any event, it was much too soon. The poor guy needed a rest; the media pressure and the constant criticism of his acting talents must have been unbearable to him. McKay had a dark vision of life, a tendency to brood, and an abiding dislike for what he called "those Hollywood people." It was as if someone had put a gun to his back and ordered him to star in a television series. He kept to himself most of the time, and we all got along. But he soldiered on, to his own detriment. It couldn't have been easy for him, as he seemed to be fighting his inner demons almost every day. Goldstone and I both rather liked Gardner, but we kept a safe distance. Years later he became a moderately successful novelist, sometime-playwright and teacher, living out his life in Hawaii.

Our series was unique in many ways. Nobody expected us to reach top-ten ratings, but we usually made the top twenty, which, for whatever delightful reason, ABC found acceptable. Ours were soft stories, lacking a great deal of dramatic tension, action, violence, or sex. We took our cue from Michener's *Tales of the South Pacific.* Our stories were often exotic, character driven, and off the beaten path.

William Self, a former child actor and Beverly Hills tennis champion, was the vice president in charge of television for Twentieth Century Fox at the time. A more agreeable and supportive boss would be impossible to find. He made life at the studio a television hyphenate's paradise. During one of our many casual conversations in his office, he told me a story that, as a lifelong Fred Astaire fan, I can never forget.

Astaire and Self were playing golf together. Astaire casually asked Bill what he was working on.

"We're doing a TV pilot with Ginger Rogers."

"Swell," Astaire replied, "just don't let her dance."

Self figures Astaire was kidding, but he was not 100 percent certain, since Astaire blithely went off to make his next shot.

One day Goldstone suggested there was no need for me to write at the office. He suggested I take a week's "vacation" but return with a shooting script for our series. He said Bill Self had approved. I accepted the deal with pleasure and holed up in a bungalow alone at the Palm Springs Racquet Club, dutifully writing every day.

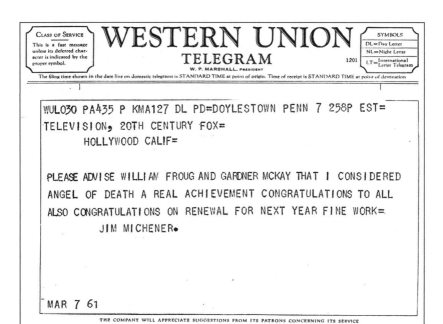

WULO30 PA435 P KMA127 DL PD=DOYLESTOWN PENN 7 258P EST=
TELEVISION, 20TH CENTURY FOX=
     HOLLYWOOD CALIF=

PLEASE ADVISE WILLIAM FROUG AND GARDNER MCKAY THAT I CONSIDERED
ANGEL OF DEATH A REAL ACHIEVEMENT CONGRATULATIONS TO ALL
ALSO CONGRATULATIONS ON RENEWAL FOR NEXT YEAR FINE WORK=
     JIM MICHENER.

MAR 7 61

I returned with a script I called *Angel of Death* as a starring vehicle for Inger Stevens, a Scandinavian actress I admired. In my story, she and her actor-husband played Swedish doctors transported by Adam Troy to the islands where they planned to test an elephantiasis vaccine. They ran into trouble with the natives, who didn't want to be part of the experiment nor would they allow their children to be inoculated.

The chief, a Yale graduate, tries to calm his people's fears, but they are unmoved and are especially angry at Captain Troy for bringing these doctors to their island. One of the inoculated children dies, prompting the natives to form an angry mob intent upon driving the doctors off the island. With the help of the chief, Troy plays peacemaker, a role Gardner McKay especially enjoyed, and the episode produced a surprising and heartwarming response in the form of a telegram from James Michener.

I had it framed and hung it on the wall above my typewriter. "So much for the critics," I liked to tell myself.

With the renewal of *Paradise* for another season came a change of vice presidents in charge of television. The new man was Roy Huggins, unquestionably the hottest hyphenate of his era. He had seemingly single-handedly created the entire roster of Warner Brothers television shows. *Maverick, 77 Sunset Strip,* and *Bourbon Street Beat* were among his many hit television series. Later he added *The Rockford Files* and *The Fugitive* to his mind-boggling list. Understandably the entire town thought his body waste smelled like gardenias. I was summoned to his office.

I discovered Roy Huggins, his feet on the desk, smiling in an oddly sinister fashion . . . called, in some circles, a shit-eating grin. He was clearly a man savoring the heady aroma of power, and he wanted me to know he knew it. I understood at once why some said he was a man of extreme self-confidence. But I quickly discovered Huggins was simply insufferably arrogant. He leaned back in his chair grinning, regarding me as a troublesome gnat he was about to swat.

"Please sit down," he said, as patient as he might have been with a naughty child. "You missed my meeting with the producers. I was told you've been writing your scripts in Palm Springs," he said, adding, "it sounds like you've got a cushy deal. I wish I had a cushy job like that." Huggins had the ability to increase his smile as he twisted his sarcasm. "But you missed the meeting, so I'm going to fill you in. There are some important changes effective immediately. From now on all stories for all Fox series must be approved by me before the writer can go to script. All scripts must also be approved by me, as well as all casting, including all spoken parts, even if it's two lines. As to *Adventures in Paradise,* I am not at all happy with it, the stories are too soft. We're going to change that. I want natives with war paint, I want tribal warfare, battles, more war paint, spears, slaughter, blood and thunder, *action.* Do you understand me?"

"But we were just renewed for our third season," I protested, dumbfounded by his frontal assault.

"I know," he said, "but your ratings are slipping. We have got to improve them and we will. Action and more action, war paint, spears. No more sleepy lagoon stories. Do you understand me?" He never raised his voice, he merely widened his condescending smile.

I told him I understood perfectly and beat a hasty retreat. I had no interest in debating our different visions of the series. While bicycling back to my office I realized I simply had no desire to write or produce the series Huggins wanted, much less work with him. He was right about our stories, but they were *our* stories, told the way we wanted to tell them. Goldstone and I had kept this series alive and well, in our own fashion. We had a strong audience of loyal followers, millions of viewers, and we had just been renewed for another year.

As soon as I got back to my office I phoned my agent and said, "Get me out of here now. I'm leaving this office as soon as I can collect my stuff. Huggins wants a series I don't want to write or produce. Contract or no contract, I'm the wrong guy for this job."

Dick Goldstone gave me a genuinely sad farewell. "I'm sticking around," he said, "these guys come and go. It will pass."

My fuse was lit. I was in no mood for reason. I was out of the studio by close of business that day. Roy Huggins, superstar-hyphenate, created many highly popular TV series and some of them turned into hugely popular features such as *The Fugitive* and *Maverick.* But *Paradise* was canceled after another season. Huggins created no winners for Fox. I left with no regrets. I had had a two-year run. How many television hyphenates have ever had a chance to experience paradise? I left feeling like a lucky man. I was gaining a reputation as a producer of soft shows, and enjoying it. Obviously, violence is all around us. Being aware of it did not obligate me to devote my creative energy toward creating more of it. The movies were just beginning to lift off into an era of gratuitous ultraviolence and more and more television was pushing the limits far past those of common decency. I figured there ought to be a tiny pocket of civility in our vast wasteland of mayhem and carnage. I was obviously out of step with the American mainstream, which suited me just fine. My views had nothing to do with any high-minded morality or religious convictions (I have none) but were purely a matter of my personal taste.

The Century Plaza Hotel now stands where our sleepy lagoon was once home to this hyphenate's fantasies. You can't brown bag a peanut-butter-and-jelly sandwich at the Century Plaza, but for a few hundred dollars a night you can enjoy whatever fantasies appeal to your taste. L.A.'s posh Century City occupies the entire acreage of what was once Twentieth Century Fox studios back lot. What a loss.

7

Skinny Knows

My agent phoned to tell me that Dick Powell had offered me a one-year contract to write and produce one-hour shows for his *Dick Powell Show*, one of the few remaining anthologies in television. What distinguished this series was Powell as the ongoing host. His was a likable, down-to-earth persona, and he had a rich history as a popular movie star.

This job had a very special attraction for me. I had hoped to meet Dick Powell one day because, like me, he was from Arkansas. He had been a big movie star when I was growing up and the idol of all of us locals. (We all assumed he was a Little Rock boy, though he was actually born in Mountain View.) A "boy tenor," Powell had starred in many Warner Brothers musicals such as *42nd Street, Gold Diggers of 1933, Footlight Parade,* and at least a dozen others. Today they seem ridiculously corny, but to us small-town preteens back then they were movie magic. Even as we mocked his tenor voice and the silly stories he was in, Powell was an awe-inspiring figure. He had made it big in Hollywood, that mythical kingdom far, far, away; a place like Oz that a Little Rock kid could only wonder about.

Powell had morphed from musical comedy tenor of the thirties and early forties into playing tough private eyes. His 1945 performance in *Murder My Sweet* had seized the attention of Hollywood. From baby-faced crooner to hard-boiled private eye was a turnaround nobody expected. But that was only the beginning of this actor's ability to re-create himself. After more tough guy roles, he became a director, then a producer. It was as a television entrepreneur that he evolved from kid tenor to tough business man (which apparently was not role playing). He brought together several other popular stars and created the *Four Star Playhouse,* a rotating half-hour anthology series with Charles Boyer, Ida Lupino, and David Niven. Later other big-name stars were added to the lineup. Powell hosted the series as well as directing several of them, but he was becoming more and more interested in the entrepreneurial aspect of television programming. He was widely regarded as a shrewd businessman who nonetheless maintained his status as a big-name actor-producer, albeit in television. It was a remarkable reinvention of himself.

I reported to Powell's offices on the CBS Studio Center lot in North Hollywood, in the San Fernando Valley. He had hired a top advertising executive, Tom McDermott, as his business affairs manager. Studio Center was a renamed and somewhat renovated updating of the old Republic Studios, site of the filming of many of the old Herbert Yates Westerns, starring the young John Wayne, Roy Rogers, Tom Mix, and others. CBS had added a modern high-rise office building and a couple of soundstages designed for three-camera sitcoms filmed live before studio audiences. Otherwise, it was pretty much the same—dusty, aged studio soundstages standing like testaments to days gone by. Walking around the old buildings one could almost hear the echoes of the horses hooves and the plunking of those "git along little doggie" guitars.

After meeting McDermott on my first day on the new job, I never saw him again, except to glimpse his back as he hurried into offices. After a brief introduction that first day, he had sent me down the hall to meet the boss, Dick Powell.

Seeing Powell seated behind his desk was a bit unsettling. Perhaps I thought he would still be the baby-faced tenor of the Warner musicals of my childhood. But Powell was solidly in middle age,

Movie and TV star Dick Powell *(right)* guest stars on CBS Radio's *Hallmark Hall of Fame,* with producer-director Bill Froug. Later when Froug went to work for the Dick Powell Theater neither remembered they had worked together in radio. (from the author's collection)

thickening at the waist, graying at the temples, wrinkles galore, all the trappings of a man in his late fifties. He was smoking a cigarette, talking on the phone, making deals, oblivious to his newly hired hyphenate. He waved me to take a seat. I waited and waited, as he put out his cigarette and lit another without interrupting his conversation. When he hung up I introduced myself, telling him of my Arkansas background, my schoolmates, and my pride in an Arkansan becoming a big Hollywood star. Even saying it I felt foolish, but the urge to make that connection with my childhood was uncontrollable. Powell was totally disinterested, perhaps even put off by my reminding him of his passing years.

"Let's get down to business," he responded, cutting me off. "I brought you here to write and/or produce segments of our one-hour series. We are open to the idea of buying properties to adapt, but we would prefer original material. Have you any ideas you're working on?"

I told him I did, which was a half-truth. I had some ideas but hadn't done any work on them.

"I have several hyphenates under contract just now and all of you have the same assignment. Come up with good shows. I will play the lead in a couple of them if I like the part, but frankly, I prefer to function as executive producer of this operation. Your office is in the same building as the others. My son, Norman, will show it to you. I trust you will find it satisfactory. I don't mean to seem rude, Bill, but I have a large operation to run and I'm a very busy man." He lit another cigarette and reached for his phone, indicating our conversation was over.

Outside I was greeted by Norman Powell, a warm and friendly young man who resembled his father but was as gracious and welcoming as his father was not.

Settling into my new office, I immediately went to work listing various notions for projects that might be worth developing. Dick Powell had established himself as a no-nonsense boss for whom work was the be-all and end-all. I wondered if he had had an especially hard climb getting to the top. Certainly his credits as star or co-star in more than sixty movies, and his outstanding success in making the transition from movies to television stardom both as personality and independent producer, seemed, at least on the surface, a smooth rocket to the top. But appearances and reality are often a great distance from one another. This is especially true in Hollywood where creating make-believe looks easy but is very difficult to bring off successfully.

My fellow hyphenates generally remained in their small offices. Next door to me was Richard Alan Simmons, a Canadian from Toronto, who was already known as an extraordinarily talented writer. (He had written an outstanding *Adventures in Paradise* teleplay I had produced. I vividly remember his story to this day.)

A hapless agent had dropped by my office with a coverless copy of that teleplay, claiming he represented an exciting new talent who had written it. The cover with its credits on it "had been lost" was the ridiculous explanation. I couldn't believe the guy hadn't even bothered to note that I had produced the same Richard Alan Simmons teleplay on *Adventures in Paradise.* It was a rare instance of an attempted con that was doomed from the start. However, wannabe con artists are not rare in Hollywood, and many succeed.

Simmons's new script, "The Price of Tomatoes" for the *Dick Powell Show,* would win Peter Falk an Emmy. Simmons was far and away the most talented of the lot of us. He soon developed a screenwriting career. It is a characteristic of most professional writers that we don't talk about what we are writing while we are in the process of doing it. This is not because we fear another writer will steal our stuff, but rather because we don't want to dissipate our energy verbally, when we need it for the actual writing. In truth there is not nearly as much thievery in Hollywood as many imagine. What few conversations we did have were in the commissary at lunch. There were rare moments when we would gossip about a fellow hyphenate who kept himself apart from the rest of us. We were actually somewhat dismissive of him as well as his talent because his scripts tended to be corny, old fashioned, and empty of ideas. Aaron Spelling was such a loner, which seemed odd in our busy workaday world. He did not hobnob with his fellow hyphenates. Indeed, he remained aloof.

Spelling, a young actor-turned-writer from Texas, arrived at the studio each day in a long black limousine. His chauffeur stopped the car directly in front of our office building, so each of us glancing out of our office windows overlooking the building entrance could see his arrival. As he got out of the limo, his then wife, actress Carolyn Jones, would sometimes follow him holding their French poodle as she and Spelling bid a theatrical farewell to each other. It appeared to be a staged ceremony for our benefit. It was noteworthy because none of us were driven to work by a chauffeur with all the movie-star trappings. Spelling created the distinct impression that he was superior to the rest of us journeymen. And, as it turned out, in terms of income, he was right. Aaron Spelling was, and remains, in a world entirely of his own creation. Yet to the rest of us ordinary mortals at Dick Powell's company, Aaron Spelling became a sort of an inside joke worth a couple of laughs over lunch at the commissary.

Fellow hyphenate Walter Doniger dropped by my office with a teleplay he had written about a World War II bomber crew, asking if I would read it and produce it for him. He wanted to direct it and didn't want to do both. He was already working on another script.

I read his script, liked it, and agreed to produce it. It turned out to be a good, if not outstanding, show. Powell was happy with it, and we all understood this was our first goal.

I began to work in earnest on my own spy story. During my radio days I had liked to experiment with two-character scripts, a man and a woman inadvertently caught up together in difficult and conflicting circumstances from which they could not extricate themselves. It had been a successful platform for thirty-minute radio plays and I wondered how far I could take it in a one-hour format.

My story was about an American CIA agent traveling by train to London on a secret mission. I liked the privacy and feel of European trains, so I decided that after my spy was seated, a woman would join him with a ticket for the seat directly across from him, facing one another. She was a British spy. I would play the story as a cat-and-mouse game. Each suspecting the other, each on similar but conflicting missions unknown to the other. It would be a play about secrets within secrets between two people dedicated to their work but sexually attracted to one another. I was determined to write a script that would compel my boss, Dick Powell, to play the lead.

When I finished I had a seemingly simple premise with a complicated backstory worked out, and the writing went well. My usual style is to let my characters lead me into unexpected directions. I like to be surprised by my own stories. If I'm not, there's a good chance they're boring. I try to avoid that by making only a few important story notes before starting, rather than a detailed outline, leaving plenty of room for improvisation. If I'm surprised by the turns the story takes, maybe the audience will be too. Writing by the numbers bores me to distraction; I begin to think of other things I'd rather be doing.

When the story was completed, I took the teleplay to Dick Powell with the comment that I hoped he would consider playing the lead.

"I don't know," Powell replied warily, drawing on his cigarette with another one still burning in his ashtray, "I really don't feel I'm looking good enough to get in front of a camera anymore."

No doubt emboldened by my confidence in the script I said, "You're going to kill yourself smoking two cigarettes at the same time."

Powell shrugged, "So my doctor tells me." Then he added tersely, indicating my script, "I'll run it by Skinny to see what he thinks." He made it clear that he did not wish to elaborate on who Skinny was.

A few days later I was summoned back to Dick Powell's office. Chain-smoking his Camels as usual, he had my script open on his desk.

"I like it, so does Skinny. I'll play the lead."

"Who is Skinny?" I felt bold enough to ask him.

"Skinny is Aaron Spelling. I don't do any script without running it by Aaron first." No doubt seeing my look of surprise he felt compelled to explain.

"You see, Aaron started out with me, writing the introductions to our *Four Star Playhouse* series, and he did them so exceptionally well that I asked him to let me read one of his scripts. I did and liked it. Over these last few years I've learned to trust his judgment. I find his opinions invaluable. The fact is, Skinny *knows*." Powell's private phone rang, with a look of annoyance he answered, "Sweetheart, I'm in a meeting." He pleaded, "Junie, darling, I can't talk to you now. You know I love you, sweetheart, can't I please call you back? I've got to go, darling, goodbye, sweetheart, love you, talk soon." His was no longer the voice of the hard driving CEO. He hung up the phone and glanced somewhat sheepishly at me, "My wife. You know how it is?"(He was married to former MGM star June Allyson.)

"I did know," I replied. "I'm divorced."

"Who do you see for the girl?" he said, snapping back into his business voice.

"Hazel Court," I answered, "a British actress, she's been in a lot of BBC productions. There is film available on her. She's the most beautiful woman I've seen in a very long time, and she has a lovely understated English style," I told him. "Her agent says she's available but we'll have to fly her in from London."

"Arrange for me to see her film, and I'll get back to you," he responded.

Two days later I received a call from Powell, "I agree with you about Hazel Court," he said. "Have business affairs make a deal and after you have it settled, we'll go into production. Talk to Norman. I'd like to get going on this one, I haven't been feeling too well lately."

Within two weeks, I received a phone call from Hazel Court's agent saying she'd just arrived in town from London and suggested she and I have a lunch. We agreed on a time and place.

The following week I walked across the street to the Polynesian restaurant where we hyphenates often took our guests to lunch. When I entered the dimly lit restaurant, I saw this extraordinarily beautiful redhead seated in a booth facing the entrance. As I hurried across the room to greet her, a tall, very handsome redheaded man stepped out of the shadows, hand extended, with a huge grin on his face.

"Hi," he said, with a smile too big. "I'm Don Taylor. Thanks so very much for bringing my fiancée in from London."

I recognized him at once. He had been one of MGM's young contract players. When I mentioned I'd seen his work, he said, "That's me, all right, I'm the guy who gave Elizabeth Taylor her first screen kiss."

The three of us had a delightful lunch and began a close friendship that was to last many years until I moved out of Los Angeles.

The show came off rather well; I was pleased that Powell and Court seemed to have some on-screen chemistry. Powell was pleased with it, so was Court. Powell later thanked me for bringing her in for the show.

Dick Powell's belief in the infallibility of Aaron Spelling proved more prescient than I suspect even he might have imagined. Alas, Powell died in 1963 at the age of fifty-nine of lung cancer and did not live to see the full magnitude of Spelling's success.

It has been said with some justification that Aaron Spelling single-handedly created the third network, the American Broadcasting Company. ABC was having problems competing with the twin giants, NBC and CBS, until they made a deal with Spelling to provide one or more new series every season. He did, and every one of Spelling's shows became an immediate hit.

Spelling's uncanny ability to produce winning series after winning series for all networks is unmatched in the history of broadcasting. In short order, he presented *Dynasty, The Love Boat, Charlie's Angels, The Mod Squad, Sunset Beach, Titans, Hart to Hart, Beverly Hills 90210, Melrose Place, Burke's Law,* and *Malibu Shores,* more series than any other entertainment company in history. Spelling has produced or been directly involved in almost *two hundred* television series and motion pictures. He rarely misfires; almost all of his company's television series become hits. He has not, however, had the same degree of success with his features.

For several years, Spelling's *Charlie's Angels* was my rent-money series. Between producing gigs, I'd write a *Charlie's Angels* episode. It was good pay for a week's work. We all approached this series as a bubble-headed comedy where corny puns were the substitute for wit. One evening at a Writers Guild meeting I ran into affable Ben Roberts. Roberts, along with his highly successful screenwriter partner Ivan Goff, had created *Charlie's Angels* and sold it to Spelling. I got the distinct impression from Roberts that, after seeing what the boob tube was showing, he and his partner created *Charlie's Angels* as a what-the-hell-it's-only-TV idea. Although many of us privately pissed on the medium, all of us enjoyed the bounty it brought us.

What is the secret of Spelling's remarkable success? What Aaron likes, the American public and, indeed, the entire world likes. He has what is sometimes called a "golden gut." But there is another factor that can't be overlooked. Success breeds success.

Producers with projects take them to a company that has a track record of producing successful shows. Thus, just by being Aaron Spelling, his staff has only to filter through the truckloads full of material, metaphorically speaking, that are unloaded at his office every week. He has readers whose sole function is to sort the wheat from the chaff. (The truth is that 99.5 percent of unsolicited material is chaff and the remainder is worthwhile—and that may be a generous estimate.) When you read what comes in from the public, you are reminded that what the professionals are doing night and day is sheer genius by comparison. There is a false idea that there exists a great untapped well of undiscovered creative talent, writing, acting, directing, and so on, hidden in various places in these United States. There isn't. Those with the unquenchable urge to express themselves creatively through the performing arts eventually make their way to places and cities where opportunities exist to show their wares. The cream still rises to the top.

Those of us who have spent many years evaluating artistic talent know what a rare gift outstanding talent is. For a further understanding of the reality, ask yourself how many truly gifted doctors, lawyers, or teachers you've encountered? Only in Lake Wobegon are all the children above average. Average (by definition, mediocrity) is all around us. We are swimming in a sea of it. That is the answer to the question of why is television predominantly "a vast wasteland"?

There is simply too much of it, too many hours of the day on too many channels, and there are not nearly enough talented people in the world to feed the insatiable appetite of the medium with original, outstanding work. The entire works of Shakespeare could be presented in one season on one channel, and then what do you do after wet T-shirt wrestling . . . watch a tank of swimming tropical fish, as the Danes do during station breaks?

My father liked to tell me (quoting H. L. Mencken), "nobody ever went broke underestimating the taste of the American public." Except for the news, my father loathed most of television. Mencken has been proven right most of the time on the TV screen, seven days and nights a week, but audiences couldn't care less what the Bard of Baltimore had to say. Worldwide, people of all age groups, rich and poor alike, remain tuned in to TV many hours of every day. Paradoxically, the public can become transfixed by countless hours of around-the-clock mindless crap and then become unexpectedly interested in programs of good taste and high quality. (Public broadcasting survives by addressing its programs to the discerning minority largely ignored by the networks.) What the public wants on a higher level, we have hyphenates Norman Lear, Aaron Sorkin, and Steven Bochco to consistently provide it. Their work also reflects their own quality tastes. Giants likes these men are all too few and far between.

In a recent interview the president of NBC was asked if, starting from scratch, he could present an entirely new program schedule and how would he begin? "Give me thirty-nine Aaron Sorkins," he replied. But there is, of course, only one and only one *West Wing, Sports Night, American President,* and *A Few Good Men.* Sorkin is in a class by himself.

In my experience, most producers produce programs or films that they themselves would like to see, while hoping for mass appeal. At least the wise producer does. If their taste happens to coincide with the taste of the majority of the public, they will succeed beyond their wildest dreams; if not, they have to settle for less.

Far and away, the most successful producer in the history of television is Aaron Spelling. He loves his shows as much as audiences love them; he's as big a fan as any of his fans.

I knew Spelling casually in those early days when he would boast his personal taste was more elevated than his shows suggested. He presented himself as a man of much greater sophistication than his audience. But with the enormity of his success, he has come to a point in his life where the critics' frequent negative judgments of his shows are meaningless to him. (What he thinks in private could be another matter altogether.) Maybe if you were worth a billion dollars you would ignore their judgment as well.

In his early days in Hollywood Spelling was a quiet, unassuming, even shy, man with a soft Texas accent. He said he grew up a poor boy in Dallas and he came to Hollywood to become an actor. He and I were among the founding members of the Hyphenates Lobby, which turned into the Caucus for Producers, Writers, and Directors. Like me, Aaron was a long-time member of its executive committee. We were both on the Producers Guild Board of Directors as well, and I rarely missed a meeting during the twelve years I served. Spelling rarely attended a meeting. He was busy becoming Aaron Spelling, and it was not an easy job. He has worked tirelessly to achieve his pinnacle position in Hollywood.

The last time I saw him was at a general membership meeting of the Producers Guild of America. He came walking down the aisle, skinny as always, his close-cropped gray hair dyed orange. Maybe he was making a billion-dollar statement. Naturally, gossip about Spelling has never suffered from want of material.

One of my favorites was the story of his building his mansion in the flatlands of Beverly Hills. It was alleged that when this incredible edifice was under construction, Spelling's wife Candy was looking out the framed-in window one day and complained she could see the sign of a nearby department store in downtown Beverly Hills. Spelling, so it's been said, immediately ordered the building taken down, the foundation raised a few feet, then construction started all over again so his wife would have a better view. The cost of this mansion, which is said to contain a bowling alley as well as a large ballroom, was several millions of dollars. All of these rumors only add to the Aaron Spelling lore of Tinseltown.

Closer to home, I once dated a beautiful young Italian actress who said she had been engaged to Spelling. She told me of his screaming night terrors that drove her to break off the engagement. Her descriptions were graphic. Can a man with success beyond all imaginings and worth a billion dollars be miserable in private? Of course not. Her story must have been nonsense.

However, only Skinny knows.

8

Bombs on the Left,
Cannon on the Right

In April 1962 I was asked by my old college roommate, E. Jack
Neuman, to produce *Sam Benedict,* an MGM Television one-
hour series for NBC. Neuman had created, written, and produced the pilot, which NBC bought with an extraordinary order for
thirty-five new episodes.

The network had slotted the program for Saturday night opposite CBS's *Jackie Gleason Show*—a suicide time slot. The network
called this counterprogramming, but there was no way a serious
drama series about a high-powered lawyer could steal an audience
from the popular comic.

But I had signed on because I liked Jack's pilot, and I wanted to
work with my old buddy again. Our paths had rarely crossed since I
had roomed with Jack and his mother back in 1946, when we had
collaborated on radio scripts. Since our radio-writing days our careers and our personal lives had gone in different directions; we had
seen little of one another. Yet we knew our friendship was lifelong.

Jack asked me to produce his series because he preferred to write.
He also realized that producing thirty-five new one-hour episodes in

a little less than six months would be an enormous undertaking (it came close to taking *me* under before the season was over). He needed a pro, as he put it, and we had always enjoyed an excellent working relationship.

Going back to work at MGM still held the same thrill of working for Hollywood's most illustrious studio, only now I wasn't merely working in Yankee Stadium, I was now *playing* for the Yankees. My disastrous experience with Mark Goodson did not dim my happy memories of the glorious ghosts of my movie-going youth. I was to lunch for the next couple of years at the MGM commissary, sometimes sitting at the table the waitresses proudly told me was where Clark Gable used to sit. It was clear that the movie magic of glories past rubbed off on everyone who worked there, including me. I had my haircut in the MGM barber shop in the chair where Spencer Tracy had his haircut, at least so the barber said. (Stars generally had their hair styled by a specialist, but who was I to contradict a romantic?) The shoeshine man, when prompted, proudly told of shining the shoes of stars Van Johnson, Walter Pidgeon, Gene Kelly, and Frank Sinatra, momentarily reliving the moments of his glory past. I understood that most of these tales were imaginary, but it mattered little. I was thrilled to be in the Kingdom of Let's Pretend. Metro-Goldwyn-Mayer was the ultimate dream factory. I never lost my feeling of excitement and privilege of being able to work on the MGM lot. As we may have learned from our experiences with President Bill Clinton, you can take the kid out of Little Rock, but you can never take Little Rock out of the kid.

One day at the commissary as Neuman and I were having lunch, Jack invited famed screenwriter William Bowers to join us. Bowers had been nominated for Academy Awards for both *The Gunfighter* and *The Sheepman*. Jack and Bowers were friends, so naturally he asked Bowers if he'd write an episode of *Sam Benedict*.

"Not on your life," Bowers replied, laughing. "Leonard Hanser would have me for lunch."

"Well," Jack urged him, "at least ask him."

"I already did," Bowers replied, chuckling. "You know what he told me? 'My clients don't *do* television!' He said it like he meant we don't do windows," Bowers explained, laughing. We all understood that Hanser, perhaps the premier screenwriter's agent in Hollywood, believed if his clients wrote a TV episode for very little money, it would not only undermine their status but hurt his bargaining position when negotiating for them as screenwriters. Television episode writers received $4,500 per episode in those days for a one-hour show. Today it is more than quadruple that amount. However, Bowers's established price for a screenplay was $100,000, even then. Today it would be it least $1 million or more.

Major Talent Agency was founded shortly after World War II by army paratroop major Leonard Hanser, or the "little major" as some called him. Hanser stood an inch or two above five feet tall in his GI boots. On the Fourth of July he always gave a chili-recipe contest party. Big stars would come bringing their chili in hopes of winning recognition. The party gave Hanser a chance to dress up in his army paratrooper uniform sporting his major's oak leaves and his battle ribbons. He stood in the driveway entrance to his huge backyard, in full dress gear and polished boots, wearing his pistols à la General George Patton.

Hanser was widely considered the toughest negotiator in the business. He managed to corral a client list of the finest screenwriters in Hollywood, and he liked to crack the whip on them as well as the companies with whom he was negotiating.

Bowers had received a writing credit on more than twenty movies, but he was also widely known as a great raconteur. Telling Hollywood tales seemed to be his obsession, and he was very good at it. His stories always began the same way, "Did I ever tell you about the time that I . . . ?" It was likely you'd heard the story before, but it didn't matter, the fun was in Bower's own great joy in his telling. Bowers had a well-worn face with deep pouches under his eyes and a perpetual hangdog look. His strong Missouri twang growled like an out-of-tune banjo and lent a special quality to his yarns. This acclaimed screenwriter loved Hollywood and its craziness more than any other man I ever met.

Bowers was only about five years older than Neuman and I me. Like us, he had attended the University of Missouri. Following graduation he went to New York, sold a Broadway play, and became a wunderkind. Soon he was offered a job in Hollywood. He fell head over heels in love with the business and, unfortunately, with alcohol. "I became the town's leading drunk," he would boast. "But not anymore. I use Antibuse; it's this tiny, little pill I take every day because it tells me if I drink I'll die."

Jack and I needed to get back to work, but Bowers was working on a screenwriter's schedule: deliver four pages a week and you're okay. We were working on television time: write ten pages a day and you're okay. Bowers drank coffee by the gallon, apparently replacing alcohol addiction with caffeine addiction. Once Bowers was on a storytelling roll, no force on earth could stop him.

"Did I ever tell you about the time Rod Serling asked me what pilots call that time of day when it's too light to use instruments but not light enough to rely on visuals? That's what we call the twilight zone, I told him. So, who knows, maybe I'm the guy who named Rod's show? Of course he never thanked me, so maybe I didn't. I used to be an army air force pilot, you know. One night during landing practices the fence on the cow pasture next to our base landing strip went down. Horses and cows were all over the landing strip. While landing, I ran into a horse! Damn near killed me. When they got to me the cockpit was covered with blood, not mine, thank God, the horse's. Who else could fly a plane into a horse! I was pretty banged up. I've still got the scars to show for it. Don't run off, guys, let's have another cup of coffee."

"So anyway," Bowers continued, even though Neuman and I were now standing, checks in hand, "one day I decided to ignore that little pill and I took a drink. Put me in the hospital. I damn near died. I've never been so sick in my life. So now I take the damn thing every day and believe me, guys, I never touch a drop. Did I ever tell you about the time . . . ?"

"Sorry, Bowers," Jack said, as he and I were leaving the table, "we've got a screening of the pilot in about two minutes."

For a new series like *Sam Benedict* we began by screening the pilot in one of MGM's many projection rooms for a carefully chosen half-dozen writers, followed by a brief talk about how we saw the series going, then a Q-and-A about the kinds of stories we were looking for and how we wanted to develop the characters.

Sam Benedict was loosely (very loosely) based on the career of

Jake Erlich, a flamboyant, high-powered, much-publicized San Francisco attorney. Sam was played by the well-known character actor Edmond O'Brien, who had won a Best Supporting Actor Oscar for his work as a press agent in *Beat the Devil*. Eddie was a nice, unpretentious guy, hard working, always on time, knew his lines, and gave his best. It was clear from our first meeting that Eddie would be a pleasure to work with, a charming, self-effacing, good-natured man, or so it appeared at the beginning.

Neuman, as the show's creator, was executive producer, the boss. In the course of developing the show, Jack and Jake Erlich had developed a jovial camaraderie based upon mutual respect.

Erlich had obtained from Neuman the right to approve and consult on every script. So part of my job was going to be to commute to San Francisco every week, sit down with Jake in his office law library, and go over the current preproduction teleplay with him line by line, scene by scene. This was after the script had been rewritten and finally polished by me and/or Jack and our story editor. In defense of the freelance writers, it must be said that none of us can get inside the heads of the hyphenates running a series. Only they know exactly what they're looking for.

Neuman had hired as story editor Joseph "Doc" Calvelli, a delightful little five-by-five guy with a huge smile, easy laugh, and a sense of humor bigger than he was. He was called Doc because, when he and his father, a doctor, walked down the street, people would say, "Hello big Doc and little Doc."

Jack, Doc, and I got along wonderfully from the start. We lunched together almost every day and talked stories. (Actually we talked stories many hours of every day.) What kind of cases would be interesting and challenging? How could we get Sam Benedict deeply involved in them? Sam was not primarily a criminal attorney, which was a mixed blessing. We could avoid all the Perry Mason clichés, Sam as detective, and the like. Civil cases were his field and they had to pique his interest. We wanted personal stories.

Shortly after I signed my contract with MGM Television in April 1962 I was invited to a dinner party by one of their brass. The evening was quite formal and stuffy, but I got to sit next to the famous concert pianist and MGM star Oscar Levant. He was also a composer and the leading interpreter of the music of his friend George Gershwin. Levant was routinely cast in movie musicals (such as *An American in Paris*) playing an urbane, witty, mordant cynic. He wisely didn't try to act. He usually played himself, at which he was at best adequate. Levant ended his career hosting a Los Angeles local TV series. He sat at the piano and amused the public by being himself, rarely playing the piano but telling stories about himself, a talented but hypochondriacally neurotic, seemingly freaked-out concert pianist. Sitting next to him for an evening, I can personally attest that he was in fact a hypochondriacally neurotic, seemingly freaked-out concert pianist. His conversation focused on how many shrinks he had seen and the long list of medications he was on. "I take more pills than there are keys on the piano," he boasted to me as he jiggled in his seat, his shoulders twitching, his eyes blinking constantly. He was, in a word, a mess. But he was a great storyteller, and he was funny.

Oscar Levant story: "You know, every summer George Gershwin and I took the *Super Chief* to New York for the annual Gershwin Concert in Central Park (I played the piano, of course). So George and I are getting on the *Super Chief* from L.A. to Chicago; we go into our stateroom and I toss my bag on the upper berth. George comes in behind me and says, 'No, no, Oscar, upper berth genius, lower berth talent.' So I take my bag off the upper berth and throw it on the lower berth; he then puts his bag on the upper berth. And he was right actually. I'm just an outstandingly brilliant concert pianist, but George was a genius. The guy was the rarest creature in Hollywood, a genius who actually *was* a genius. Every trip thereafter I assigned myself the lower berth. I really liked George, a very nice guy. Go to a party where George was also a guest and, with no coaxing at all, he would head for the piano. An evening with Gershwin was an evening *of* Gershwin. The guy practically invented the 'and then I wrote . . .' routine. He could go on for hours without repeating himself . . . and did."

It was no surprise that I was going to spend much of my time on *Sam Benedict* at my typewriter hunched over a keyboard rewriting scripts. As every hyphenate knows, our trade guarantees shoulder-muscle aches as the price of doing business. I had heard stories of the legendary MGM chiropractor, Doc Mitchell. He was reported to be one of MGM's oldest and most successful employees. So as scripts that needed working on began to come in, I decided to get an early read on Mitchell's alleged magical manipulations. It turned out that his treatments came with an added bonus.

The best storyteller of them all was Mitchell, whom studio chief Louie B. Mayer himself had installed in a wood-paneled suite of offices on the top floor of the Thalberg Building. Doc told me that one day while taking a driving trip Louie B. found himself in Riverside, California, with an aching back, so in searching out help he came across Mitchell's office. So happy was Mayer with the results of his treatment that he offered the chiropractor a job on the spot. He would pay Mitchell's moving expenses, install him in splendid offices at the studio, pay him a handsome salary, and guarantee him that he would be treating the most famous movie stars in the world.

"I couldn't pass it up," old Doc told me, "I packed my bags the next day."

When I was his patient, back in '62, he must have been in his late seventies, yet he was lean, muscular, and vigorous. As he worked on me he told me tales.

"Mr. Mayer was a sly character," he said, "he insisted only his secretary could make my appointments. It was in my contract. Over time I learned why. One day Clark Gable phoned me for an appointment. He was in terrible pain having hurt his back on a picture. I explained Mr. Mayer's policy. Gable had to phone Mayer's secretary to get an appointment."

According to Doc, a few minutes later Gable called back, "That son of a bitch won't let me see you until I sign a new contract," Gable yelled. "I oughta kill the son of a bitch."

Doc Mitchell was indeed a master of manipulation. A couple of sessions with him and I was able to return to my desk, pain free, my head filled with MGM lore.

Lou Gray, the head of television production for MGM and a long-time veteran of features, dropped by my office to introduce himself and offer his services. Lou was a delightful gray-haired, very soft-spoken little man who knew the Metro lots (there were three) like the back of his hand. He suggested that I set aside some time to walk the back lots with him and look at sets. He told me he would read each week's script and suggest sets Metro already had available that might suit a particular episode to save the cost of building a new one.

Our budget for each episode (almost all of TV was broadcast in black and white in those days) of the one-hour series was $185,000 (in 2005 dollars that would not finance a thirty-second commercial), which included an MGM overhead charge (about 15 percent of the entire budget). In addition, MGM, like the other Hollywood studios, charged an overhead fee for each department used in the series (i.e., for the makeup department, camera department, wardrobe, set construction, casting, editing, and so forth), then added the overall production fee on top. Every series shooting at MGM paid the same overhead fees plus each department's overhead charge. Our budget was also being charged for every set we used. Multiply this times the half-dozen series shooting on the lot using the same facilities and services, and you begin to understand why making television series for the networks was turning into a gold mine for the Hollywood studios.

One afternoon on one of our walking tours Gray said, "I thought maybe you might find some terrific standing sets worth writing stories around." I thought that an unlikely possibility until one day I happened to look into a great soundstage and see a particularly lavish set with a winding stairway, a two-story enormous living room. A home of the most wealthy. I told Lou that I would keep it in mind for future use; maybe we could write a story involving a very wealthy client of Sam Benedict. "Don't do it," Lou replied, "This set is reserved for feature films."

Thus I learned that while Metro had finally gotten its foot in the door in television, the company was not ready to fully embrace the enemy. Again and again, Lou would respond to my interest in particular locations with the comment, "Yes, it's very nice, my boy, but it's for features only."

"But here's another one I think you might like to see," Lou added, leading me toward one of the biggest soundstage of all these giant soundstages. The great doors were open and looking in I saw a truly amazing sight. Here on the stage floor, tilted at about a twenty-degree angle was a vast sand-colored, roughly textured Mount Rushmore! There, laid out before me were the faces of the great presidents, dead ringers for the real thing. It was an extraordinary example of movie magic.

"Hitchcock used it for *North by Northwest,*" Lou told me. "It's built to about a hundredth scale or maybe much less. It doesn't matter because in the movie you can't tell it from the real thing. The reason is that when you go to a movie you *want to believe* what you're seeing on screen is the real thing. If we're doing our job, we've got you from the minute you sit down to watch the show. Can't you just see Cary Grant and Eva Marie Saint scrambling over the faces of the presidents on Mount Rushmore as they're trying to escape the bad guys?" I could, indeed. It's film's first and foremost trick: creating the audience's willing suspension of disbelief. It must start with the first foot of film.

"I don't think you'd have much use for it," Lou said, "but even if you did, I'm certain the studio wouldn't allow television to use it."

Lou, always accommodating and sweet natured, insisted on completing the walking tour out the back gate, across busy Overland Avenue onto Lot number 2, which was very different from Lot number 1. Here we had the generic city square, the town hall, a park, store fronts, a barber shop, beauty shop, candy store, and the like. Not far away, around the corner was a lovely neighborhood with a tree-lined street, which I recognized immediately as where Andy Hardy lived. There was his house, fronted by a white picket fence, lawn and garden, ready to move in.

"We call this the Andy Hardy Street," said Lou, proudly, "there's been many a picture shot here, not just for Andy Hardy. It's the ideal neighborhood for Everytown, USA. Did it ever occur to you," Lou continued, "that a few Jewish immigrants from the old country created the America that every *goy* thinks is his birthright?"

One glorious spring afternoon I drove alone, top down, out Overland south toward LAX to Lot number 3. It was completely different from Lots 1 and 2 but just as impressive. Here was the classic movie-western street, only bigger and better. But driving farther into the lot I came to a startling sight—a cobblestone street bordering a graceful curving row of Victorian homes with manicured lawns and hitching posts for the horses! It was the *Meet Me in St. Louis* street, St. Louis, circa 1900. Judy Garland in one of her many great roles, singing "Clang, clang, clang, went the trolley!" and "I just adore the boy next door." If you've seen the movie, you've seen this magnificent set. Driving along this street I felt what it must have been like to be in St. Louis for the 1900 Exposition. No, I actually felt I *was* there. It was a magical, thrilling, moment.

Having worked on three of the major Hollywood studio lots, it became obvious to me why Metro was, indeed, the crown jewel of Hollywood. It wasn't merely their roster of movie stars.

Driving on I came to a small harbor dock where a steamboat from the MGM classic musical *Showboat* was moored facing a realistic waterfront town, which, of course, was only a one-dimensional wooden facade. The harbor was designed so that the "Mississippi River" leading into it was around a curved bend with no end in sight. All outdoor locations always end in a curve around which your imagination tells you where the rest of the river, town, or city lies. Your mind wants to believe it's really there. In movies, as in radio, the imagination of the audience must become a willing partner in the deception. And it does, unless the deception is too crude, as sometimes happens in low-low-budget movies.

I told Doc about the steamboat and suggested he drive out and take a look. Calvelli later wrote an episode in which we used this remarkable set.

At lunch, Jack talked about an episode he was planning to write. Doc and I did the same. So that meant we were sure of three of the thirty-five scripts we needed. We settled into our own offices to write, oblivious to the ceaselessly ringing phones. Agents were calling all day, every day, selling writers, selling directors, selling actors, or just selling their agency, just in case we found a new talent who needed an agent.

Simultaneously I was booking directors for some of our thirty-five episodes. By now, I had seen the work of very many and knew who I wanted for the series. Good directors were in such demand that they came in only to shoot their episode, then moved on to another series. They were rarely involved in casting, viewing either dailies or a so-called director's cut. They were generally off to direct another TV series episode on some other lot. The good ones were usually booked solid. Thus both the pre- and postproduction chores fell to me. Today these chores are handled by assigned postproduction personnel.

I had the MGM carpenter shop make me a big production chart and mount it on my office wall with blank spaces for episodes one through thirty-five, boxes in which to fill in episode titles, the writer, the director, and, of course, the airdates.

Bill Bowers dropped by my office to insist we have lunch at the commissary and, during the meal, brought up the idea of reestablishing "the writers table" there. Bowers was a man who would not take no for an answer. He said that he was going to try to recruit every writer working at MGM to convince them to become regulars. He could not seem to grasp that we were working under a high-pressure television deadline. The concept was unimaginable to him. He not only didn't do television, he had never done television. He had an insatiable appetite for socializing and telling his fascinating tales of the old days. For him, the whole scene was Disneyland for grown-ups. He had been an enthusiastic player since he left the University of Missouri.

Once we were seated in the commissary, he started: "Writers used to sit at tables according to their salaries," Bowers told me, "Seven-hundred-and-fifty-dollar-a-week writers sat over there," he indicated a table across the room. "You and I are sitting at what used to be the thousand-dollar-a-week writers' table. Don't you feel more talented, already?" he added, laughing. "It's not that we weren't friendly with each other, we were. But there was this pecking order everybody just sort of slipped into."

Bowers was a man you could not possibly dislike—a genuine, open, gregarious soul with no hidden agenda, a rarity in Hollywood. With his big Missouri drawl and his laughter recalling his own adventures, he had the ability to make his stories last the entire lunch and keep you laughing.

One of my favorite Bowers tales was his story about how he came to rewrite *Night and Day,* the life of Cole Porter.

Bowers had been under contract to Columbia Pictures when, one day, two writers, Charles Townsend and Charles Hoffman, appeared at his office with an intriguing problem. They had signed on to write composer Cole Porter's life story. But they told Bowers they couldn't lick it and they wanted his help.

He read the draft they gave him and saw the problem at once. Porter was born a wealthy man, he graduated from Yale, married his college sweetheart, and started writing hit song after hit song. Soon his wealth increased from being a millionaire to being a multimillionaire. Porter's was seemingly a carefree life of fame and luxury. Bowers told them he wanted no part of this picture because he couldn't see a way to fix the problem. (In 1946 nobody dared mention Porter's homosexuality.) It was boring. Noted character-actor Gregory Ratoff was scheduled to direct *Night and Day.* He summoned Bowers to his office.

"Dun't tell me, Beel?" the heavily Russian accented Ratoff shouted at Bowers, "You are refusing to rewrite my peekchure!"

Bowers said he told Ratoff he couldn't save the script; it was a story without conflict. Porter's life was a progression from being born wealthy to becoming internationally famous and even wealthier. "It's a bore, there's no conflict," he told Ratoff.

"No conflict!" shouted Ratoff, who apparently could not speak in anything softer than a shout. "Vell, my boy, you mess de point! Dis is a story about a great American songwriter who is born with *seex* million dollars, then graduates collitch, marries the girl of his dreams, writes "Night and Day," "Begin the Begun," "I Got Chew Under My Skin," "Chew're de Tups," and mebbe a hundred more of the best songs ever wreeton. Dis iz a story of a man born with a seelver spoon in his mouth, who marries his childhood sweetheart, writes heet song afta heet songs, and becomes worth *four hundred meelion dollars.* Can't you see, Beel, it's a story of *struggle, struggle, struggle!*"

Bowers said he laughed so hard he agreed to rewrite the screenplay. "That Ratoff was funny, but he was a good director.

"And then, wouldn't you know?" Bowers continued, "Ratoff left the picture and Michael Curtiz took over. Mike and I got along fine but nobody was as funny as Greg Ratoff, especially when he was being serious.

"Did you see the picture?" he asked me, but before I could answer, he was off and running. "Well, I thought it was just terrible. The next time I was in New York I called Oscar Hammerstein and said, 'Oscar will you ask Cole Porter to please have dinner with me; I want to apologize for that terrible movie.'

"So Cole and I had dinner at the Stork Club. He was a very nice man, you know. I called Oscar the next day and told him, 'Can you believe this; Cole Porter liked the picture!'

"'Of course he did,' Oscar told me, 'why wouldn't he? The movie had about thirty or forty of his most popular songs. And Cary Grant was playing him. What was there about it he wouldn't like, Bowers?'

"I guess I've got no taste," concluded Bowers, "but I thought it was a terrible movie, just terrible."

When I returned to my office I found Neuman hunched over his keyboard writing, a Camel cigarette burning in his ashtray. I was horrified by the thought of my chain-smoking buddy constantly inhaling this stuff into his tuberculosis-scarred lungs. However, my lectures fell on deaf ears. Jack had made it clear from the start that he intended to spend his time writing or rewriting episodes, which he did while sitting behind his enormous desk, in his enormous, high-ceilinged office. There were two big couches facing each other in front of an almost walk-in fireplace. This had been the office of the legendary Irving Thalberg during MGM's heyday. Thalberg, who had been the number-two man at MGM under Louis B. Mayer and had invented the role of the hands-on studio producer, was also said to have been the model for F. Scott Fitzgerald's fictional Hollywood producer Monroe Stahr in *The Last Tycoon*.

My small office was across the reception area from Neuman's in our *Sam Benedict* suite. We were at ground level on the main street of the studio. Outside my office window technicians, sets, actors, movie people of every stripe and size moved back and forth all day long. I was facing soundstage 25, where we would be shooting *Sam Benedict*. This was convenient because several times a day I had to go to our stage while we were shooting to confer with our assistant director as well as the actors and the director. For the actors it was either to soothe their nerves or just reassure them that they looked good in the footage I'd seen so far. No matter how professional or how important a star or actor is, their insecurity during a shoot almost always lurks beneath a calm exterior. There is enormous stress in putting your face in front of a big 35mm Mitchell camera as forty to sixty people on the set stand in total silence—staring at you— while hot lights expose your every pore. The film actor gives his or her performance to dead silence and often to little or no response. The experience can be unnerving. Film actors are naked with their clothes on. Small wonder that I was almost constantly being summoned to the set to douse small emotional fires.

We were working in the greatest movie studio of all time, surrounded by glories past, but history was no longer in our minds once production began. We were totally focused on making thirty-five quality episodes of a new one-hour series while meeting our airdates. Airdates were the Sword of Damocles that hung over us every working hour of the day and some nights. When we began shooting we had four months of lead time . . . time to get episodes ready for our premier date, September 15, 1962. It was too late to even think about whether the audience would like our show or not. All we had going for us was our creative instincts ("our guts," as we like to say). Either we would connect with the audience or we wouldn't.

I hired a young assistant to go to the mixing stage and supervise postproduction, but I always went to the music-scoring stage to hear the score for each episode. Jack had hired the extraordinarily talented big-band-era arranger Nelson Riddle (who had scored Jack's pilot). I had been a big fan of his since college when we danced to his arrangements for Tommy Dorsey and his orchestra. Riddle was one of the swing era's top arrangers. However, he insisted on composing romantic dance-band-style music for our dramatic episodes and refused to change it. We had serious disagreements, but I could not dissuade him. It was to be his style or else. He left me no option. After getting Jack's approval, I fired him. Though our paths sometimes later crossed he never spoke to me again. I understood and accepted that as the price of my authority and his pride.

The problem for the television producer is that while these episodes are aired every seven days, each one takes eight or nine days to film. (For many years Hollywood had filmed six day's a week until film unions, after long intensive bargaining, finally won the five-day week.) So although we started early we lost lead time every week; the pressure to produce episodes on schedule was relentless. Everybody who worked on the show felt the enormous weight of it. Once production began we were a high-speed train driving down the track, with no brakes, no stops for refueling or rest. We were at the mercy of the calendar, airdates clicking by every week, followed maddeningly by yet another airdate, and on and on. Everyone working on a television series from secretaries to studio head to stage crew felt the constant pressure. "You guys gonna meet your airdate?" was an ominous question posed to us frequently by the network and studio executives, like inquisitors tightening thumbscrews. We prayed for preemptions, a political event, a national crisis, or anything that would give us a week off the network schedule and a little breathing room . . . but it rarely happened.

Though Metro obviously had mixed feelings about this new upstart medium, they could not allow themselves to be further embarrassed by the other studios. They demanded an MGM movie-quality look to anything that had their logo on it. They assigned our series the very best personnel they had in each department. Our cameraman, our sound man, and members of our crew were of the first rank, and a few were veterans of the glory days of MGM.

A young Don MacEllaine reported to my office to introduce himself as my casting director assigned by MGM to our series. Don quickly proved that he was tops in his field. We clicked from our first meeting. To say that I was impressed by these knowledgeable folks, all of whom knew more about making movies than I did, would be an understatement. I had told MacEllaine I was open to the idea of finding new actors for the series. Thus, one Wednesday, having sold me on the idea, he brought in a slim, teenaged, red-haired girl from San Francisco to audition for us. She was no great beauty, but she was interesting looking, with big searching eyes and a freckled face under that tumble of lush red hair. The reason he had flown her in for the reading was, as he put it, "she has no film," meaning she had never appeared in a feature or on television. We had her read an important jail scene from the upcoming episode. Katherine Ross gave an excellent cold reading, and we cast her without a moment's hesitation. She was later featured in *Butch Cassidy and the Sundance Kid* and *The Graduate,* among many other films.

The older MGM pros were amazed by the new TV people. Lou Gray often expressed his astonishment. "How do you guys do it? You're shooting the equivalent of thirty features in four months!"

We had started production when there was no way we could delay a day longer without missing our airdate. My NBC contact, an executive in their Burbank studios, phoned weekly to ask when he would see story outlines and then later, when would he would see scripts, and later still, when would he see a rough cut? NBC kept the pressure on, always letting me know I worked for the network primarily and only secondarily for MGM, which was not the case. My contract was with Metro, which MGM management wouldn't let me forget, either.

One day as Jack, Doc, and I entered the commissary we passed the check-out counter manned by a cute blonde with a pert nose and a sweet smile named Dottie. Beside her cash register she had placed a white cardboard cylinder with a slit for donations cut in the top. Wrapped around it was a boldly lettered label: HELP STAMP OUT TV. It was the perfect metaphor for the studio's contempt for the new medium that had destroyed their old way of doing business, yet had given them an entirely new, if unwelcome, way of remaining in the film business.

Inside the commissary, lunch business was always booming, the huge room packed with players and extras from *Dr. Kildare, The Man from U.N.C.L.E., The Twilight Zone,* or whatever television series was shooting on the lot. I would guess that at least two-thirds of the customers were working in television. (Television production had long since overtaken feature production. Like it or not, MGM was rapidly becoming a television production studio.) There was the usual assortment of costumed cowhands, nurses, doctors, and the like. The food was good and inexpensive. Though it was noisy and crowded, we felt at home in this milieu and ate there a couple of times a week.

Jack and Doc and I would find an empty table amid the mob and settle in for lunch. The menu never changed: Clark Gable Steak, Judy Garland Salad, Great Garbo Soup, Spencer Tracy Burger, all the big legendary MGM stars were on the menu. If you couldn't see them you could have a taste of them for lunch. Such was the strength of glories past that every studio employee on the lot seemed in denial that it was over and gone, murdered in the first degree by television, aided and abetted by the breakup of the old studio system and the subsequent release of contract players, many of whom were the most famous players in Hollywood. Major stars, no longer under contract to studios, were forming their own independent production companies, leasing studio space on whichever lot gave them the best deal. Hollywood was undergoing radical changes and was not entirely comfortable with the brave new world it faced.

Jack Neuman remained in his huge office most of the day, a dark brooding figure smoking while hunched over his typewriter; pecking away behind his gargantuan desk, working on his own script about which we knew little.

At the end of each day Jack, suddenly jovial, would insist that Doc and I come into his office for drinks. Jack made certain the office had a well-stocked liquor cabinet, if not a bar, and liked having the three of us hang around and laugh about the whole insanity of our business and the work we each did. To work successfully in Hollywood was to understand the madness, absurdity, and difficulty of the entire enterprise.

During production of *Sam Benedict* we encountered a behind-the-scenes human tragedy on a magnitude we could not have imagined. Among the many writers with whom we met was a young man I will call Butler Brewster, a tall, handsome man with credits on many shows. Jack suggested we meet with him and see if he might have any ideas for our series.

When Brewster showed up, we met in Jack's big office. Butler was wearing a suit and tie (most unusual for a writer), and he seemed extremely nervous. His face was bathed in sweat as he fidgeted in his seat. He had a couple of very good story ideas and we gave him the go-ahead to outline one of them on the spot, confirming the deal with his agent after the meeting.

When Brewster's story came in, we liked it and sent it along to NBC for approval, which was quickly granted.

When the time came and went for delivery of the script, I phoned Brewster. He was evasive on the phone, sounding nervous and unsure of himself.

As it turned out, we never saw Brewster's script. He apparently went mad, and murdered his wife and children in a blind rage. He was found not guilty by reason of insanity. He was hospitalized for some years, undergoing extensive psychiatric treatment. When he was released he resumed his successful career writing episodic television and movies for television under a pseudonym. Anybody doubting the stress of making a living fighting the deadly television deadlines need only look to Brewster's extreme example.

On the other hand, we had writers like George Eckstein, a lawyer who became one of our best contributors. Eckstein later became a hyphenate and produced several popular series including the famous made-for-television movie *Duel,* which was Steven Spielberg's directorial debut.

Neuman often made a last-minute decision to hold up a script for further rewrites, which Doc and I had thought was ready to shoot. He sloughed me off when I reminded him we had to get the script to NBC for approval, as well as to Jake Erlich in San Francisco and to our cast and our casting director. He appeared disinterested.

"Don't worry about it, Willie, I'll get to it."

Days would go by. Often I had a cast and director set but couldn't begin production until Jack released the script. He had an amazingly blithe disregard for our airdates or our budget. I would end up going into his office, where he was sitting at his typewriter working on his rewrite, and pleading with him to turn the script over to me. "Don't worry, Willie, I'll get it done." Just as often, Lou Gray would come to my office desperate to get the final script so he could budget it and lay out a production schedule. Or Eddie O'Brien might drop in and ask if we had next week's pages. I would routinely reply, "Ask Jack," which really drove all of them nuts because he would tell Lou or Eddie, Jake or Doc, or anyone who asked, "Don't worry about it."

Lou and I fought the battle of the budget together, while Neuman fussed over the script. I asked Jack one night before we went home what I could do to end this bottleneck. We had had a couple of drinks, and Neuman was in one of his "black Irish" dark moods, as he sometimes called them.

"I lay in that VA hospital TB ward for over a year, Willie," he told me. "Guys were dying on both sides of me, sometimes twice a week. They even told me I was dying. Well, I showed the sons of bitches, didn't I? Honestly, do you think I give a rat's ass about the shit that goes on around here? I do my job as best I can, and that's it. Let's drop it, if you don't mind."

I never asked him about the bottleneck again. I simply continued to do my job as best I could.

Bob Weitman, president of MGM Television, had developed a friendly relationship with Jack. When it got too dicey, Lou Gray would call Weitman and Bob would phone Jack to remind him that we owed NBC delivery of these episodes on time; MGM's ass was on the line. It often took this kind of pressure for Jack to finally sign off on the script and let us shoot. Usually he had changed very little or, sometimes, nothing. Beneath this attempt at perfection was his unspoken hope that a revised scene or line or dialogue might make the show a success. It's the silent desperation that underscores producing series television.

I came to realize this was also Jack's way of letting everyone know that he controlled the show. Sure, I ran the series without interference from him. I made all the day-to-day decisions, but Jack made sure that the word went out that he was the true boss.

Early one morning Jack phoned me at home to ask me to give him a ride to the studio. We both had homes less than a mile apart in the Santa Monica mountains high above, behind, and west of Bel Air on Roscomare Road. When I arrived in Jack's driveway he came out to meet me, his right hand encased in a huge cast and bandage.

"Sorry, Willie," he said, as he hopped into the seat beside me, "can't drive." He indicated his encased hand. "Last night Irene came at me with the fireplace poker," he said, casually, "just got my hand up in time, caught it between my thumb and forefinger, ripped it open right down to the bone, she could've killed me. She had to drive me down to UCLA Emergency. There was blood all over the living room. The doc took forty or fifty stitches, whatever. . . . It was one hell of a drive down there, she was drunk out of her mind."

Then he chuckled, "She'll be on her knees all day cleaning the blood off the carpet and the living room furniture. Serves her right."

By a remarkable coincidence, Jack and I had both married women who later turned out to have deep-rooted emotional problems. And we each had four children we adored. We were each, in our own different ways, trying to resolve our domestic problems amicably with no success. Though our friendship had begun when we were college roommates and it still flourished, our work lives as Hollywood writer-producers had gone separate ways. We didn't socialize, yet we never doubted that our friendship would be lifelong.

Jack was the sole reason I became a writer and moved to Hollywood to take my chances. My debt to him was immeasurable. *Sam Benedict,* however, was putting me under almost intolerable stress. As much as I would beg and plead with Jack to stop creating the bottleneck, he was unmoved. The truth was that by the time the script got to him it had already been rewritten by me or Doc or both of us. Whatever words or scenes he tinkered with did not significantly alter the final film.

Despite the delays, shooting went smoothly. Eddie O'Brien and the rest of our regular cast were pros, they showed up on time, knew their lines, and delivered first-rate performances. NBC liked our scripts, so did MGM and the cast. And they liked the finished films they were seeing. Hope against blind hope, they felt these shows had a real chance of knocking off Jackie Gleason.

With production underway, I had a whole new set of problems. Every day there would be some minor glitch on the set and the standard routine was, "call the producer." So I would hurry over and fix it with an obvious solution to these often simple problems. When you have thirty to fifty people on a soundstage trying to turn out a film under tremendous time pressure, problems were as certain as the air we breath.

One of the most unusual calls I ever received from the set was when our script supervisor (called "script girl" in those days, even though they were usually mature women) asking me to rush over at once.

"We're running short," she said, "at least two or three minutes,

E. Jack Neuman: "our leader," radio-writer-turned-TV-hyphenate who launched William Froug's career as well as several of television's prime-time series—*Dr. Kildare, Sam Benedict,* and *Mr. Novak.* Emmy Award–nominee for *The Rise and Fall of the Third Reich.* (courtesy of Marian Collier Neuman)

and we're shooting our last scene." This woman, who had more filmmaking experience than I would likely have in a lifetime and was generally the only person on the set who knew exactly what was going on every minute of the shooting day, beckoned me to follow her toward the brightly lit area next to the makeup chairs where she had set up her "office," a tall, director's chair, draped with canvas bags for her leather notebook containing her copy of the script currently shooting, pens, her stopwatch, and whatever else she needed for her demanding work. (It is the invaluable notes of the script supervisor that the editor uses when cutting the film. Without her notes, transcribing how many takes of a scene were shot and which were ordered printed by the director, all would be chaos.)

"Here's the problem," she said, opening her notebook and indicating the scene we were shooting, "our director is pacing this episode very fast. We are going to be at least three minutes short of my estimated time. I checked our printed takes, they still add up to a completed episode considerably short. We have nothing left to shoot after this scene."

She was right, we had ourselves a big and immediate problem. We could not deliver an episode to the network two or three minutes short. There would be hell to pay, not only from the network but from MGM management. We had a contract with MGM to deliver a specific length of film for each episode. The network was not about to fill the empty space with a test pattern. And we had neither the time nor the budget to go back later and shoot added scenes. Our script supervisor pointed out that our company was, at that moment, almost half finished shooting the scene in the restaurant following our principal character's meeting with Sam Benedict. The company had stopped to relight. The stars were in their dressing room.

As it happened our guest stars for this episode were Ida Lupino and her husband, Howard Duff. They were playing a married couple in deep financial trouble who seek out Sam Benedict because the husband, a developer, is being sued by several homeowners for shoddy construction as well as overcharges. The wife feels certain that her husband is guilty. The couple was being squeezed emotionally as well as financially. Sam Benedict had just told them that there was a strong likelihood they would lose the case and be in for severe financial losses. Bankruptcy was staring them in the face. Their marriage was falling apart.

I found a set on our stage with a desk and a chair and studied the pages they had been filming. Since the characters' situation was loaded with conflict and I had two highly professional actors playing one on one against each other, the answer quickly popped into my head: expand the scene, explore some of the issues that have been eating away at their marriage. I realized at once that I could add at least three pages with no sense of padding, even though that is exactly what I was doing. I rationalized that the material was already there begging to be written (desperation is sometimes the mother of self-delusion as well as invention).

I asked my secretary to bring me a couple of legal-sized lined pads and some pens. Meanwhile, I told the director what I was planning to do and suggested that the company take a half-hour break. Then I met with Howard and Ida, telling them what I had in mind. They were delighted, looking forward to the new pages and promising to be ready to shoot on a moment's notice. (I could not have known that the marital conflict I was about to write was, in fact, somewhat a mirror image of the martial conflict Duff and Lupino were actually suffering through.)

Writing the new expanded scene turned out to be remarkably easy. I knew the characters, understood the core conflict of the scene, and was able to let the characters dictate the new pages to me. Among the great experiences of writing drama are those periods when inside your head your characters speak to you. I often speak the dialogue out loud to see how it plays. There is sometimes a euphoric sense of being almost a bystander, fascinated and even surprised by what your characters are saying. These are magical but hardly rare moments. It seems to me that the dramatist is not really connected to the material until his characters begin to talk to him.

In less than an hour we were shooting the new scene. It went better than we could have hoped for. The minor tempest illustrated why almost all television series, then and now, are produced by writer hyphenates. Last-minute rewrites were no doubt born when the first Greek drama went into rehearsal. Certainly last-minute rewriting is an integral aspect of producing every television series.

That *Sam Benedict* episode was completed with more than enough footage. Looking at the scene in the dailies the following afternoon, it was seamless. The episode was completed and delivered at the required length and on budget. NBC was happy with it. MGM management liked it.

Sandwiched between writer meetings, casting meetings, director meetings, production meetings, rewrite meetings, and emergency trips to our set, I had to look at the dailies every afternoon and discuss with our film editor my choices of which camera angles I preferred. That done, I hurried over to the set to discuss what I had just seen. It seemed I was always being besieged by the cast, cameraman, set dresser, and everybody on the stage to tell them how the film looked to me, but the director was always my first priority.

While writers were working on their teleplays, I had time to enjoy lunches with friends. One day I got a call from screenwriter Eleanor Perry, who asked me to meet her for lunch in the commissary. There was an urgency in her voice.

Eleanor and her then husband Frank had been living in an upscale neighborhood of Cleveland when Eleanor, an avid reader and theater and film buff, happened across a little book titled *Lisa and David*. Written by a psychiatrist, it was the story of two young people confined to a mental institution who gradually discover and help each other. Eleanor knew at once it was a potential film, and she was the person to write it, which she did. The Perrys went knocking on doors, making phone calls, hitting up their wealthy friends, and several doctors in particular, until they raised enough money to make the film. Frank directed Eleanor's screenplay of what was now titled *David and Lisa*.

Released in 1962, their "little" low-budget movie took the arthouse scene by storm. It became an instant classic. Frank and Eleanor's careers moved them triumphantly to Hollywood, where they were fêted, wined and dined, and made instant celebrities. After their divorce they continued to write and direct movies, separately, with mixed results.

As soon as we sat down in the MGM commissary, Eleanor told me her story, in a gush of emotional frustration. She had been contracted to write *The Man Who Loved Cat Dancing*.

"I'm about halfway through the screenplay. So I decide to take a break. I walk down the hall a few offices from me, and I see this guy pounding away at his typewriter. 'What are you working on?' I ask him, casually.

"'I'm writing *The Man Who Loved Cat Dancing*,' he says.

"Of course, I nearly blow my cork and I head into the producer's office demanding an explanation. He tells me the other guy is merely writing a back-up script in case mine doesn't work! What a hell of a rotten trick to do to a writer!" she fumed. But as usual, the writer is powerless. All I could do was commiserate.

Eleanor later wrote the book *Blue Pages* about being a screenwriter in Hollywood. Thanks to her and other screenwriters' complaints, the Writers Guild added a stipulation in their next contract with AMPTVP (Association of Motion Picture and Television Producers, in effect, the studio owners' union) making it a rule that any writer working on any picture or series must be notified when and if another writer is employed to write the same story.

Meantime, there were my weekly commutes to San Francisco to go over the current preproduction script line by tortuous line with Jake Erlich who, so far, had been a lamb. He was proud to have his name on the end credits "based on the career of Jake Erlich." He loved the publicity. Jake was a cocky little guy, standing about five feet five in his high-heeled, highly polished cowboy boots, which he wore every day. He alternated his dress from tailored, solid brown suits with a starched high collar shirt, solid brown tie, and brown boots, or, on alternate days, a solid black suit, white shirt, black tie, and black cowboy boots. (I figured the boots were to give him a couple inches more height.) He was so crisply and precisely dressed that he might have been a department store manikin.

Yet he was anything but wooden; he was a highly animated little man with a big, powerful personality and an ego to match. He had made a reputation in San Francisco handling headline-making cases. Flamboyant was the word the local press always used to describe him, and it was accurate. As easy as he was for me to deal with in our weekly meetings, I was always aware of a darker, more ominous side of him lurking in the background, and he made certain that I knew it.

I hereby appoint
William Froug
Chief Deputy Master
for MGM-TV.
Jake Ehrlich
The Master
Himself

From *left:* high-powered San Francisco attorney Jake Erlich (the real-life Sam Benedict) on the set of the NBC series *Sam Benedict* with star Eddie O'Brien *(center)* and the author. (from the author's collection)

Gradually, one episode at a time, we were building a series, even though we were working in the dark. NBC and MGM were happy with the episodes, but we had yet to hear from the audience. Jack and Doc both finished their scripts, both were good and they were shot—which left me as the lone exception to our script agreement.

However, on weekends in my spare time, I wrote a script about an older lawyer who was facing disbarment for frequently appearing in court drunk. Sam Benedict, an old friend, decides to defend him. I was delighted when veteran English actor Claude Rains agreed to play the starring role. Meeting him was a pleasure, and the show was well received.

Ben Conway, a tall, handsome, young agent who stood out from the crowd and who was new in the game, dropped by my office. He had decided upon a very low-key approach. It was wise, and I appreciated his wisdom. He didn't have a big client list, but he had a talent for the soft sell. He never tried to overpower me as some of the big agency guys would. They routinely struck out. So when Ben finally asked for an appointment, I agreed. After he sat down on the couch across from my desk, he started his pitch. He had signed this new young director from New York (we all knew agents used "New York" as a code for exceptionally talented people, as in he or she is "a New York actor" or a "New York director"). It revealed Hollywood's awe of Broadway, the theater, the world of publishing, and whatever emanated from the city. It was the unspoken capital of showbiz. Like the song says, with considerable truth, if you can make it there, you can make it anywhere.

"This director," Ben was saying, "has shot a couple of *Wanted Dead or Alive*'s with Steve McQueen and they want him back for more. However, I want to show you some of his film, when you have the time. His name is Dick Donner and you're going to hear a lot about him; he has a few openings now, but you'd better get him early before I have him booked on every show in town."

I had some of the best directors working in Hollywood TV. I had booked Ida Lupino to direct two episodes. She was a pioneer, having directed a couple of independent features. Women directors were rarer than snow in August. But Lupino was very good at it. Abner Biberman, an actor-turned-director, was down for two episodes;

actor Paul Henried (who had a featured role in *Casablanca*) was down for one. Don Medford was consistent and reliable. By and large, I was satisfied, but being careful about whom I hired, I told Ben I would let him know.

One day I told him, "Okay show me some Donner film, I have a couple of hours Friday afternoon."

I liked what I saw, phoned Ben, booked Donner for an open date I now had due to a director cancellation. Dick Donner was obviously exceptionally talented. The episode Donner shot for us was beautifully done. I was struck by the freshness of his camera angles and the crisp performances he got from the cast, and I booked him for additional episodes. He became one of our trio of rotating directors—Ida Lupino, Abner Biberman, Dick Donner. Not surprisingly, Donner went on to an extraordinarily successful career in features. It is no small matter that under the pressure of completing television episodes on time, a director who could shoot superbly while keeping a happy, relaxed set was a major asset. No one accomplished this better than Donner.

Before the season ended Donner came bursting into my office waving a screenplay.

"See this," he said, gleefully, "this is my ticket out of television!"

The name of the screenplay was *The Omen*. Donner's forecast for his future career in features was right on the money, in more ways than one.

A writer named John Bloch came in with an unusual story idea: Sam Benedict defending an avowed communist while at the same time defending a neo-Nazi. Parallel freedom of speech First Amendment cases that end up getting him in trouble with both extremes while being squeezed by the middle. He was in a no-win situation. John called it, *Bombs on the Left, Cannon on the Right*.

At lunch that day, both Jack and Doc agreed it was for us. The story won quick approval from the network, and we sent Bloch home to write the script, unprepared for the crisis it would ignite.

We were running along smoothly, turning out our shows on schedule with only the usual day-to-day problems, mostly from Jack holding up the final draft. Lou Gray took to coming into my office with the same plaintive cry, "When's he going to finish the damn thing? I can't get a final budget made out. Is he changing any of the sets or locations? We've got to shoot tomorrow; doesn't our friend know what pressure he's putting us under? Ask him, please!"

John Bloch's teleplay came in and needed very little rewriting. My casting director and I went to work. I knew I wanted Nina Foch for the part of the communist, an actress with a long history of solid performances, both in leading roles and, later, aging into character parts. Foch had an edginess, an unpredictable quality that was ideal for the character. Don agreed to go after veteran actor James Gregory (I vividly remembered him from *The Manchurian Candidate*), for the neo-Nazi. We cleaned up the minor parts zapping through the Players Directory.

Don felt certain he could get both actors. "Nina will have to see the script first," he said, "but it's not going to be a problem because it's a hell of a good part and a good script."

At lunch Jack and Doc and I were congratulating ourselves on finally getting an excellent first draft that we didn't have to massively rewrite. Our euphoria was misplaced. Later that week I got a phone call from Jake Erlich that began, "I'll be goddamned if I'm going to defend a fucking communist! This script I've just read has got to go." It fascinated me that Erlich, a Jew, had no problem with defending an anti-Semitic neo-Nazi, but drew the line at defending a communist.

Then I got a visit from Eddie O'Brien, in makeup for the episode currently shooting but holding next week's script in his hand. Friendly, agreeable Eddie was quick to get to the point, "I'll be goddamned if I'll defend a fucking communist," he said, "I won't do this episode. I've talked to Jack and he passed the buck to you. Worst of all, he said he likes it just the way it is, so, my friend, we have ourselves a big problem."

My NBC contact phoned with a variation on the same story: "I don't think it looks good for your series or the network, either for that matter for Sam Benedict to defend a communist." When I explained that he had approved the story himself, he was unconvinced, "Sure, but he's made the script a lot tougher than I thought it would be. Get rid of the communist, or the script is not approved for production." (When network executives realize that they may have inadvertently been thinking outside the box, they tend to lapse into denial.) Bloch had followed his network-approved outline exactly, but without NBC's script approval we could not shoot.

This sudden rebellion was a total surprise to us all. We thought the nightmare of Senator McCarthy and his communist paranoia was long past. Obviously, we were wrong.

Doc and I met in Jack's office that night after work, having the obligatory scotches. "I say, fuck 'em," said Jack to us, "fuck 'em, we're going to shoot it like it is. I told Eddie that if he didn't like it he could take a walk. And I explained patiently to Jake, who was off the ceiling, that it isn't *him* defending a communist, it's a fictional character named *Sam Benedict*. Somehow, he can't tell the difference." The three of us got a good laugh, but my laughter lacked enthusiasm. I was the guy who had to produce the show, get something on the soundstage, meet an airdate.

The next afternoon, Jack, Doc, and I had lunch to discuss the crisis. Neuman had mellowed. Bob Weitman had phoned him at home the previous evening saying he personally liked the script a lot, it had a very strong civil liberties theme he related to as a Jew, and he thought that the show could even win us an Emmy . . . but he had to think of MGM first and its relationship with NBC. This extraordinary thirty-five-episode order alone put MGM Television on the map. MGM was occupying it's rightful place among the major studios. As much as he liked Jack, Weitman could not allow him to destroy that relationship. The script had to be changed until it met with NBC's approval.

"Eddie O'Brien, Jake Erlich, and their like come and go," Jack said Bob Weitman told him, "I don't give a damn what they think though I'll admit it'll make life easier if you humor them, but the network is something else, they'll be around for a long time and we have other series we'd like to sell them."

Being at root a pragmatist, Neuman said, "Okay, guys, we've got about twenty-four hours to change the script and get this thing into production." Suddenly I saw a new and different E. Jack Neuman.

It turned out to be ridiculously easy. We cut all references to the female lead as a communist; the word was eliminated from the newly revised script. Now she was simply a "left-wing nut case." We sent it out to all concerned by the next day. Eddie, Jake, and NBC withdrew their objections and we set a start date. Don told me that Foch had loved the original script and agreed to play the communist, but now she was thinking of backing out. We were in danger of losing our guest star. "However," Don said, "she's willing to meet with you and discuss it."

Nina Foch, a tall, quite attractive, sophisticated blonde, appeared in my office the next afternoon. She cordially announced her displeasure with the rewrite. She was not looking for a fight, but she was unhappy. She had liked the part, she told me, and had therefore agreed to star in it for less than her usual fee. She had been impressed by its stance on civil liberties. Now it was mushy and vague, "ordinary" was the way she put it. She wondered if she still wanted to do it "in this version." I had admired her work for years, and now I discovered I also admired the woman.

We had a friendly open discussion; I told her the reasons for the changes. She felt as I did—we had taken the guts out of a damned good script. It became clear that she and I were on the same page politically. What she wanted was reassurance that the script would not be further weakened. She left agreeing to accept my word that she was safe. She would report for shooting as scheduled.

Eddie O'Brien dropped by later in the day to apologize for his temper tantrum and to tell me that he was happy with the new pages and was certain it would be a great show.

I didn't hear from Jake Erlich, which meant that he and Jack had reached an agreement and there was no further problem.

Somewhere toward the end of production I began to get severe headaches, a kind of burning pain down the center of my head.

Coming back on the plane from San Francisco one afternoon, I felt as if my head would split open. By the time I got to the main entrance of MGM, the pain was unbearable. As I entered our office suite, I ran into Dick Donner picking up revised pages for his upcoming episode.

Donner took one look at me and said," My god, what's happened to you?" I described my headaches and he instantly replied, "Get in my car, right now, I'm taking you to the leading neurologist in Beverly Hills! And don't argue!" Donner has a big, commanding voice. In desperate pain, I got in his car.

We raced to Beverly Hills, Donner took me by the arm and led me to the offices of two neurosurgeons. Their secretary looked up, startled, but Donner didn't let her open her mouth, "I've brought my friend here in to see Sandy *right now.*" She persuaded Donner to let me wait on the couch, assuring him that Dr. Rothenberg would see me just as soon as the patient in his office left.

In minutes I was in a dark room. Dr. Rothenberg and his partner, using pins, began to prick my scalp searching for the path of the pain. I was surprised by their grave concern. Gradually they discovered that the pain formed a line directly down the center of my head, from front to back. "I want you in the hospital immediately," Dr. Rothenberg said. "Is UCLA okay for you?"

Dumbfounded I said, "Fine, but what is it?"

"Virus, probably," replied Dr. Rothenberg. "It's probably not serious, but we've got to be certain."

Donner drove me to UCLA Medical Center where I was admitted. Within a few hours I was subjected to blood tests, EKGs, everything imaginable. But the final indignity was when the doctor himself came in at the end of the day with a very, very long needle.

"Roll over on your side," he ordered, "we're going to do a spinal tap."

By the next day I was told it was all clear. As Donner drove me home he explained, "There's been a couple of cases of encephalitis recently, as a matter of fact, a patient in a room down the hall from you died. That's why Sandy wanted to get on top of it right away."

After being released from UCLA, I discovered that when fluid is drained from your spine, it's the cushion that protects the brain from banging into your skull. The headaches that followed made my original headaches seem like a soothing head massage. I couldn't sit up for six weeks. MGM put a cot in my office and one in the projection room, so that I basically worked lying down, even watching dailies from my cot. I was told by the doctor that if I thought these headaches were bad, I would not be able to endure them if I so much as sipped anything with alcohol, so I didn't touch a drop of the stuff for six months. Slowly, my life returned. Dr. Rothenberg had also suggested that I should avoid stress, which gave me the only laugh of the entire experience.

The series debuted to good but not great notices. Jackie Gleason really whipped our ass. We never did win our time period. However, we did get one Emmy nomination for noted feature-film actor Joseph Schildkraut, who played a rabbi in our Jewish wedding story. Nonetheless, we slipped quietly beneath the sea without a trace. Color television was clearly on the horizon, thus a black and white series faced little likelihood of being syndicated (or ever being shown again, as indeed, it hasn't been). But the extreme stress of that experience gave me the impetus to realize that producing television series was not the way I wanted to spend my life.

One weekend I wrote a thirty-nine-page outline for a proposed course in producing and writing television. I introduced myself to film historian, author, and critic Arthur Knight at a Writers Guild screening the following Sunday evening. I had learned Knight was a professor at the University of Southern California's Film School. I asked him if he would look it over. Though I was a total stranger to him, he readily agreed.

The next morning he phoned to tell me how much he liked it, promising to give my presentation to USC Film School chairman, Bernard Kantor.

Monday of the following week Kantor phoned. "I like your course outline very much. How soon can you start?"

The following semester I began teaching one night a week for USC's Film School as an adjunct professor. But I could not support my family on seven hundred dollars a month. My career as a television hyphenate still had many more surprising thrills and spills as I continued to reluctantly ride Hollywood's bucking broncos, but as they say in the rodeo business, you have to get back on the horse that threw you. Besides, the money was good.

Soon after our television work together, Donner's career took off at light speed, after he directed *The Omen,* a megahit that spawned several sequels. He eventually directed and/or produced seventeen feature films, including the most successful buddy series in movie history, *Lethal Weapon, Lethal Weapon 2, 3,* and *4.* Our friendship endures.

9

Chew Vass Hexpectin Mebbe Too Loose Latrek?

In the spring of 1963, as NBC's one-hour drama series *Sam Benedict* was unspooling on the nation's screens every Saturday night, I was cleaning out my desk at MGM making ready for whatever job would be available. I had completed the production of thirty-five episodes for MGM Television and had brought the show in considerably under budget. While the series was well received by both MGM management and the network, it did not generate the kind of audience popularity that gave it even a marginal possibility for continuing into another season. MGM had queried NBC about that possibility but received an official cancellation as a response.

Our story editor, jovial Doc Calvelli, had been the first to pack his briefcase and head for home. It is a wise rule of thumb when you produce a television series to never have more personal belongings in your office than you can throw in a briefcase or a cardboard box at a moment's notice. I had heard of many cases of TV producers who had been ordered "be off the lot by noon" at ten in the morning, as I had learned firsthand while in preproduction for the ill-fated *Philip Marlowe* series.

There is a somber silence that settles over the offices of a television series that, while still playing on the air and alive in homes all across America, is, in fact, dead in the production offices. The phones stop ringing, agents no longer pester the secretaries, actors looking for work no longer drop by. People move about listlessly. It's life in a ghost town. We were apparently alive and well to the few million people who watched us every Saturday night at 7:30, but we were DOA to the industry and to anyone who walked into our suite of offices on the main street of MGM's Lot number 1.

On his way out Doc wandered into my office, briefcase in hand but full of good cheer. "Can you believe that guy?" Doc laughingly asked me, "Here we are closing down and our leader has already sold another series to NBC! That guy is amazing."

"Our leader," as Doc often mockingly referred to E. Jack Neuman, who had created, executive produced, and written the pilot for the *Sam Benedict* series, was one of the most prolific hyphenates in Hollywood. He had also written the pilot for MGM's highly successful TV version of that studio's popular motion picture series, *Dr. Kildare.*

I walked through our reception area where our secretaries were sitting, glumly awaiting their pending unemployment or hoped-for reassignment by the MGM secretarial pool to another series. I found Jack in his huge office, seated behind his desk, hunched over his typewriter, smoking as always as he pecked away. He beckoned me to come in.

"You busy this afternoon?" he asked me. "I've booked Room One at the Thalberg Building. I've got something I want to show you."

We walked out the front gates and down the narrow sidewalk into the basement of the Thalberg Building, continuing down the noisy, narrow corridors where rows of mimeograph machines were busily printing scripts for MGM's various television series and whatever movies were in production. Here was the pulsating, clattering center of it all. As they loudly spun away, Jack and I paused to watch.

"Without the scripts, my friend," he said, "nothing would happen, no movies, no television series. Those sons of bitches who tell us directors are the *auteurs* of movies, pardon me, *film,* don't have a clue. Let any director get on a set with one hundred and ten blank pages and let's see what he *auteurs*."

Deeper in the basement we came upon a lush, red-carpeted area leading down some steps into the lobby of the MGM executives' screening room. It was like entering the empty lobby of a commercial sized theater with a lower ceiling.

Once inside, walking down the plushly carpeted aisle and settling into the large, leather-upholstered chairs lined up beneath the projection room, one could not help but imagine Louis B. Mayer, Irving Thalberg, and his chief executives watching the dailies or rough cuts of one of the many movies they had in production during their halcyon days, when they were producing three hundred features a year. The huge auditorium could seat a bit more than a hundred people. The back two rows of deeply cushioned matching maroon-leather chairs were obviously for the seats of the privileged. There was rich Hollywood history here, you could almost taste it.

We watched the pilot for a new series called *Mr. Novak,* which Jack had quietly written and produced during the previous Christmas holidays. Although I had been aware of it, I had little time or inclination to discuss it with him. Jack had a habit of keeping his own council. I knew that if and when he sold the pilot, he would tell me about it.

Jack's pilot story was about a young high school teacher, Mr. Novak, played by handsome young actor James Franciscus. The school principal, played by Dean Jagger, was the featured actor. We are meant to understand that Jagger will be Franciscus's foremost adviser, boss, and sometimes critic; a strong, even tough but essentially kind father figure. The sort of father figure that Jack, educated in Catholic schools by Jesuit priests, longed for but lost too early in his life.

When it was over Jack turned to me. "Do you like it, Willie?"

"Very much," I replied. "Dean Jagger is terrific."

"He's going to carry the show, all right," Jack assured me. "NBC has given us an order for twenty-six one-hour episodes, and I want you to produce them."

I hesitated, remembering those harrowing days when the entire production company from the head of MGM Television on down waited anxiously for Jack to finish his final polish of each script before we could shoot.

"MGM wants you," Jack said, in his brusque manner, "and NBC wants you. I guess that sort of makes up your mind, doesn't it. Frap?" During our lifelong friendship we never ceased to invent outrageous nicknames for each other. Keeping in mind that I sometimes thought my old college roomie behaved like a goose-stepping Nazi, mine for him was "Goosebaum." It was also intended to remind my Catholic-raised Irish friend that he had had a half-Jewish great-grandfather. Jack had won an Emmy for his teleplay of *The Rise and Fall of the Third Reich*. During his research he claimed that he and former Nazi chief architect Albert Speer had developed a genuine friendship. I had no trouble believing it.

I wasn't worried about MGM or NBC; it was Jack's eternal last-minute rewriting that I was thinking about as I hesitated to give him my answer.

"How about it, Frap?" Jack insisted.

Neuman affected the abrupt, militaristic mannerism of a Marine. What the Marine Corp had not implanted in him in authoritarian behavior, the Catholic priests (whom he called "the Jebbies") who educated him during his formative years surely had. He liked to give terse orders, which he understood nobody was going to follow while under the stress of producing a television series. Still, he just liked the feel of giving orders. Yet there was no meanness in him, nor did he expect that any of us would do more than shrug them off or laugh in his face. For all his bravado, he was a sweet-natured, gentle man, which he tried unsuccessfully to hide. He always went along with any decisions I made, and I ran the show . . . except for those infernal last-minute rewrites of his.

Though our paths had gone in different career directions after we each married, we remained genuinely fond of one another and had a strong mutual respect. Jack was as close to a brother to me as any man I have ever known. I loved the stubborn son of a bitch, and I admired his talent. I agreed to produce the series.

"Let's get to work," Jack said, "start getting some writers in here. As usual, we are under the gun."

It was an easy transition; we all stayed in our same *Sam Benedict* offices, the three secretaries remained at their desks. But we lost one member of our team—Doc had had a heart attack. Though he was recovering, his doctor told him joining the staff of another television series could be hazardous to his health.

Jack hired a new story editor, Robert Thompson, an excellent writer with strong credits. Suddenly we were off and running.

Preproduction is always an exciting time. I wiped clean my wall-mounted production chart; it would be a fresh beginning with a few holdover writers and directors but all new actors.

Boris Sagal, born in Russia, who directed the pilot and had been nicknamed "the mad Russian" by Neuman, was unable to stay on a regular rotation due to prior commitments and a desire to build a career in features. Dick Donner agreed to direct a couple of episodes, as did Ida Lupino. I called several of my favorite writers to come to Metro to see the pilot and talk stories.

For a few foolhardy moments I began to think that this was going to be a piece of cake. Dean Jagger and James Franciscus came in for wardrobe fittings. Franciscus dropped by my office to meet me. He was a tightly wound but handsome young man, blond haired, with strong jaw muscles that rippled above his tight-skinned chin. I liked him, but realized he did not have the personality that would make girls swoon. The secondary actors Jack had chosen as other high school teachers for the pilot were all top-drawer players and solidly professional. Jack and I continued our commissary lunches, now joined by Bob Thompson, a tall, stoop-shouldered, ruddy-faced redhead, who was a serious, rather foreboding, Yale drama school graduate. Of course, his nickname was Red. He had an odd habit of speaking slightly above a whisper while glancing over his shoulder furtively, as if he was being followed.

We all understood it was not going to be easy to develop strong dramatic stories in our high school setting unless we dipped into juvenile crime stories, clichés we were anxious to avoid. We were also tightly restricted by being scheduled in the so-called family hour time slot: 7 to 8 P.M., seven nights a week on all three networks. (ABC was slowly beginning to emerge as competition for CBS and NBC.)

One afternoon Emma, my secretary, announced, "Mr. Jagger is here to see you." I had been looking forward to meeting our co-star whose busy career as a character actor was well established in Hollywood and had included an Oscar as Best Supporting Actor for *Twelve O'clock High*.

I looked up from my desk to see a very tall, lean, bald-headed man of about sixty standing over me, his mouth set in an angry crease, his eyes blazing.

"Look at this!" he commanded me by way of a greeting, as his right arm snapped across his chest in military fashion, his finger pointing to his left shoulder, "this is a disgrace, you hear me, an absolute disgrace!" He wanted me to know that he was trying to control his all too apparent anger.

I stared at the offending shoulder and saw only a well-fitted, newly tailored, handsome tweed jacket with leather elbow patches. His introductory greeting left me speechless. But the silence was quickly broken.

"Is this what you call MGM wardrobe?" he demanded, his voice filled with contempt, "this shoulder is unacceptable, this tailoring is deplorable."

"It looks like it fits to me," I replied, blandly, "but if you don't like it, it can easily be altered before we shoot."

"I call it shoddy workmanship," the imperious actor proclaimed, "especially from Metro-Goldwyn-Mayer," he added, spitting out the studio name. "And I haven't seen any scripts."

"They are in work," I replied, "and we have some good ones." I was stalling, trying to figure out how to deal with this onslaught.

"Let me tell you something, Mr. Froug," Jagger said, "I've appeared in many feature films, and won an Oscar, but I've had to write every line of dialogue I've ever spoken in every motion picture I've ever been in; I just can't work with the crap they've given me."

I'd had enough of this guy, but I didn't want to start a war before we had even begun shooting. Life in production was obviously going to be even more difficult having to deal with Dean Jagger on a daily basis for the next year. There would be enough stress to go around, so I tried to neutralize this rageful actor.

"It's been nice meeting you, Mr. Jagger," I said, politely, standing to indicate the meeting was over. "I wish us all good luck with our new series."

"Yes, it was nice meeting you, too," he replied tersely, taken off guard. He walked out of my office. As he exited I thought "My god, what am I going to do with this narcissistic egomaniac?" At lunch I told Jack about my first encounter with Dean Jagger. As always, Jack was sanguine.

"Do what I do," Neuman advised me, "tell the prick to fuck off."

"Did you?" I asked Jack. Suddenly a smile broke out on his face, "No, I told the s.o.b. to talk to you, you're the producer. I'll stick to the scripts."

My heart fell into my shoes; it was going to be *Sam Benedict* all over again but this time with a nasty-tempered star. Jack would be hunched over his typewriter endlessly rewriting, while I had to deal with every problem involved with producing a television series. At that moment I knew I had to figure out a way to get out of this job, even as I realized that I was under contract to MGM who had guaranteed NBC that I would produce the series.

As we went into production and I began my many trips across MGM's main street to our soundstage, I made it a point to greet Jagger and Franciscus with brief but polite hellos, and keep my distance. It turned out to be easy. Jagger performed his scenes, spoke briefly to a few people, then made his retreat into his onstage trailer dressing room. Many years later actress Marion Collier, who played one of our teachers, told me Jagger was helpful and courteous with her. I attributed that to Collier's winning smile and generous, ebullient personality. But Jagger did not hobnob with the crew; they respected his work but kept their distance.

On the other hand, James Franciscus dropped by my office to ask if I was satisfied with his work and to tell me that he was a Yale graduate and had aspirations as a writer. I found him to be a polite, intense, soft-spoken, introspective young man, eager to do his job without fuss or bother. Though unspoken, it was clearly understood that Jimmy, in the title role as Mr. Novak, was going to play second fiddle to the principal played by veteran Dean Jagger. But if Jimmy had a problem with that he never said it to me. He had considerable respect for his older, more experienced co-star. He said he hoped to learn from Jagger.

Looking at the early dailies confirmed this was the Dean Jagger show. Contrary to the actor's assertions, he delivered his lines as written, adding only minor touches that gave them an unexpected and arresting panache. The man's performance in each episode was compelling; it was difficult to focus your attention on any other actor in the scene.

"He's the actor you hate to love," Jack would quip as we watched the dailies.

NBC and MGM expressed contentment with what they were seeing, but in our offices, Red, Jack, and I increasingly realized that in order to create a more exciting show we needed to get into heavier subject matter. But being in the so-called family-hour time slot, we would be tightly monitored by the network. Thus, in the early shows, we did a story about a young student who refused to take ROTC on the grounds that he was a conscientious objector; another about a teacher who cheated, upgrading his student's exam scores in order to make himself look good. In this one, Hershel Bernardi had delivered an understated yet outstanding performance.

As was my custom, I dropped by the scoring stage to hear the music composed for each episode, especially when working with a composer new to me. Thus I listened to Lynn Murray's score for our cheating teacher episode. I was dismayed to hear him conducting background music based on *The Anniversary Waltz,* giving it a *hora* flavor. I asked him why he had chosen this music for the episode.

"Don't you get it?" Murray shot back, offended by my question, "I've given the music a traditional Jewish flavor because Hershel Bernardi is Jewish!" His anger astonished me.

"But this story isn't about the actor being Jewish, it's about a teacher who cheats," I replied. "Ethnicity has nothing to do with it."

Lynn, who had a long successful history as a composer and arranger, especially for vocal groups, turned on me, "Then I'm not the musician you want for your series! Get yourself another boy!" and he stalked angrily off the podium but not before turning to the orchestra and shouting, "That's it, fellas, we're finished for the day. Go home!"

I was stunned. Dealing with temperamental artists is high on every producer's misery list, but our weekly deadline dictated that production move ahead like a high-speed train. There is no turning back. I quickly replaced Murray with Leith Stevens, a solid, reliable, professional.

A couple of years later my wife and I attended a formal dinner party at composer-conductor Jeff Alexander's home. Jeff and I had worked together when I was producing and directing CBS Radio's *Hallmark Hall of Fame.* He was an MGM regular and a highly regarded studio musician. As we were all being seated I spotted late arrivals Lynn Murray and his wife entering; at the same moment he saw me. For a brief moment our eyes met.

"I will not have dinner in any room that has Bill Froug in it!" he shouted to the assembled group. He took his wife's arm and headed for the door. Alexander hurried over to mollify his guest, but it was futile. Murray was out the door, slamming it behind him.

In our ongoing *Mr. Novak* story meetings, our worst fears were being realized. The stories were lacking dramatic tension. We had to find stronger dramas.

We struggled to develop more in-depth personal stories, exploring our characters' inner conflicts as production proceeded on schedule. One day I received an urgent call from the set: "We've got trouble, we need you over here." It was our assistant director, Teddy Butcher. The AD functions as the top sergeant on any set, making certain that everyone knows where they ought to be and when, and making sure they get there when needed.

When I entered our soundstage it became immediately clear that the company was shut down. The big lights (the "brutes") were out. People were standing around aimlessly in the semidarkness, the director was chatting with the script girl. Butcher, a young, good-looking, savvy pro hurried over to greet me.

"It's Dean," he said, "he's locked himself in his dressing room and nobody can convince him to come out."

Jagger's dressing room was in a large trailer wheeled onto the stage. I walked over to the director and asked him what Dean's behavior was all about.

"He claims Jimmy insulted him. I didn't hear it, maybe he did, maybe he didn't. But we're shut down and I'm not going to beg him to come out again."

I crossed to Jagger's dressing room and knocked on his door.

"Who is it," came an angry voice from inside, "and what do you want?"

I identified myself and asked him to come out and finish the scene. He refused, "I am not going to let that youngster insult me."

"Who insulted you, Dean?" I asked him.

"James Franciscus," he replied, "that young man can't talk that way to an actor of my stature and get away with it," said the voice from behind the door. I turned to Butcher standing beside me and asked him what Jimmy had said to offend Jagger.

"I have no idea," our AD replied, "I didn't hear anything, and I was standing next to the camera and saw the entire scene shot."

I found Franciscus chatting amiably with a few members of the crew. He was telling them that he had no idea what Dean was angry about. He was as amused as he was genuinely puzzled. I went back to Dean's trailer and knocked again.

"Who is it?" Dean's voice answered.

This time I decided not to play his game, "Dean, nobody seems to have heard the insult. And if Jimmy offended you, I'm certain it was unintentional. Please come out and finish this scene, we are falling behind schedule."

"No," Dean's voice replied, "I will not. James Franciscus ought to be ashamed of himself addressing a man of my stature like that."

"May I come in and talk to you?" I asked.

"No," he replied, "I have made my position perfectly clear."

"Suppose I ask Jimmy to apologize, would that be acceptable?"

"I'll consider it," came the cautious reply. Something in his voice suggested that he might be looking for a way to get out of the trouble he'd created while saving face.

I went back to the camera where, as usual, everyone on a soundstage was gathered. There were a number of confused people in the crew. Nobody had heard or seen anything that James Franciscus had done or said to set off this tempest that was gradually turning into a crisis. I took Jimmy aside, filled him in on my discussion with Jagger, and asked him for help.

"Sure," Franciscus told me, "I'll apologize, but first we have to figure out what I'm apologizing for?" Jimmy was trying to keep from laughing. Franciscus was now finding the entire situation amusing, but for a television producer, once production began the meter was running, several thousand dollars a day were going down the drain and our production schedule was dissolving along with it. We had to get moving.

"Please help us out," I implored Franciscus.

"Sure thing," replied our agreeable title star, and together we walked over to Dean Jagger's dressing room, standing at the foot of the stairs to his door like school children about to face the principal.

"Dean," Franciscus called to the door, "it's Jimmy. Please come out and let me talk to you."

There was a long pause, and then the door opened revealing Dean Jagger at the top of the stairs frowning down upon us—the stern principal preparing to deal out punishment to naughty students.

"Dean," Jimmy said, "I honestly have no idea what I've said to offend you, but if I did offend you I am genuinely sorry."

Jagger pondered this apology for a moment, then said, "That's not good enough," and closed the door firmly in our faces. We heard the door lock click.

I'd had enough. I hurried back to my office and phoned Jagger's agent reminding him that Jagger had a contract to deliver his services as an actor, and unless he was ready to perform within one hour I would turn the matter over to MGM's legal department. Jagger's agent seemed familiar with this problem and guaranteed his client's services promptly.

Within an hour the set phoned to tell me that the cameras were rolling, Jagger was delivering his usual superb performance, and Franciscus was playing his role, unfazed by it all.

But for me it was a seminal event. I knew it was only a matter of time before I would retire from producing television series and, as of that moment, I would not continue to produce *Mr. Novak.* Period.

I phoned my agent and told him my feelings, concluding with, "Get me out of here."

Much to my surprise he was delighted. "Rod Serling and CBS are looking for a producer to take over *The Twilight Zone*. They need someone who can start immediately. We represent Rod and I know CBS approves of you, so how soon can you report to work?"

I had one little problem, I was under contract to MGM Television and had been guaranteed to NBC to produce *Mr. Novak*. The key to both problems was E. Jack Neuman.

I went into his office as soon as possible and asked him if I could get a release from my contract. He had heard the Dean Jagger story, of course, and he laughingly said, "The problem, Frap, is that you didn't tell him to go fuck himself."

But I pressed on, pulling out all the stops, telling him I didn't have it in me to produce another season of one-hour dramas, especially with a temperamental star. I also told him I felt producing *The Twilight Zone* was an exciting opportunity. Producing half-hour shows was half the work and ten times less stress than producing a one-hour series. I knew because I had done both. After explaining to me that he was disappointed that we wouldn't be working together, he promised to go all out to win my release.

Meanwhile, Jack had struck up a close friendship with one of our teachers, actress Marion Collier. We were all pleased to note this had mellowed him a great deal. He was, in fact, falling in love and his sense of humor was returning.

Out of the blue, I got a call from Bernie Kantor, head of USC's Film School. "I've been getting excellent feedback from both students and faculty on your course. How would you like to teach an additional course one afternoon a week in Short Film, and if you're available, how about teaching a screenwriting course this summer?"

I couldn't say "yes and yes" fast enough. I was thrilled. I knew I was looking at my future and it looked terrific. In a few days Neuman came into my office and said, "You're okay to go, Frap, but don't ever say that I didn't do anything for you."

The offices of *The Twilight Zone* were located in a two-story stucco building just inside the main entrance to MGM. The series merely leased office space and soundstages on an as-needed basis. It was a CBS–Rod Serling (Cayuga Productions) series.

I had never met Serling but had been a fan of his since the golden age of television. His *Requiem for a Heavyweight, Patterns,* and *The Comedian* were but three classic examples of his outstanding talent. I had seen *The Twilight Zone* a few times and liked it, but I would not describe myself as an ardent fan. In truth, I had not been much of a television viewer since the era of live drama out of New York ended. I rarely turned my set on except for news and special-events programming. I found most TV programs unbearably boring.

I reported to work the following Monday. Strolling down MGM's main street toward the building that housed *The Twilight Zone* offices, I had a sense of excitement and possibilities that I had not felt since my days of producing *Alcoa-Goodyear Theatre*. Anthology television! Different characters, different stories every week. And Rod Serling scripts! If you were a producer of television series, it seemed to me this was the best venue in all the TV world. It would be a chance to stretch my creative muscles. With Rod Serling as the key writer (he had written 80 percent of the scripts for the series), I felt we could produce some good work.

I was warmly greeted by venerable *Twilight Zone* production manager Ralph Nelson, who had been with the series for years. He showed me to my office, which was a long, narrow room whose windows looked down on the flow of foot traffic moving on and off the lot. Nelson told me that Serling had phoned and would be coming down soon to meet me.

My first visitor was our casting director Patricia Rose, a sunny, charming blonde who, after a few introductory exchanges, told me that she was looking for another job and asked me if I knew of any openings for a casting director. I was nonplussed. The word was out that this was going to be the show's final season. She thought that was the reason producer Bert Granet had left the series. By the time she left my office I had the feeling that I had been hired on to take command of the *Titanic.*

Later in the morning the secretary buzzed to tell me that Rod Serling was here to see me. Immediately there was a knock on my office door. I called "Come in."

The door opened. Rod Serling entered on his knees, hobbling the entire length of my long, narrow office until he reached my desk, his face beaming with a welcoming smile, his outstretched hand offered up to me. In this position he was about three-and-a-half-feet tall. He was fully enjoying his own prank.

"Chew vass hexpectin mebbe Too Loose Latrek?" he asked me. His comic Yiddish accent was flawless.

We made an easy transition to a serious discussion of the series status. Rod also believed that this was the last season of *The Twilight Zone*. He said he was burned out. He had exhausted his enthusiasm for the show and was finding it more and more difficult to come up with scripts. He was going to write only about half-dozen scripts at most, "or when I get an idea that intrigues me," was the way he put it. My heart sank. Rod Serling was *The Twilight Zone* and *The Twilight Zone* was Rod Serling. Without his scripts, I'd be thrown back into the freelance market, which was not a place any TV series producer wants to be.

I had, indeed, inadvertently signed on as captain of the *Titanic,* and it was already seriously leaking. I knew I liked Rod Serling immediately, but I could not have guessed that we were going to become close personal friends or that I was going to cause him so much pain.

10

The Sunset of *The Twilight Zone*

Throughout the summer of 1963 I discovered that Rod Serling seemed to have total recall of every joke he had ever heard and an unmatchable range of ethnic accents to use in telling them: Greek, German, Italian, Russian, Chinese, Japanese, Yiddish, Cockney, English upper class, all were in his memory bank. I am a born straight man, capable of great guffaws, easily collapsing with laughter, tears pouring down my cheeks, begging for mercy until I can get my breath. I realized that nobody could tell a funny story better than Rod Serling.

He made it a point of dropping by my office whenever he came to the studio to film his intros. We quickly discovered we had a great deal in common. We were only two years apart in age, we had both been in service during World War II, we had both begun our careers writing radio dramas. And we both had daughters. We began to exchange stories about the worst radio scripts we had written, cracking each other up as we tried to top one another on how bad we had been as writers. Over time we bonded as writers, but I never lost my awe of his extraordinary talent.

He invited me to his large two-story brick home just off Sunset Boulevard in the Pacific Palisades, showed me his large swimming pool and beautifully furnished poolside office suite at the western end of the pool, where his secretary typed his scripts. Entering the reception room, a visitor is greeted by six highly polished Emmy statuettes standing like golden sentinels on a glass shelf, guarding his private office, the inner sanctum. Other plaques and honors, including four Writers Guild awards, were tastefully placed about the deeply carpeted offices and reception room. I had never met a writer with more elegant quarters, or more richly deserved awards.

Serling told me he dictated his scripts to a tape machine while sunning himself on a chaise by his pool. He had become an authentic California sun-worshipper, keeping a deep brown tan all year round. During my few visits to his home I was struck by the oddity that we rarely left poolside. I met his wife only once that I recall and was put off by her lack of warmth and congeniality. He and Carol appeared to have little connection. Rod seemed to prefer his life outside the house, by the pool or in his office.

Rod was a small, trim athletic man who kept himself in excellent shape in spite of his addiction to cigarettes. Like my friend E. Jack Neuman, Serling chain-smoked Camels and kept a persistent, dry smoker's cough. Like every reformed smoker (I had smoked three packs a day for fifteen years until I quit cold turkey one day in 1959), I lectured him on the dangers of smoking but met my usual success. I soon ceased my lectures.

Scripts would arrive by messenger at *The Twilight Zone* office from Serling's secretary. They would run anywhere from thirty-five to forty-five pages in length, though Rod knew we needed only twenty-nine pages maximum to fill out our half-hour format. It became a pattern: I would phone and complain about the length and he would always respond the same way, "Cut whatever you need to, *bubbie,* I trust you." (Serling called people he liked *bubbie,* a Yiddish term for nanny.) And that was that. He was apologetic that his scripts were often not up to his own high standards. These were not vintage Rod Serling scripts, but who could blame him? After writing scores of *Twilight Zone* scripts over a three-year span, the well had to run dry sooner or later. It was inevitable.

One afternoon Rod dropped by my office with a script in a sealed envelope. "It's a screenplay I've been toying with and I'm stuck. Would you mind reading it? I'd welcome your suggestions." I was honored that he had faith in my judgment.

The closer I came to knowing Serling, the more aware I was of a deep sadness within him. There is usually a tragic aspect to most people who can be very funny, and Rod was no exception. But I began to puzzle why.

That night I read what was the first third of an unfinished screenplay about a murder that took place in Yankee Stadium during a ball game. While there was the urgency and power of Serling dialogue and scenes, the story went nowhere. The characters had page-long speeches that, powerful as they were, did not progress the story. While reading this embryonic screenplay I began to suspect what might be the source of Serling's angst.

He had been a king in New York live television, had come to Hollywood, written a couple of movies, and created his own long-running television series. But now it was over. Serling, approaching fifty, though highly respected and even admired, was no longer on top, king of the hill. He was of another era. In Hollywood, fifty is dinosaurian.

Many of the better New York live television writers went to work in Hollywood television, but most quickly vanished into the mainstream of the studio/network assembly line system. Some of them got jobs working on screenplays or writing episodic TV series (a lowly status in the Hollywood writing hierarchy). These writers were making a living without big money, glory, or recognition. Today most TV series are staff-written by highly skilled professionals who work out stories and rewrites in meetings with fellow writing staff members' input. (The freelance market is drying up. Hollywood has never been a place to explore the human condition or to challenge the status quo, precisely the territory in which Serling did his best work.)

One New York live television writer, Paddy Chayefsky, rose far above the others, adapting some of his TV plays into films and for the Broadway stage. Chayefsky perfectly expressed his contempt for what network television had become with his brilliant tour-de-force film *Network*. But Chayefsky's career had been cut short by a fatal heart attack.

Serling had some early success writing movies, but few were Rod Serling movies. They didn't offer him the chance to demonstrate his powerful talent. Then he came up with a way to beat the system. He created his own filmed-in-Hollywood television series. It would be aimed at the mass audience, but he would have a chance to say what he wanted to say, the way he wanted to say it. He wrapped his considerable gifts in the guise of fantasy or science fiction. He could be the real Rod Serling and nobody would send him into the trash heap of ordinary "vast wasteland" television. Serling accomplished what few New York golden-age television writers could in Hollywood. He beat them at their own game. But he paid a high price.

Now the game was up. *The Twilight Zone* had ceased to be an oasis. It was now a vehicle for his celebrity, if not his talent, and a source of considerable income. In four years of writing television, albeit *The Twilight Zone,* he had gradually become yesterday's news. He was painfully aware the parade had passed him by. But, while he jokingly denigrated his celebrity status, he loved being recognized, having fans ask for his autograph. It was an interesting paradox: as his status as a major writer diminished, his stature as a celebrity increased. He laughed about doing commercials, voice-overs, and filming his introductions, making feeble self-mocking jokes about being famous. Yet he was totally seduced by fame. Now in his middle years he was becoming a celebrity, period.

Under my contract to produce *The Twilight Zone,* I owed the show an original script and two storylines. The original script I came up with had to do with the famous three monkeys, Hear No Evil, See No Evil, Speak No Evil. People desperately rushed to hospitals as a thick substance was mysteriously closing over their eyes, rendering them blind. Doctors could find no explanation, and the disease was spreading. It's easy to look back now and see that all three monkeys were me. With twenty-twenty hindsight, it is clear to me now I had my belly full of television and could not see working in it anymore.

In any event, it was a poor script. It had no satisfactory resolution, the reason these people's eyes were being covered by a mysterious disease was never explained. (I myself didn't fully understand it.) Both

CBS and Serling turned it down, although Rod suggested I do a major rewrite. He was intrigued but saw its weaknesses. Years later during a Writers Guild strike some enterprising producer, turning out one of the several resurrected *Twilight Zones* sans Serling, found the "Many, Many Monkeys" script in the files and put it in production. I chanced upon it while channel surfing one evening. I wanted to crawl under a rug as I watched, decades later, this feeble effort of mine coming into my living room. I hated it. In which venue other than film and television are writers, actors, directors, and others doomed to see their sins endlessly recycled? Perhaps it is a modern-age purgatory. I have found a way to combat it. I never view reruns of any series I've written or produced. Why suffer for the same crime twice?

One day, after filming an intro, Rod dropped by my office with the look of a man trying to balance pain and relief from pain, "I've blown it, *bubbie,* I've blown *The Twilight Zone.*"

True to predictions, CBS had formally notified him that they had canceled the series. Press notices had gone out that day. But right on cue, Rod had received a call from Tom Moore, president of the American Broadcasting Company, offering to put *The Twilight Zone* on his network. Rod told me why he turned him down.

"He wants me to turn the show into ghosts, ghouls, graveyards, monsters, every week Halloween. I just can't see myself doing it," Rod said. "I told him no thanks."

"Did you know," I asked him, "that before becoming president of ABC Tom Moore was a cemetery plot salesman?"

Although Rod was aware of Tom Moore's pre-showbiz life, somehow juxtaposing Moore's offer with his idea for revamping *The Twilight Zone* gave the story new life and both of us a good laugh. We started improvising an ideal "Tom Moore Twilight Zone," blood dripping off corpses as they struggled to crawl out of their graves to join other newly freed corpses who were cheering them on.

"Not to worry," Rod said, "I've got a new series idea and I'd like you to produce it."

"I'd be delighted," I heard myself saying. "What's it about?

"I'll tell you on the plane, "Rod replied. "We're going to New York tonight for a meeting with Jim Aubrey tomorrow afternoon. I'll pick you up at your home at 6:30 tonight. We're taking the red eye because the only time Jim has open is tomorrow afternoon at three. Ted Ashley has it all set up for us; he feels strongly that we'll walk out with a deal."

On the evening of November 21, 1963, Rod Serling and I boarded a plane for New York. For the early part of the four-and-a-half-hour flight Rod ran through his joke repertoire and kept me doubled over with laughter, but when I pressed him about the new series idea he was going to pitch to Jim Aubrey he became evasive. At one point he told me it was going to be about a reporter-at-large on assignment all over Europe. "We'll shoot it on the continent, *bubbie*," was about as definite as he got. I had a feeling that he would basically improvise whatever he told the president of CBS during our meeting the next day. He would go with the flow.

We arrived a bit groggy early that Wednesday morning, as anyone who flies across the country all night can understand. It was sometime during the sleepless night that I realized that Serling didn't need to have a show idea when we met with Jim Aubrey. He would come up with an idea that he sensed Aubrey was willing to buy. All he needed was to present himself as the creator-writer of any series idea he thought Jim was interested in, and he would have a deal for Cayuga Productions. I was merely an added attraction, since our mutual agent knew that CBS approved of me as a producer.

We arrived at Ted Ashley's office at about one o'clock that afternoon for a brief preparatory discussion with our agent before our meeting with television's currently reigning king, James T. Aubrey. Aubrey had a kind of power that almost equaled the magnitude of the famous studio-founder-owners of Hollywood. There was one thing lacking: unlike the Hollywood moguls, Aubrey did not own his network. William S. Paley did. In retrospect it's clear this detail had escaped Aubrey's attention.

We had just settled in across the desk from Ted Ashley, beginning our discussion of what we would say in our afternoon meeting with Jim Aubrey, when a secretary burst into the office shouting: "The president's been shot! The president's been shot!"

The three of us rushed into the next office where a small group of people was focused on a tiny television screen. Walter Cronkite was announcing that President Kennedy was dead. During the stunned silence that followed we all awkwardly drifted out, Ted, Rod, and I back to Ashley's office where he turned to us and said quietly, "That's it, fellas, you guys might as well go back to L.A."

Rod and I reacted as I suppose most of America did. We were speechless as the cab driver took us back to LaGuardia.

During the flight back to L.A., we began to speculate on the circumstances of the murder of JFK and on who did it and why. But there was no energy left in us. We were almost overwhelmed with despair. Kennedy had meant so much to the United States, if not in substance most assuredly in presentation. He was a president we could proudly show the world and say, look how intelligent, sophisticated, and grown up we've become. We could stand tall among nations with John Fitzgerald Kennedy in the White House. Rod dropped me off at my home on Roscomare Road and continued on to his in the Pacific Palisades.

My wife (I had remarried three years after a particularly bitter divorce) greeted me at the front door, and it was clear that something dramatically new had happened.

"They've arrested the guy who did it," Marie said, "it's on the bedroom TV." We both hurried in to watch the Dallas police leading a handcuffed Lee Harvey Oswald out of their headquarters. Suddenly a heavy set man pushed himself through the little knot of onlookers, a gun in hand. The "pop pop" of his pistol was instantly followed by Oswald slumping to the pavement, his face distorted with pain, then all hell broke loose.

Our phone rang within minutes. I answered. It was Rod. "How would you like to fly to Washington tonight? The United States Information Agency just now phoned me. They want us to do a half-hour documentary on Lyndon Johnson. They want it immediately, if not sooner. I told them we would be in Washington tomorrow morning to meet with them. I'll write it, you produce it. Is that okay with you? Hate to do this to you, pal, but you've just about got time to shower, eat some lunch, maybe take a nap, repack. USIA has made all the arrangements. God knows what we're getting into, but it's clear we have to do it. This is *pro bono* work, of course. I'll explain as much as I know about it on the plane, which isn't much. Gotta go, see you around six o'clock."

It was almost unbelievable, turning around, rushing back East that night to do something the government wanted immediately. "I'll write it, you produce it, but I haven't a clue as to what 'it' is," he said, his voice filled with excitement and anticipation of the challenge that lay ahead. I took a shower, then lunched, and tried but failed to ease myself into a nap. My mind was spinning, I had never produced a documentary in my life and knew nothing whatsoever about how to go about it. But I was buoyed by knowing I would be performing a service for my country. For a deeply patriotic Hollywood hyphenate this alone was enough. The details of how we would do the work required were of secondary importance. Lyndon Johnson, suddenly the president, was already known by everyone in America as a congressman, a Senate majority leader, a presidential candidate, then as vice president. But he was apparently relatively unknown to people in the far reaches of the world. I made up my mind not to speculate further on the bizarre mission Serling and I were about to undertake. We would be doing work for our country that was important and necessary, that was the greatest reward of all.

Meantime, I was also producing the final episodes of *The Twilight Zone*. I had a freelance script ready to shoot, but I had yet to cast it. I didn't like the script and had planned to ask for a major rewrite or, if time didn't allow, rewrite it myself. But time had run out. I phoned my office at MGM and explained to our production manager that I wouldn't be in the office until god-knows-when and that, meantime, we would have to shoot the script as is, forget the rewrite I'd promised. *The Twilight Zone* would have to fend for itself.

Rod's limo picked me up at 6 P.M. on the dot. Almost exactly twenty-four hours later we were taking the same American Airlines red eye as we did the night before, but this time into Washington rather than New York.

"Here's the deal," Rod's voice was intense with suppressed excitement as he began his explanation when we were airborne, "USIA says our embassies all over the world are getting panicky phone calls, especially from third-world countries, demanding to know who is this guy Lyndon Johnson? They know he's a southerner, but they don't know where he stands on racial issues. They're afraid we've got a bigot in the White House. What we've got to do is introduce President

Johnson to embassies, foreign offices, and to the world, while proving he's not a bigot. In fact, that he will have a benign foreign policy. Don't ask me how we're going to do it, but they want a half-hour film they can ship out as soon as possible. Actually they've given us three weeks. Meanwhile, they've got an editor pulling newsreel clips on LBJ. There' s no time to shoot new film. We're meeting with a guy named Carter tomorrow afternoon in his office, he's head of something or other in the USIA. It would be a good idea if we had something to tell him."

As we flew through the night, Rod and I kicked around ideas. We could only speculate on what might be available on preexisting newsreel film.

We kept coming back to one core idea: we would begin with a montage of the United States—familiar scenes, the Statue of Liberty, the Empire State Building, the Yankees in mid-game, scenes of pro football, golf tournaments, tennis matches, busy cops and cab drivers, churches, synagogues, farms—a montage of shortcuts to give third-world countries a mosaic of life in this country. We knew we'd have no problem finding these bits and pieces of film with which to weave America's portrait. We were two lifelong dramatists being asked to become overnight documentarians and propagandists. We both found this new challenge stimulating and exciting.

Rod's narration would briefly explain the meaning of these scenes, which we assumed already existed in film-stock libraries. He was talking along the lines of "We are a nation of builders, not only materially rich but rich with freedom, democracy, and diversity . . ."

Following our montage the camera would very slowly move in on the White House, then inside to an empty chair in the Oval Office. (We might have to shoot this in a set, but it was simple, a half-day max.) Rod's narration would say that though the chair had been briefly and tragically made empty, it was immediately filled by a new, experienced leader committed to the same spirit of freedom, democracy, and diversity. The U.S. Constitution remained bigger and stronger than any one leader . . . and so forth.

As we talked, our confidence and excitement built. We could bring this off, we could have a strong half hour that would do credit not only to LBJ but to our country.

When we had exhausted ourselves of ideas we tried to take brief but restless naps. For me sleep was impossible. When we landed the next morning I had never felt so excited about the job before me. All the miseries of producing television were gone from my mind.

At the Washington airport we were met at the curb by a driver who hurried us into a limousine with nothing but the briefest identification, "Welcome to Washington, gentlemen, I'm taking you directly to the United States Information Agency offices. They are expecting you, please get in." Obviously he had recognized Rod Serling.

During the high-speed drive to our destination, not a word was spoken by our driver, nor did Rod and I exchange more than a few whispered observations. The mood in Washington hung like a shroud over every face we saw, this entire city was in mourning. You could feel the weight of the silence.

The limo pulled over to the curb and the driver handed us our bags. Armed Marine guards stood by the entrance as we were escorted into the building by the driver. An escort whisked us up the elevator to the offices of USIA.

A trio of somber dark-suited men seated in a semicircle faced us as we entered the offices of the man in the middle, who introduced himself as Carter. I did not catch his first name.

In the near distance we could hear horses' hooves clattering on the pavement and the chains of the caissons clanging a dirge tempo along Pennsylvania Avenue as JFK's funeral cortege slowly passed by. It cast a pall over this emergency meeting; the body and the memory of John Fitzgerald Kennedy passing into history as Rod Serling and I were deeply involved in presenting a new president to the world. For me, an uneasy sense of sacrilege created an eerie background score for the remainder of the brief meeting.

"Gentlemen," said Carter, "thank you for coming here on such short notice. Even as we sit here, there is a film editor in New York scouring the file footage of Twentieth Century Fox News for anything and everything they have on President Johnson that might help reassure world leaders that our new president will be a fair-minded, unprejudiced, and compassionate future world leader. We have got to convince the people of distant countries and different political systems that they have no reason to fear LBJ. Our embassies and foreign offices are clamoring for this film. We must show the world we have a leader they can trust. Guys, we need this film as soon as humanly possible. Do you both understand that under USIA's charter nothing we produce can be used for domestic distribution? This film will not be seen in the United States."

Carter took only a brief pause before adding, "I presume you've been talking about ideas. If you have, we'd certainly like to hear them."

Rod took the lead and began to describe our opening montage of America in all its diversity, the towers, the fields, the teeming cities, the churches, the synagogues, the ballgames . . .

"Stop right there," Carter said, abruptly "No synagogues. We can not send a film to our foreign offices in the Middle East with a Star of David in it. We'll lose the Arab nations before we begin. They simply won't distribute it. I like your opening montage idea, but you have to leave out the synagogues."

"In that case, no montage," Rod responded in his crisp, clipped manner. "We'll just open with the camera moving very slowly into the president's empty chair in the Oval Office. Our narration will describe rather than show America's diversity. It will not be as effective, but it will work. Then we will slowly dissolve into whatever film you have in your vaults."

"Very well," said Carter. Turning to his companions he added, "How does that sound to you guys?" They both nodded their approval.

"Fine," Carter concluded. "We've booked you into a suite at the Plaza in New York. I've made arrangements for you to fly up there immediately after this meeting. How do you plan to work it?"

"Bill is going to view the films, select what he thinks will work for us, and I'll write the narration, "Rod responded.

"Anyway you two want to work is fine with me," Carter concluded.

We exited the building into a waiting limousine. The city had grown as silent as a tomb. The funeral cortege had passed on toward Arlington Cemetery, but the streets remained nearly deserted.

Aboard the commuter jet to New York, Rod and I decided upon a simple but expeditious plan. I would spend my days at Fox

Movietone News viewing whatever footage of LBJ the editors had found that would serve our purpose. Rod would remain at the Plaza at his typewriter. As I chose film, I would phone him with what I had and how long the footage ran in minutes, and he would begin constructing a script to fit the film.

Early the next morning I entered the basement projection room of Fox News where an editor sat with a lighted clipboard in his lap, waiting.

"I've been up half the night looking at this stuff," he said, wearily, "and I think I've found some usable footage. What you use is up to you. I've got enough to keep us going for a couple of days. By the way, in case nobody told you, we won't print anything until you decide what you want. You're going to have to look at negatives."

For the next three hours I sat alongside the editor, the control stop-start switch panel between us, as we looked at scores of short cuts of film negatives of LBJ: shaking hands with tribal elders in New Guinea, walking with black school children, addressing a black church congregation, shaking hands with the black pastor outside, mingling with Latinos along the banks of the Pedernales River bordering his Texas ranch, and so forth. Frequently I would stop the projector, ask the editor how many feet he had of a particular scene (90 feet equals one minute), and tell him to print it or mark it in case we needed it for a backup or reject it. As the hours clipped by we began to construct a coherent narrative of LBJ as a man who was comfortable with people whose skin was not white. At a midday break I phoned Rod with the information he needed to start writing the narration.

The editor and I took a short lunch break and continued on into the afternoon until my vision became blurry. The editor had done a superb job. When the day was over I knew beyond a shadow of a doubt that we had made a helluva case for LBJ as world citizen. But I still had only about twelve minutes of useable film; eighteen minutes to go.

That night, after discussing our progress and concept of how to bring this project to a successful conclusion, Rod and I treated ourselves to a night on the town. We had a fabulous dinner with our usual lively nonstop conversation. At dinner or in a bar, Serling was often greeted by fans who recognized him. He assured me that these interruptions were bothersome, but quite obviously he loved the recognition. As our encounters broadened through our work, I began to look upon Rod as a close friend. On this project we were collaborating like composers, words and music. I was choosing the music, Rod the words.

By the end of the second day my mission was accomplished. I knew that the finished film would turn out quite well. Rod was still working on his words. By that evening I had a message from the hotel operator to call Carter at home, no matter what time of night it was.

When I returned the call, Carter's response was both positive and insistent. "Our editor tells me that you've completed your work, so I've set up a screening tomorrow afternoon for some people here at USIA. Ed Murrow and his group want to see it. Be in Washington tomorrow morning." It was not a request, it was a command.

"But Rod is still working on the script," I protested, "I've just finished telling him about the final footage we've chosen."

"No matter," Carter said, "he can tell you what he's going to write, and you'll describe it to us as we look at the film. Be here tomorrow afternoon in time for a three o'clock screening. I'm counting on you." He hung up.

Rod and I had dinner in the room as he prepped me for my debut of the film the next afternoon in Washington. We had gotten to the point where we could talk a kind of shorthand. In a few minutes I had the gist of his words and felt confident that I could somehow muddle my way through what I now thought of as the Edward R. Murrow screening. I had idolized Murrow since I was a teenager. Along with my parents I had stayed glued to his *This Is London* CBS Radio broadcasts during the savage bombing of that capital in the early days of World War II. Between Murrow and Norman Corwin, William S. Paley had made his CBS Radio network an often glittering cathedral.

I arrived promptly the next afternoon in the basement projection room of the USIA building in Washington. Carter came out to greet me. He was understandably nervous.

"I don't know if Ed Murrow can make it," he told me, "but we'll proceed on schedule."

The editor and I took our seats in the elevated back row just under the projection room lights. The editor had his metal lighted clipboard, pencil poised, ready to take notes. About a dozen men filed in. In the darkened room I hadn't a clue as to who they were or who they represented.

The door opened and Edward R. Murrow entered, accompanied by a couple of his aides. Even in the dim light I noted how slouched he stood, his hacking cough was alarming. He was smoking a cigarette. Few of us were aware that chain-smoking Murrow was dying of lung cancer.

I adjusted the mike toward me as Carter ordered the film to be run. The room went pitch black.

Suddenly there was a movie on the screen that I had never seen in its entirety. I began my spiel. I did not try to imitate Rod Serling's voice, but I did try to get his words as exactly as he had told them to me. I was surprised to discover I felt completely at ease.

The audience sat in silence, only their cigarette smoke curling up through the projected light told the editor and me that we were not alone. When it was over I said into the mike, "Well, gentlemen, that's it. It's the best we could put together in less than a week," then added apologetically, to Murrow, "It's a house of straw."

The audience was silent. Then Murrow stood up, fixed me with his famous heavy browed piercing eyes, and said, "Some straw."

That's all he said, and he was escorted out the door with his associates. However, I was thrilled. I felt this was the highest accolade of my career. As the lights came up, Carter hurried up to me, hand extended, "It's brilliant, simply brilliant. You and Rod have my heartiest congratulations and gratitude."

"Thanks very much," I responded. "I'll tell Rod at dinner tonight. I'm flying back to L.A. on the red eye. I've got *Twilight Zone* work to do."

"I understand," replied Carter, "but I want you here to oversee the music and sound. Of course, we don't have time to create a score. So you and our music editor will have to choose music tracks. And I'll want you and Rod here for the screening of our answer print, if we have a screening for the President."

It couldn't have gotten any better than this. The entire process had been completed in a little over a week, everybody was happy, and now I could go back to Metro and do the work I was being paid to do.

The next day, sleepless and groggy eyed I made my way into my *Twilight Zone* office on the MGM lot and settled in behind my desk to survey the situation. How fast could I get some scripts to keep us from shutting down and missing airdates?

The first phone call, as expected, was from Boris Kaplan, my CBS program supervisor. He wanted to assure me that CBS was pleased Rod and I were doing this service for our country. However, he had received no story outlines in the past two weeks. He said the quality of *Twilight Zone* must not fall between the cracks. This was ironic in that CBS had officially terminated the series at the end of the present season. But when you work in television, irony is your life's companion.

My return to work was interrupted by my secretary advising me that a *New York Times* reporter was in my outer office wanting to ask me a couple of questions about the LBJ film. This was not surprising since *Daily Variety* had front-paged "Rod Serling–Froug Speed USIA Film on New President" a couple of days earlier.

An impeccably dressed, middle-aged man in sport coat, sweater vest, and tie, appearing to fit the mold of a *New York Times* reporter, entered. After a brief intro he sat alongside my desk and took out a pad and pencil. "How did it go with your USIA film?" he asked, pleasantly. I was sleep deprived from too many red-eye cross-country flights. I knew I should ask him to please leave, but my mind was not sharp and I was physically exhausted.

"It went great," I told him. "We're almost finished and everyone seems pleased with it."

He didn't move a muscle. "So there were no problems?'

"None," I replied, "none whatsoever."

"That's unusual, isn't it, when dealing with the government?"

"We didn't have any problems," I insisted, "the whole experience was better than we could have hoped for."

He remained seated, looking at his notepad, pencil poised. (I have since been told by my reporter friends that this is a reporter trick: sit in silence mid-interview until your victim, growing uncomfortable, blurts out something that might make a story.)

I was, indeed, growing increasingly uncomfortable and too tired to simply tell him to leave my office I fell into his trap. I was finding the silence unbearable and felt saying something would get him out of my office so I could get to work. "We did have a minor incident," I told him, "when we suggested opening the film with a montage of America including churches and synagogues. They said no synagogues because Muslim nations would ban the film. But it was unimportant. We easily figured out a way to get around it. The whole thing came off much easier than Rod or I expected. They left us alone; it was easy working with them."

He stood up. "I'm glad things went so smoothly," he said. "Sorry to have taken up your time."

As the door closed I went to work phoning writers. The ten-minute inconsequential interview vanished from my memory as soon as he was out my office door.

Later in the day Rod phoned to ask me how everything was going with *Twilight Zone.* He also told me how really grateful USIA was for the job I'd done. Carter had called him to personally express his pleasure with the film, and to ask Rod how soon he would have his narration and be able to record it. Rod told him the narration was finished, but he would not be the narrator. He suggested they hire an actor. But Carter wanted me back in to New York to supervise the narration recording, the sound, and the music tracks for the film ASAP. I agreed to take yet another red eye to New York that night. Rod meanwhile would return home to L.A.

That night I flew to New York and checked into the Hampshire House the following morning. As I got into the elevator I happened to glance down at the stack of fresh *New York Times* beside the elevator operator. The papers were folded face down so my eye caught the front-page headline just below the fold: TV PRODUCER CHARGES USIA WITH ANTI-SEMITISM.

The first thought that popped into my mind was, "who could that be?" I knew almost every television producer in Hollywood, having been a member of the Producers Guild of America's board of directors for the past six years. I had to find out who had made the charges. I picked up the paper and read:

"Hollywood television producer William Froug today charged the United States Information Agency with blatant anti-Semitism . . ."

I was dumbfounded. I had said nothing of the kind. I tucked the paper under my arm and entered my room, so filled with rage that I was speechless.

My phone message light was blinking furiously. The telephone operator informed me that a senator had phoned to advise me that he was considering launching an investigation into the USIA, and he would be calling me as his first witness. I had two other calls, one from Rod and one from Carter.

I returned Carter's call, He said, "You're fired, go home." Then he added, "By the way, I happen to be Jewish." He slammed down his phone before I could tell him the story was a lie. I had never in any way, shape, or form charged the USIA with anti-Semitism. I had merely mentioned a comment they had made at the beginning of our first meeting but assured the reporter it was of no consequence. I'd made it abundantly clear that both Rod and I had a good experience with enthusiastic support from USIA.

Next, I returned Rod's call, and he was quite angry and upset. "Bill, I've got god-knows-how-many TV reporters outside my door with cameras, it's a mad house. How could you have done this to me?" I tried to explain but he, too, angrily hung up on me.

I did the only thing I could do. I phoned and made a reservation on a late afternoon flight back to Los Angeles, another red eye. At LaGuardia I picked up an afternoon paper. On page two of the *Post* was a six-column banner headline that read: SERLING DENIES USIA ORDERED 'NO SYNAGOGUE.'

Sick to my stomach, I glanced through the rest of the story, Serling, by lying, had in effect called me a liar. I threw the paper in the trash as I boarded the plane. How could he have done it? I was angry and bitterly disappointed.

I had a long night alone on the plane to think over the incredible events of the past forty-eight hours. The *Times* reporter had created a story where there was none; it was the kind of sleaze journalism that I had never expected from the *New York Times*. This was tabloid trash. Rod's response left me furious at him and at myself for my own stupidity. But rightly blaming myself wasn't going to help the situation.

When I got home my phone was ringing off the hook. A local news reporter wanted to know if I was "one of those professional Zionists." I answered that I didn't think so in as much as my wife was Presbyterian, my birth mother was Catholic, my birth father was Jewish, and I was not a member of any organized religion. He hung up.

By the next afternoon I was back at work, scrounging for scripts. What I eventually was able to come up with only reflected the time I had spent away from the show. We were shooting pretty much whatever came in. The final episodes of *The Twilight Zone* were winding down in homes across America, and they were poor.

However, Boris Kaplan was on my back about the budget, we had not eliminated the overage, and, Kaplan said, Aubrey was furious. Thanks to my absence I had nothing to shoot for our final episode.

Desperation can be the mother of invention—and in this case it was. During my semester of teaching short film at USC's Film School, I had shown students scores of short films, but far and away the best of the lot was "An Occurrence at Owl Creek Bridge," a French adaptation of an Ambrose Bierce short story. Written and directed by Robert Enrico, it had won a Palme d'Or at the 1962 Cannes Film Festival. I recalled that it was about twenty-four minutes in length, a bit longer than most of the short films I'd shown in class. Bierce's story was a perfect *Twilight Zone*. Had Enrico shot the film for the show itself he couldn't have done it better.

Before mentioning it to Rod or Kaplan, I immediately set about to discover if the television rights were available. Anne Nelson, now at CBS TV business affairs, reported back that we could buy the TV rights for a one-time showing for ten thousand dollars. If I could sell the idea to Serling and Kaplan, *The Twilight Zone's* deficit would be erased in one airing. We would end the series right on budget.

I arranged a screening for the three of us: Serling, Kaplan, and myself. I was not surprised by Rod's enthusiastic response. Kaplan, on the other hand, worried about showing a French film on American television, especially CBS (what would James T. Aubrey think?).

In reality, the film was almost entirely silent with only some brief lyrical lines sung in English. Ever the fearful bureaucrat, Kaplan finally gave in. He would notify his business affairs department to buy the rights, and we would close the series with a bang, esthetically as well as financially.

Now came the hard part. When a copy of the print was delivered to our editor, he advised me that the film was ninety feet too long. We had to cut it to squeeze it into our format (time needed for our commercials, for Rod's opening, mid-break, and closing filmed comments).

Going into the editor's cutting room, staring down at the tiny movieola screen alongside the editor, running the film back and forth, we both searched for places to nip out a few feet here, a few feet there, until we had enough cut to make it fit our tight time requirements without marring the masterpiece. It was akin to figuring out what you could cut out of the Mona Lisa without destroying its beauty. We finally found the deletions we had to have, and yet felt certain we had not marred the masterpiece.

Rod came to the studio to do his intros as always, but he no longer stopped by the office to say hello. We spoke a few times. He was cordial but distant. He was not interested in my attempts to tell him the truth of what had actually happened with the *New York Times* piece nor did he want to know what I actually had said to the reporter. He cut me off, "I don't want to discuss it." At that moment I realized how deeply my misquoted comment in the *New York Times* had embarrassed him. A fundamentally honorable man, I knew he had not forgiven himself for calling me a liar in the *Post*. I had inadvertently caused his guilt and pain, and I was wracked with my own guilt and shame. Suddenly we had nothing to say to each other.

When the season was over we gave a special wrap party on the set. It was the end of a five-year run of one of television's most distinguished series. Dick Donner and I had our pictures taken standing over a prop gravestone that said "R.I.P. Twilight Zone," alongside was a huge, fake funeral bouquet that read "Good Luck, Rod. Tom Moore." Some champagne and forced laughter marked the end of this illustrious television series.

Wrap party for *The Twilight Zone* series. Producer William Froug stands over Rod Serling lying on "grave," mocking ABC's offer to turn the series into weekly tales of ghouls and ghosts. *Twilight Zone* director Richard Donner looks on. (from the author's collection)

Rod and I never really spoke to one another again. I ran into him once at a Writers Guild gathering. He was embarrassed and noticeably uncomfortable.

"You know, that *Night Gallery* series," he said, confidentially, "it's crap, I've got nothing to do with it. I only come in to do my stand-ups." I knew it was his awkward attempt to put things right between us.

However, I left the brief encounter feeling a deep sadness for him. His career had shriveled after *The Twilight Zone*. He had become a victim of his own celebrity. But in spite of his family history of heart disease, a previous heart attack, and warnings from his doctors, Rod would not give up smoking. He died at age fifty-one following bypass surgery. I felt it was a conscious decision he had made, a kind of unstated suicide. He had won more Emmy Awards for dramatic writing than any other writer. He had been elected president of the Academy of Television Arts and Sciences. He had created a series that might be in reruns as long as television survives. And he was a good man, a decent man. He had been king of the hill for longer than most writers would dare to dream. Where did he have to go from there? He discovered teaching, and enjoyed it, but he had once been a king.

Even today I can not shake the terrible sense of guilt I have about the incident. Nearly forty years later, I want to reach out to him and say, "Rod, I'm terribly, terribly sorry."

After production of *The Twilight Zone* was completed, I got a job offer from CBS to become executive producer in charge of dramatic programs at CBS Hollywood.

Nowhere in that job title or in my contract could I have anticipated that shortly after reporting for work, I would be given an S.O.S. order to rescue *Gilligan's Island.*

11

Banished to Gilligan's Island

James Thomas Aubrey Jr. stood more than six feet tall, was thin as a reed, handsome in an angular way, and born to privilege. He graduated from the prestigious Phillips Exeter Academy and Princeton University. Yet he had the surest feel for the mass audience's taste in TV programs of anyone in broadcasting history. In a remarkably short period of time he became the most powerful president of a television network in the history of the medium. Soon, the press dubbed him "the smiling cobra"; books and movies were made about him, depicting him as a cold, ruthless, arrogant tyrant. I was soon to discover that all of them were accurate.

Aubrey began his meteoric career in 1948 as an account executive ("spot ad" salesman) at CBS's Los Angeles radio affiliate, KNX Radio, where I met him briefly one day as he rushed out of the building to see a Los Angeles Dodgers game. Aubrey, high spirited and full of youthful enthusiasm, had been a test pilot in the Unites States Army Air Force and was honorably discharged as a major. By all accounts he was a good salesman, very bright, and quite aggressive.

198

Aubrey, trim in his pinstriped Brooks Brothers suit, kept himself physically fit, exceptionally neat.

After a brief stint as program director and then general manager of a local Los Angeles TV station, his career took off like a comet. In 1957 he and a young CBS-TV Hollywood executive named Hunt Stromberg Jr. helped launch a new program called *Have Gun, Will Travel.* It became an overnight hit, ranking among the top five shows in its first season on the air. It was the beginning of a tumultuous and scandal-ridden collaboration between the two opposites, who were to rule CBS for a decade, lifting the network's ratings into first place and increasing CBS's annual profits from $25 million to $49.6 million.

Aubrey in New York, not Stromberg in Hollywood, was in complete command of the network. Eight or nine of his personally picked series were among the top-ten rated shows, year in and year out. He was dubbed "The King of Television" by the media press. At the height of his powers Aubrey was also making other kinds of headlines: JIM AUBREY, CBS PRES. 'BROKE MY ARM' SAYS N.Y. MODEL or CBS'S AUBREY, JACKIE GLEASON IN MIAMI SCANDAL. William S. Paley was allegedly asked by a reporter how he could keep such a disreputable man on as president of his television network. Paley is said to have replied, "As long as my stock keeps going up, Jim Aubrey is my television network president." Paley may or may not have said it, but it was a logical explanation of his acceptance of Aubrey's ruthless, scandal-ravaged reign.

When I reported for work at CBS's mammoth glass-and-steel building called Television City, on the corner of Fairfax and Beverly Drive in Los Angeles, Aubrey (officed in New York) and Stromberg, then vice president of programs at CBS Television, Hollywood, were at the height of their powers. The front page story in *Daily Variety* had headlined FROUG TO EXEC PROD CBS DRAMA.

My agent had negotiated a one-year contract and a substantial pay increase with an option for a second year at more money with pilot incentives. I had no idea what the executive producer in charge of drama actually did, but felt I'd get a break from the constant pressure of being what was beginning to be called a show runner.

My vision of my new assignment was that I would sit in a posh office and make infinitely wise decisions without ever going on a set or setting a finger to a typewriter. In short, I was fully prepared to rest on my laurels, or so I imagined. I foolishly did not include the Aubrey-Stromberg axis in my thinking. Though I'd come across Aubrey once or twice, I had not met Stromberg.

My first inkling that my fantasy was far out of line with reality came when I reported to work at my new headquarters. When I arrived on the third floor a woman who introduced herself as Mr. Stromberg's assistant took me down the hall and pointed to an empty office. "This was Boris Kaplan's office," she told me, "he's been moved down the hall, around the corner. It's now yours."

I was chagrined to learn they'd kicked my old CBS program supervisor from *The Twilight Zone* out of his office for me. I had rather liked Boris in his quiet, gentle, bureaucratic way. The idea of his being humiliated by my arrival was actually a hint of unpleasant things to come. When he dropped by his former office to pick up a few items he'd left behind, I apologized to him. He merely shrugged.

"Crazier stuff than this goes on around here," he said, with only a hint of bitterness. "You'll get used to it. I have."

I knew no one at Television City except my old friend Anne Nelson. Nelson was as rock solid as you can get, and just as reliable. I had admired her from the day we met in the late forties at CBS Radio. It seemed a lifetime ago.

Soon I was summoned to Hunt Stromberg Jr.'s office just down the hall. Stromberg was the son of the highly successful MGM movie producer responsible for many of that studio's biggest hits. Stromberg Sr. had worked there for seventeen years. It was said that his son had inherited several hundred million dollars worth of real estate, which included vast ranches in Texas. Young Stromberg was already building a reputation in town as high-strung, impetuous and unpredictable. Not a man you wanted to mess with.

When I entered Stromberg's office he stood up to greet me with a warm welcome. He was a dark-haired, handsome man with a youthful face, a naughty-boy grin, and quite effeminate mannerisms.

"Welcome aboard, as they say. Jim and I are delighted to have you with us. Please sit down." He moved about his office with almost constant nervous gestures, as if uncertain of what he was going to do next.

As I sat across the desk from him he said, "Your job here is to produce shit." His grin was intended to convey that while he didn't really mean it, he wanted me to know that he understood that he and I were intellectually superior to the fare on television. In all of our conversations, Stromberg referred to Aubrey in such a way as to make it clear that Jim Aubrey was running CBS—and he was Jim's man in Hollywood.

Stromberg, fidgeting nervously in his seat, opened his desk drawer, took out some pills and popped them in his mouth, with a self-conscious giggle. His pill-popping was a fixture of almost every meeting I was to have with him.

"You are in charge of our dramatic programs. I want you to read the scripts for all our dramas, meet with the producers, tell them your ideas, and see if you can't help them make their shows better. I know you're not going to find that easy, but they respect you, so I'm sure you'll accomplish a great deal. From time to time I'll be calling on you for advice on any and all our shows. Have you met Sol Saks yet?" I replied that I hadn't but knew his reputation as a top comedy writer.

"He is," Hunt continued, "and he's going to be your counterpart in comedy, overseeing our comedy shows, as you will our dramas. He's a very nice guy, I'm sure you will like him. His office will be next to yours, as of today.

"We're developing a sitcom with Cara Williams," Stromberg continued with sudden enthusiasm. To my blank stare, he added, "Cara and her husband and I play bridge together," as if this added bit of important new information would bring recognition. He went on, "Mike Garrison and I are working on a new one hour series, it's going to be James Bond in the West; we call it *The Wild, Wild, West*. I'd like your input on that one later on when we get a pilot script."

Try as I might, I could not get a handle on who these people were, nor was I excited by 007 in western costume.

"And Jim has made a deal with Keefe Brasselle to develop some series," he summed up, adding, "Jim and Keefe are old friends."

I left his office, more than somewhat bewildered. It was as if I had somehow wandered into an alternative television universe. Cara

Williams, Mike Garrison, Keefe Brasselle? Was I really supposed to know who these people were, much less get excited about their upcoming series at CBS?

By ten that morning Sol Saks wandered into my office. He wore a big, friendly smile, and an obviously brand-new sharkskin suit.

"Do you like the suit?" Sol asked me, his eyes twinkling with delight, his Chicago accent thick as shoe leather. "It's sharkskin. I've always wanted a job where I had to wear a suit; I bought three of them this weekend. And I also get to wear a tie, I usually dress like a slob," he laughed, "this is the big time, we're *executives!*" His demeanor made it clear that he actually could not have cared less. We were going to have a good time together.

Sol's humor made him a delight to be with. He was a man utterly without pretensions, completely at ease with himself. I suspected from the start that we would become lifelong friends, which we have. We shared a sense of the absurdity of Hollywood, and we refused to take the town or ourselves seriously.

Soon we began walking around and behind the Television City building, having lunch outdoors at the Farmers' Market. We began reading scripts for the series each of us were assigned. Sol put into words the conclusion we both had quickly come to. "If we tell the producers we don't like their scripts, they won't change them. If we tell them we like the scripts, they'll say 'So what do we need your opinion for?'"

Saks and I began our separate meetings with the series producers assigned to each of us. After comparing notes we discovered our hunches were correct. We each received the same hostile receptions. It was no surprise that producers did not want an executive from the network telling them how to run their shows.

Nonetheless, I felt obliged to fulfill my assigned task: meet with producers of CBS series and talk about their shows. All of them were about as pleased to see us as they would have been at seeing an IRS man coming out to audit their income tax returns. One of the series I was supposed to supervise was the CBS hit western *Rawhide*. On the face of it the idea was ludicrous. Bernie Kowalski and Bruce Geller were both hyphenates (Bernie was also an outstanding TV director, Bruce a top TV writer) and had been producing the series

Sol Saks, former radio writer, creator of *Bewitched,* former executive producer of comedy for CBS Television, who may or may not have marooned the author on *Gilligan's Island.* You be the judge. (courtesy of Sol Saks)

flawlessly. The scripts I'd read were first-rate, if not inspired, their casting was consistently outstanding, and their ratings were good. I had nothing to contribute to what they were doing quite capably without me.

Feeling more than a bit ridiculous, I made my way out to their *Rawhide* production offices on the CBS Studio City lot. Entering Kowalski and Geller's office, I found the atmosphere even more hostile than I had expected. Although Bruce, Bernie, and I had met casually on various occasions, their icy reception could have created a rink in the simmering hot San Fernando Valley where Studio City was located. I made a few opening remarks to the effect that I'd read several of the series scripts and found them of good quality. They were obviously disinterested in my opinion.

Quickly we moved on to a discussion of their cast, young Clint Eastwood in particular. We were unanimous in our opinion that this young actor was going to be a very big star. Of course, none of us could have predicted that Eastwood would have to go to Italy and be cast in a series of Sergio Leone's so-called spaghetti Westerns in order to make the leap from TV series actor to major movie box-office star.

Geller and Kowalski told me Eastwood had the kind of all-out determination it took to make it to big screen stardom. Apparently the young actor sometimes lived in his car during filming.

After a brief interlude of meaningless conversation, I beat a hasty retreat to my office in Television City. My worst fears had been realized: being a network program supervisor was a useless and redundant job. But the networks have never accepted the concept of hiring the best producer for a series and letting him or her do their job. Every network continues to deem it their responsibility to second-guess their series producers until they either drive them out or cripple their own shows. Only a few TV producers acquire the clout to tell them to butt out. Spelling, Lear, and Bochco come to mind.

On the other hand, I had been "supervised" by Boris Kaplan on *The Twilight Zone.* I hadn't wanted him to tell me how to do my job any more than these guys with whom I was dealing. I like to think that, unlike this bunch, I had felt no hostility toward Kaplan; he was merely a consummate, loyal, one-dimensional company man dedicated to his job.

During one of our many lunches I learned that Saks had been a writer on the hit radio comedy series *Duffy's Tavern.* He told funny stories about the star, Ed Gardner, holding his story conferences with his writers while walking about the room stark naked, expounding on the art of comedy and especially on the artistry of Ed Gardner. Saks had been head writer and story editor of Howard Duff and Ida Lupino's TV series *Mr. Adams and Eve.* Saks had also written the pilot for a new series, *Bewitched,* which quickly became ABC's number-one-rated show and remained in the top ten or fifteen for almost eight years. Saks was the hottest comedy writer in television at the time, but he was totally unfazed by his status, even though CBS had given him a ten-year contract calling for him to submit at least one comedy series idea per year. The contract was for a minimum of twenty-five thousand dollars a year, much more, of course, if CBS went into development with any of his series ideas.

Sol and I quickly grasped that we had no-brainer jobs. If we told the producers what we thought about their scripts and they ignored our ideas (as they usually did) and our show ratings went down, we could always say to Hunt Stromberg Jr., "Well, we told them what to do, but they didn't listen." If our shows rating went up we could say, "You see, they did what we told them to."

CBS had initiated a new weekly musical starring Judy Garland, even though the former MGM star, now in the closing stage of her career, had already developed a history of emotional problems.

One day I heard Hunt Stromberg outside my door, calling somewhat frantically, "Judy Garland's locked herself in her dressing room! Somebody get her out of there!" Hearing the crisis being broadcast in our hallways brought a smile to my face. I realized that wherever I worked in Hollywood, there were at least a few certainties one could count on. Stars locking themselves in their dressing rooms was one of them.

Stromberg's secretary phoned me one day to request my presence in our basement projection room for a screening of a new pilot titled *Hogan's Heroes.*

About a dozen executives sat watching the antics of clever American prisoners of war in a German prison camp during World War II. Like many television series, this one was a spin-off of a popular movie, in this case *Stalag 17*. And like most TV sitcom adaptations of features, the genre was changed from tragicomedy to lighthearted silliness. In the sitcom version, the Nazis, no longer menacing killers, became lovable buffoons. I was deeply offended, no doubt still rooted in my own World War II–generational thinking that the Nazis were the most dangerous political organization in the history of mankind. At that time, POW compounds or concentration camps were not the stuff of fun and hijinks, or so I thought. Millions of Americans were to prove me wrong.

When the screening was finished there was almost unanimous agreement—*Hogan's Heroes* was going to become a hit series. No one in the room felt any of my compunctions.

I aired my feelings to Stromberg later that day; he dismissed me as a man out of touch with my audience.

Still upset, I went back to my office and phoned a friend who worked at the Anti-Defamation League, urging him to set up a screening for his associates before *Hogan's Heroes* was put on CBS's new broadcast schedule.

A few days later my friend phoned. "Thanks for telling me about it!" he said, enthusiastically. "Actually, I brought along a couple of rabbis. We all agree it's a very funny show. None of us have any objections whatsoever."

Hogan's Heroes became another of CBS's top-ten comedies. First aired in 1965 it remained on the network's schedule for six years, a remarkable run by any measure.

Stromberg and Jim Aubrey knew their audiences. Once again, I was reminded how much my own taste frequently differed from the public's.

CBS-TV's shows were consistently rating in the Nielsen's top ten, week in and week out, without any help from the West Coast executives. The press rightfully gave the credit to CBS-TV's president, James T. Aubrey. He alone decided what went on the network's television schedule and in what time slot. Aubrey's style was openly dictatorial; he rarely listened to anyone except William S. Paley. Aubrey was said to have the Midas touch, almost every program he chose was a winner. CBS-TV came to be called the hillbilly network, or the cornpone network, and other terms less flattering by the entertainment media. Our biggest hits were *The Beverly Hillbillies, Green Acres,* and *Petticoat Junction,* all based on cornball jokes and country humor. In addition we had *Gunsmoke,* Mr. Paley's personal favorite, which was often number one in the nation and for which Aubrey could take no credit. Perhaps that is the origin of the unusual events that followed his cancellation of the series.

When *Gunsmoke* had finally run its course after ten years, with the ratings plummeting, Aubrey canceled it without consulting Paley. CBS-TV business affairs executive Anne Nelson was ordered to send out cancellation notices to the cast as well as the producer. Farewell tears flowed on the set during the wrap party, and a kind of mourning set in among cast members, most of whom had worked together for the entire run of the series. Series actors playing in family-like formats themselves often become a family.

When Paley was told of the cancellation, he immediately ordered the show renewed, leaving Nelson the extremely difficult job of going back to the many agents involved and trying to pick up the stars' contracts as if the cancellation hadn't happened. Of course none of the agents took kindly to this last minute change of heart. Their clients had suffered emotional distress, and CBS would have to pay for it. It was a nightmare for Nelson and cost the network a small fortune in increased star salaries.

Aubrey's choice of programming was especially interesting to me because personally he was an urbane, sophisticated Ivy Leaguer whose own taste, like mine, included Fellini, Ingmar Bergman, Antonioni, and the French New Wave filmmakers, Goddard, Truffaut, and others. More than once when I was in New York, I saw him standing in a ticket line to get into an "art house" movie theater.

Stromberg brought Aubrey's name into every conversation I had with him, as well as in our every program meeting, always with considerable admiration, if not reverence. It was peculiarly excessive.

There was speculation that Hunt Stromberg provided Jim with women when he came out to Hollywood. (Aubrey had married and divorced actress Phyllis Thaxter, with whom he had a daughter.) There were dark speculations suggesting Aubrey had a penchant for heavy gambling in Vegas, and that somehow actor Keefe Brasselle was mixed up in it, along with associates of unsavory criminal organizations, but there was never any verification of any of the rumors that swarmed around him like toxic bees. During one of his visits to his West Coast headquarters at Television City, Stromberg told me that he and Jim would like me to join them for lunch at the Farmers' Market.

As the three of us sat at a tiny table outside having our lunch, surrounded by throngs of strolling tourists, Jim and Hunt began to discuss their politics in reference to an upcoming election. Aubrey thought Goldwater was a dangerous liberal. He was a Clint Murchison fan. Murchison was the Texas multimillionaire oil man who published a notoriously radical right-wing anti-Semitic newsletter, which was widely regarded as neo-Fascist. Jim said, "I don't defend his anti-Semitism, but I like where he stands politically." Hunt Stromberg chimed in, an eager and consummate yes-man, agreeing with everything his boss had to say. Finally, tired of being a largely ignored spectator, I announced, "I'm a left-wing liberal Democrat." Their lack of response surprised me. They simply weren't interested in whatever I had to say. It was a bewildering lunch. Why had they invited me to join them? Neither television nor CBS was discussed. As we walked back to our offices it became clear that the only opinion Aubrey was interested in was his own.

Stromberg had a scheduled program department meeting the next day because Aubrey was in town. As we entered the large conference room, we discovered Aubrey lounging on a chaise against the wall near the head of the conference table, studiously reading the *Wall Street Journal,* his long legs comfortably stretched out before him. His back to us, he did not look up as we entered nor acknowledge our presence as we filed in past him. There were no greetings exchanged. It was as if we were not in the room. It seemed his calculated statement was intended to generate fear, I suppose, or maybe just awe and intimidation among his management team. Stromberg started the meeting, "I thought it might be a good idea to have a program meeting while Jim is in town."

Totally absorbed in his paper, Aubrey did not respond, making it clear that as far as he was concerned, we were not there, nothing was happening, there was no meeting. As Hunt Stromberg led the meeting with a desultory discussion of our program problems, clearly trying to impress Aubrey with the depth of knowledge he had about our shows, Boris Kaplan stood up. I wanted to yell out, "Boris, don't!" but it was already too late.

"If you want my opinion, Jim," Boris began, ignoring Stromberg. That is as far as he got.

"I don't. Sit down," said Aubrey, cutting him off without looking up from his *Journal,* his voice soft, underscoring the power of his command. He might have been flicking lint from his sleeve. It was a bravura display of arrogance.

The meeting was a shambles from that moment on as all of us kept a low profile as Aubrey silently remained dedicated to his *Wall Street Journal.* Stromberg, ever Aubrey's cheerleader, desperately tried to generate some program discussions, but none of us was having any of it.

As always, Sol Saks knew exactly what to say. He stood up, "Well, Jim," he said, in his thick Chicago drawl, "we've taken up enough of your time. I think we all should go back to work."

We filed out silently, avoiding looking at each other or our president. Aubrey had given a tour-de-force performance. It was the last time I was to see him before William Paley instituted his headline-making CBS-TV executive massacre.

Soon, Sol and I, fully recognizing the unimportance of our work, joined the Beverly Hills Health Club where we began taking three-hour lunches, starting with massages on the roof followed by swimming laps and a light meal in the club grill. Without exchanging many words on the subject, we now fully understood the bizarre nature of our job: we were supposed to do nothing, gracefully. We were at least to look busy during our appointed rounds. We began asking each other how long this high-paying, freeloading job could last. The end came quickly for me, and more suddenly and unpleasantly than I could have imagined.

One day Hunt Stromberg called me into his office. I thought perhaps he was going to make note of our three-hour lunches. Instead he told me how happy he and Jim were with Sol's and my work.

Then he sprung a surprise on me. "By the way," he said seemingly as an afterthought, "there's a pilot I want you to see. It's set up in our screening room in the basement. They're ready to show it to you as soon as you get down there." Without being able to pinpoint it, there was something in his voice that troubled me.

"What's the pilot?" I asked him, warily. Like most of my fellow executives, I had developed a deep-seated distrust of Stromberg.

"You'll see it when you get down there. And when you're finished come back up to see me. We'll talk about it." Now I really didn't like the tone of his voice.

I sat alone in our tiny basement projection room watching a pilot titled *Gilligan's Island.* When I returned to Stromberg's office, he asked my opinion. I told him I thought it was a good comedy and might even be a hit.

"Jim and I are certain of it," Hunt replied. "That's why we want you to produce it."

I was totally flabbergasted. I could not believe what I was hearing.

"But it's Sherwood Schwartz's series," I answered with growing apprehension. "He created it and he's the producer."

"Sherwood Schwartz is an incompetent idiot. He's sent us only three scripts in six weeks and only one of them is usable. The other two Sol Saks says we can't use. We're not going to meet our airdate. And we want this show on our fall schedule. Schwartz doesn't seem to have any idea what that means. He's out there dithering around, he can't even find a location where we can shoot the series. He can't produce a series, even the thought of it is ridiculous. Jim and I feel strongly we have a possible hit, and we've got a nincompoop out there wondering what to do next!" Stromberg was getting himself worked up pretty good. "I just got off the phone with George Rosenberg, Sherwood's agent. I told Rosy to tell his client that he's fired. I want him off the show."

It was the opening I was looking for. "Sol Saks is your head of comedy," I told Hunt. "Assign him to do the show." I felt I was being backed against a wall. Desperation was creeping into my voice.

"We spoke to Sol, but he has no producing experience and you do. Jim and I agree you've got to take over the show. Jim is high on this show, Bill, we both believe it's going to be a hit. You can save it."

"But, it's Sherwood's series, he created it, wrote and produced the pilot," I pleaded. "Hunt, please leave me out of it!"

"Our minds are made up. We want this show on the fall schedule, but that idiot can't make it. If we weren't convinced it could be a hit, we'd cancel it today and send everybody home. Schwartz has only one script, which his brother wrote. He can't find his ass in a toilet! I'm ordering the gate guards to keep him off the lot. Sherwood is an idiot." Stromberg was getting really warmed up now, "You're taking over the show Monday morning. Report to Studio Center, get some writers, hire some directors, and, for god's sake, find a location for shooting. If Schwartz gives you any trouble let me know. I've told his agent to send him to Mexico, and I mean it. I don't want any interference from him. I don't want him on the lot, or anywhere near the series. Don't even allow him in your office." Having finally finished off Schwartz, he turned his attention back to me. "Jim and I have confidence in you, we know you'll save this series."

I was a drowning man looking for a life jacket. "But my office is here, my secretary is here," I pleaded again. "I don't want to produce *Gilligan's Island,* I don't even like it. It's dumb. How about sending Sol Saks?"

"Sol thinks it's a great idea you're going to produce the show, and he volunteered to drop by your office from time to time, in case you want his help on the scripts." Stromberg rose to indicate the conversation was over. "Besides," he said, "we just want you to get the show started. Help us meet our airdate, produce a few shows, then you can come back to your office. Meantime, we're keeping your office and your secretary here. You can come back just as soon as you get the show off the ground. That's a promise."

Realizing that there was no way out, I finally gave in. I didn't need a lawyer to tell me that producing a comedy series was not in my contract, but fight the King of Television? No way. I left Stromberg's office in a state of disbelief. It had happened with the suddenness and finality of a guillotine.

I headed straight for Sol Saks's office where I found him reading a script. "You son of a bitch!" I began as politely as I was going to get, "You put me in this damned *Gilligan's Island* mess. I thought we were friends."

"I had nothing to do with it," Saks replied, blandly. "They mentioned the show to me, and they asked if I minded if you produced the series, because you have producing experience and I haven't. It was all their idea, Hunt said Jim insisted on it. I swear to god, I'm innocent. I promise you. Look, Sherwood has been out there for at least two months and all he's got to show for it is three scripts, two unusable. He hasn't even decided where he's going to shoot the series. He's in over his head."

(To this day, Sol Saks and I continue to argue over whether or not he set me up to be marooned on *Gilligan's Island*. While we have remained close friends over the years, and will continue to be until the end of time, our Gilligan argument is never-ending and has become a comedic dialogue all by itself.)

I reported to work Monday morning at CBS's Studio Center in the San Fernando Valley, a traffic-jammed, mountainous commute into the hottest region of Los Angeles County.

In the *Gilligan's Island* offices they might as well have hung black drapes. Their hostility was right out there for me to witness. The secretaries barely spoke to me or even acknowledged my being there. Sherwood Schwartz was there silently cleaning out his office, his back to me. John Rich, the well-known director scheduled to become co-producer of the series, put on an especially impressive performance. Rich, a large figure of a man, looked down his nose at me silently, sniffed, and turned away. Rich had developed pomposity into an art form. He was obviously unaware how ludicrous his performance was; I suppressed a laugh and walked around him.

Sherwood Schwartz, whom comedy writer Hal Kanter had once dubbed "Robin Hood's rabbi," fussed about the offices listlessly like a CPA after tax season, his shoulders slouched over, his face set in a deep, self-pitying scowl, silent, holding in his anger. Many years later, I was to discover in his own account of the series that he believed I "plotted" to take over his series.

Coventry loomed. I was to be treated as if I did not exist. They were unaware that I didn't want to be there at least as much as they didn't want me there. But I had no time for that discussion nor for their childish peevishness. A secretary showed me Schwartz's empty office. I entered, sat down, and asked her to tell our production manager I needed to see him as soon as possible.

Shortly thereafter a tall, good-looking young man named Bob

Rosen entered. He greeted me warmly, like the rescuer he knew me to be.

"Suppose you and I go looking for a lagoon and an island?" I suggested.

"Great," he replied. "I've got a location that might work, I'd like to show it to you."

We strolled the back lot, infinitely smaller than the other studios where I had worked. We came to a parking lot, surrounded by a cluster of eucalyptus trees, where Bob stopped and pointed. "Here," he said, "we can clear out this lot, dig a lagoon, asphalt it, lose the trees, and put in potted palms to hide the telephone polls. We're just far enough away from traffic, so sound should be no problem. We bring in sand for a beach and, voilà! Gilligan's Island," he proudly concluded, turning to me for a response.

"Good work. Start digging right away," I told him,

By an odd coincidence the layout was similar to our *Adventures in Paradise* lagoon on the Fox lot, only on a much smaller scale. Over the years many people have speculated about the actual filming location of *Gilligan's Island;* no one has guessed it was a former parking lot in the San Fernando Valley.

"I showed this to Sherwood," Rosen said. "He just sniffed, turned his back, and walked away. He wasn't interested. He seems to think that he'll force CBS to shoot in Hawaii, as they did the pilot. I told him no way, the cost would be out of sight."

"We're going into production in four weeks," I told him. "Start digging."

"Right on," Bob replied. "By the way, Sherwood hasn't shown us any scripts."

"We have an airdate and we will have scripts, count on it." I hurried back to the office and started calling agents and booking some of the best comedy-writing teams in Hollywood for screenings of the pilot. I needed pros who could work fast.

There's an old producer's saying in television, "I don't want it good, I want it Tuesday." Of course, we wanted it good *and* Tuesday.

For the next four weeks my life was a continuous series of meetings with writers and screenings of the pilot. Eventually John Rich vanished to other series being shot somewhere else. I was grateful to see him go. Secretaries began to acknowledge me, yet Sherwood Schwartz still wandered aimlessly about the offices like the lost soul he had become now that his baby had been taken away from him. I had no time for his childish self-pity; I was going to get this fucking show on the air and then rush back to my Television City office and three-hour lunches, with massages on the roof of the Beverly Hills Health Club and lots of laps in their indoor pool. And I was going to make Sol Saks miserable until his dying day, or so I liked to imagine.

Stromberg phoned, "I understand Sherwood is still hanging around your office. Is he a problem for you? If he is, say the word and I'll have him thrown off the lot and locked out of the building."

"He's no problem," I assured him. "He's too busy feeling sorry for himself. When can I come back to my office?"

"As soon as you get the first show on the air, I swear it," Stromberg told me. I smelled a rat, but I was neck deep in this Gilligan's stew and had no choice but to sweat it out. My three-hour lunches with Sol Saks became quick sandwiches alone at my desk or alone in the commissary chow line. No one except our production manager would have anything to do with me. When I introduced myself to the cast they regarded me as a conniving network type who had usurped the guy who had hired them. They were obviously ill at ease but, as professionals in the business, they accepted me. As production began, they gradually warmed to me. Our amiable star, Bob Denver, a most agreeable and gifted comic actor, sidled up to me one day on the set and said, sotto voce, "Hey, man, wanna toke?" I knew I had arrived.

All day, every day, I met with writers, taking as long as it took to get a storyline ready for them to write when they left my office. There was no time for going through the process of having them submit a story outline for network approval before they could go to teleplay—I was the network. Sherwood was not involved. We'd wrap up a story and I'd send them home with my battle cry, "I don't want it good, I want it Tuesday." Fortunately I had some of the best comedy writers in the business, so my work was made easy. Actually, I was driven by my considerable anger at having been ordered into this disagreeable situation, producing a series I was increasingly growing to loathe.

Schwartz had come up with an ideal escapist concept, still popular today in the various *Survivor* series. Being marooned on a balmy desert island is a universal fantasy. Schwartz had peopled his island with easily recognizable stereotypes, written and performed as almost absurdist comedy. The show didn't have enough meat on it to qualify as farce. It was just silly. Yet, it endures, probably because anybody, any age group, can watch it and instantly recognize and enjoy this cotton candy for the mind.

The story conferences were sometimes difficult because the team of writers would come into my office and horse around with gags or the latest jokes they'd heard. Eventually, I'd reach a point where I had to demand, "Enough with the jokes, guys, we're doing a comedy show, let's get serious." It's a bedrock truth of all drama, be it comedy, farce, or melodrama—the writer must provide a strong storyline with conflict and dramatic tension. Thus, for all its inanity, we still had to come up with good plots. Just like the most serious drama, no matter how stupid the comedy is, it needs a "spine" on which to hang the jokes. If you have no spine, nothing will hang together and you have chaos. Chaos is boring. I was very lucky to have several excellent teams of comedy writers who took to the show with ease. Seasoned pros in the comedy-writing field are extremely rare. They are priceless.

Once we got down to business we could quickly fill out the storyline the writers had come in with. It was not a problem. Sherwood Schwartz had gotten into trouble because, apparently, he had decided the characters had to "learn something" in each episode. The fantasy he had created was nonsensical. This was absurdist comedy on a childlike level (hence its enormous popularity among children).

Mrs. Howell (Lovey) had apparently brought along an inexhaustible wardrobe and her husband had brought his golf clubs for a three-hour cruise. The professor had access to the entire New York Public Library, yet Ginger had only her "movie star" dress and Mary Ann had about the same narrow range of wardrobe. The island itself was in never-never land, on a never-never sea in the minds of people who liked to imagine being stranded on a tropical island. It didn't matter where it was. If you're going to play nonsense, you play nonsense. These one-dimensional stereotypical characters were as shallow as they appeared to be. Schwartz's belated attempt to inject logic and reasoning into this realm of absurdity was self-defeating. Small wonder he had had so much trouble delivering acceptable scripts to CBS. He had tied himself in knots, apparently unsure of what to do with his own creation.

Our characters could talk about cannibals and dangerous beasts of the jungle with equal ease. My personal favorite, "Wrong Way Feldman," was written by the team of Fred Freeman and Larry Cohen. In it Hans Conreid (a great radio actor I had worked with at CBS) played a pilot who had wandered off course and had somehow landed on Gilligan's Island. Thanks to Freeman and Cohen, we now had a landing strip (never shown) on the island. It became fun to see how far we could push the concept of Robin Hood's rabbi. As we went into production Schwartz took to proclaiming that he had created "the greatest situation comedy in the history of television." My friend Sol Saks gave me that one to ponder.

Saks, in one of his sharkskin suits, took to dropping by my office once in a while to ask "Can I be of any help?" grinning from ear to ear. The s.o.b. was enjoying my misery. Next came the usual preproduction details, some set adjustments, wardrobe fittings, and so on. Tina Louise's movie-star dress needed some padding in her bra, but what else was new? The cast reluctantly accepted me as the conniving network idiot who was stealing Sherwood's series. I couldn't blame Sherwood for trying to save face, but I bristled at the idea that I was doing anything other than producing his series for him. This prompted me to phone Hunt Stromberg and insist I get executive producer credit for the shows I actually produced. "You've got it, you've earned it," he responded. "We like the dailies. How soon can we see an episode?"

Things were gaining a rhythm, my anger was softening into resignation. I began booking directors leaning toward those I'd worked with before and knew could deliver. The first two I set were Dick Donner and Ida Lupino. John Rich's agent wasted a phone call telling me his client was not available for the series; I replied the series was not available for him.

Donner was a director whose enthusiasm and vitality energized everyone with whom he worked. Actors always respond to the high energy, excitement, and enthusiasm he brings to the set.

Lupino and I had worked together on NBC's *Sam Benedict* series. She was a pioneer, one of Hollywood's first women directors, and quite good at her job. She was creative, serious, and efficient; she could direct comedy and drama with equal skill. Everybody in the cast and crew loved working with her. Ida was one of those actresses who called everyone, especially crew members, "darling," usually accompanied by an affectionate pat on the arm. The crew would walk through fire for her. "Darling, would you mind moving that light, it's in the way of my shot."

Ida had her own high, aluminum director's chair with multi-colored plastic webbing, which she brought with her to every job. In large block letters on the back was stenciled MOTHER. The crew on one of her pictures had given it to her. The chair also had a cup holder in the right arm, in which she kept a plastic cup half-filled with vodka. Although she sipped at her drink frequently ("mother's milk," she would insist), I never saw her drunk during or after a shoot. She was one of those rare functioning alcoholics. In any event, she turned out consistently strong episodes. We had an excellent, strictly professional relationship; I had never seen Lupino other than on a soundstage or in my office.

As shooting got underway I discovered the cast was easy to work with, all expertly cast and solidly professional. They were enjoying themselves enormously, the set was often alive with laughter. Jim Backus (Mr. Howell) kept the set loose with his jokes, sometimes slipping into his Mr. Magoo voice. They delighted in cracking one another up by playfully pushing their stereotypical characters even further into the realm of absurdity, which was actually not a big stretch. They were playing broad comedy on camera and, once in a while, even broader off camera. Bob Denver, our Gilligan, was actually a warm-hearted, sweet-natured young man. Eager to please, he always knew his lines and was ready to work, even when we sometimes wondered what he might be smoking. Alan Hale Jr., the skipper, was a dead ringer for his father, Alan Sr., the Warner Brothers contract player who played Little John to Errol Flynn's Robin Hood and was a character actor in scores of other movies. Alan Jr. was as pleasant and accommodating an actor as a producer could hope for. Natalie Schafer, playing Lovey, was a professional in every way. Playing the role of Mrs. Howell was not a big stretch for her. Russell Johnson, the professor, stayed pretty much to himself, oddly enough, reading. Dawn Wells (Mary Ann) was even prettier and sweeter than the character she played. Tina Louise (Ginger, the movie star) was a very pretty but somewhat insecure young woman who didn't have the experience of the rest of the cast members and, I think, felt a bit inferior and somewhat intimidated by the ease with which they did their jobs. Schwartz had cast all the castaways perfectly.

We were shooting on schedule, and Stromberg was leaving me alone. At our dailies the editor and I watched as Bob Denver fell over logs, bumped into the skipper, and ran frantically about like a rag doll in motion. We frequently exchanged pained winces. This is comedy? Occasionally Schwartz would silently slip into the darkened room via the side door and slump down in a front-row seat. Soon he was chortling away, as the editor and I exchanged groans.

One day I was summoned to the set. "It's Tina Louise," the assistant director told me, "she's locked herself in her dressing room. We've shot around her until we've got nothing else to shoot. We're shut down until she reports for work."

Actors locking themselves in their dressing rooms, as I had learned again and again, was part and parcel of every producer's working life. It came with the territory. I went to Tina's dressing room, nearby, and knocked on the door.

"Who is it?" her voice replied.

I identified myself, adding, "We really have to have you on the set, Tina, we're shut down. Please report for work."

"I can't, I really can't," she pleaded. "I'm just too tired."

"But we're shut down, Tina. You're needed on the set," I replied. "Please, don't make me call your agent."

"I wish I could, Bill," she answered, wearily, "but I'm just exhausted. I came twenty-three times last night. That much sex just wears me out."

With a few more pleadings, she dragged herself into the sunlight and I walked her back to the set. Actually, a very sweet young woman, she was clearly uncomfortable working with a cast of seasoned professionals, though she could never say it.

When Stromberg and Aubrey saw the first cut of that first show my fate was sealed. They loved it. Thereafter I made it a point of beginning each Friday morning with a phone call to Hunt Stromberg pleading to be released from this job and allowed back in my office at Television City. And every Friday I would be told to produce just one more show and I'd be free to come back. I could see no way out. I was trapped. The better the episodes I produced, the longer I would be forced to remain there.

The Fridays came and went, as did Sol Saks's drop-ins, and I resigned myself to producing a series I found increasingly trivial and uninteresting. But who can argue with the taste of the American public? I got my comeuppance, however, in the most unexpected place.

I was seeing a shrink at the time. One day I was bellyaching to him about having to produce this stupid series, when, suddenly, he let loose on me, "What makes you so superior? Who are you to tell the American public what to like or not like? People love this series, men come home from work, they want to flop on the couch, have a beer, and look at some undemanding, escapist entertainment. What's the matter with that?" he demanded of me. I was effectively silenced.

Weeks became months. Six months. I remained producing the first thirteen episodes. It was ridiculously easy. I had excellent writers, seasoned directors, and a cast of professionals, but I was marooned on *Gilligan's Island.* It never occurred to me that Sherwood thought I had "plotted" to take over his series.

At the end of the day following completion of an episode, Ida Lupino asked me to join her and her husband, Howard Duff, for dinner and the theater afterward. I liked Ida but had no connection with her other than our work. I had met Duff during the *San Benedict* episode in which he and Ida has been guest stars, playing husband and wife; even sober he was a taciturn man

"Six thirty at the Brown Derby," she said, "and the three of us are going to see *Boys in the Band* after dinner, at the Huntington Hartford just across the street. We'll walk over together. They've given us three seats, front row center, isn't that lovely?" Ida had a contagious enthusiasm both in her personality and in her work, so I readily accepted.

I arrived promptly at six thirty the next evening at the Vine Street Brown Derby where I discovered Ida seated in the first booth alone, nursing a drink. She greeted me with a wonderful smile and a quick peck on my cheek as I sat down beside her. "Sit down, darling," she said, with her dazzling smile, reaching out to touch my arm.

It had occurred to me more than once that, had she been single, we might have developed a beautiful friendship. I suspect it might have occurred to her, too. Moreover, we had never discussed anything other than the show on which we were working.

"Howard's always late," she said. "Order a drink."

A few minutes later, Howard Duff ambled in the front door, slightly unsteady on his feet. When he arrived at the booth, standing over me I could see his eyes were a bit bloodshot.

"You're fucking my wife!" he shouted for the entire Derby to hear. I was stunned by his absurd charge. Ida and I had a working relationship, nothing more. I was more struck, however, by hearing the voice of one of my radio idols, Sam Spade. *The Adventures of Sam Spade* was among the greatest private-eye series in the history of radio, and Howard Duff was Sam Spade.

"That's utterly ridiculous, Howard," Ida said and added, "Sit down and shut up. You're drunk, asshole."

"Fuck you, Ida, you c—t."

The entire dinner consisted of the two of them exchanging venomous obscenities of the four-letter variety. I was trapped. I asked to be excused to go to the men's room but was let out only on condition that I would promptly return to my seat. You could cut the animosity between them with a butter knife.

When the dinner was over, in spite of my pleas to beg off, they both demanded that I join them for the play. By now they were both pretty well sloshed. Howard had abandoned his idea that I was fooling around with his wife. It was the ugliest exchange between husband and wife I had ever witnessed.

As we walked across Vine Street to the Huntington Hartford Theater, I pulled away toward the Derby parking lot. Duff hooked my arm and, suddenly my best friend, said, "Come on, buddy, you're not going to miss this show. The reviews were terrific and we've got the best seats in the house."

We walked down the aisle, me in the middle, and took our choice seats. Howard maneuvered so that I had the seat between them. We were just under the lip of the proscenium. Perhaps from exhaustion, they fell silent until the curtain went up and the actors appeared.

When the performance started Duff and Lupino added new tone to their verbal assaults, leaning across me to make certain their jabs reached their intended targets while hissing their insults. They managed to keep their voice levels just low enough to avoid distracting the actors who loomed directly above us. If the performers heard the exchanges they gave no indication. Gradually, Duff and Lupino fell silent, becoming entranced members of an appreciative audience.

At intermission we filed out to the lobby. Duff and Lupino, almost cordial by now, discussed how much they were enjoying the play. Or perhaps inhaling the cool night air in front of the theater was having a pacifying effect. At least I hoped that was the case as we filed back into the theater for act two.

Indeed, we were finally able to focus our attention on the play, which, as it happened, was a very good comedy, well performed. At the final curtain, the audience gave the cast a richly deserved standing ovation. As they took their final bows I saw several of them staring down at the three of us. I wondered how much of the Duffs' venomous arguing they had heard, or were they merely impressed that two famous stars were present?

"We've got to go backstage and congratulate them!" Lupino exclaimed, full of enthusiasm, as if the evening of marital misery hadn't happened.

"And thank them for these great seats," added Duff, now jovial and sober. Suddenly they were the glamorous, sitcom couple who were soon to be seen as co-stars in their upcoming TV series *Mr. Adams and Eve*. They were not the same people with whom I had entered the theater. The transformation was astonishing.

The three of us made our way backstage, an enthusiastic trio, where we were greeted with a large sign on the bulletin board that read. "Give it your best, kids, TONIGHT IS HOWARD DUFF AND IDA LUPINO NIGHT!"

"You are darlings, and you were all wonderful!" Ida proclaimed, kissing as many actors on the cheek as she could find. "We're taking you all to the Derby Bar for drinks! The entire cast! You're all our guests."

Rounding them up with great open arms, she herded about a dozen or more actors out the door. Howard joined in with great gusto, "Drinks on us!" he shouted.

As Duff and Lupino, the gracious hosts, led the small band of actors across Vine Street to the Derby, I saw my chance to escape. In the darkness I drifted off toward the Derby parking lot and drove home. They didn't notice my departure.

When *Gilligan's Island* debuted on September 26, 1964, predictably the critics panned it, and just as predictably Jim Aubrey had another hit. But I wanted out. I phoned Stromberg and told him I was absolutely finished, and nothing or nobody could change my mind. I had produced the first thirteen episodes following the pilot, and had spent six months covering Sherwood Schwartz's ass while he was taking bows and bad-mouthing me to my peers. He had not been involved in any way, in any of those thirteen episodes. Nonetheless, Stromberg's assessment of him had been ridiculously harsh. He was simply a writer with a marketable idea who had gotten in over his head and was unwilling to admit it.

It was becoming increasingly obvious to me that the better the ratings were on the shows I produced, the more likely Aubrey and Stromberg were to keep me locked into a series for which I had no respect. It was a hit. But I was unwilling to continue dedicating a serious portion of my life to *Gilligan's Island*. I had no choice but to take a stand. It could mean that CBS's option on my services for a second year at a significant increase and my commitment to present them new series idea would be in jeopardy. I decided to take my chances, which, in essence, I had been doing throughout my career. But I had to escape this job that was boring me to death.

I phoned Stromberg and quietly explained that I'd had enough, I didn't have the energy to continue to produce another writer's series. It may have been his pride and joy, but it held no interest for me. I'd put in the six months, produced the first thirteen shows, and wanted a week's vacation with my wife in Puerto Vallarta at CBS's expense. Much to my surprise, Stromberg replied, "Yes, by all means. Leave whenever you like, just send in the expense account when you return." He was too agreeable and chipper not to have something up his sleeve, but I hadn't a clue what it was. When I found out, I couldn't have been more astonished.

That afternoon, I received a call from his assistant. "Mr. Stromberg wants a meeting with you at seven o'clock tonight in Mr. Reynolds's office. Please be there, it's most important."

What was this all about? John Reynolds was vice president of CBS Television Operations, Hollywood. He was in charge of the physical plant and was the nearly invisible man sitting quietly in his corner office on the third floor. Reynolds was solid, respectable, and straight-arrow, unlike Stromberg who was quirky, mercurial, and temperamental, with tastes that went to god-knows-what.

Reynolds had no part in any of Stromberg's machinations. So what the hell did they want with me . . . at seven o'clock on a Friday night? I hadn't set foot in Television City in months. Something was up, but I hadn't a clue as to what bizarre schemes surely awaited me.

When I arrived on the third floor, I was struck by the darkness and total silence. Busy offices were now devoid of people. I made my way to the lighted, open door of John Reynolds's corner office. Stromberg came out to meet me and escort me inside. "So good of you to come," he said, closing the door behind me. The office was lit only by lamps, the overhead fluorescent lights were turned off. John Reynolds was seated quietly behind his desk, lit only by the desk lamp.

There was no longer any doubt in my mind that something of a certain sinister magnitude was going on. Stromberg hurried to the bar and poured me a scotch and soda, while commenting on how pleased CBS was with my work on *Gilligan's Island.*

"As a matter of fact, Jim and I have picked up your option for another year, and we're looking forward to seeing the series ideas you'll be presenting."

Both John Reynolds and I were playing it close to the vest, neither of us commenting on Stromberg's monologue. Finally, Hunt pulled a chair over close beside me across the desk from Reynolds. He lowered his voice, conspiratorially.

"Jim Aubrey is going to be fired. I'm going to New York to take his place as president of the company, and I want you to take my job here as vice president, programs Hollywood." He almost gushed out the words as if he couldn't wait to get them out of his mouth. "Will you do it?" he concluded.

"Sorry, Hunt," I responded immediately, "I'm not the least bit interested. I've already been a vice president of CBS. I hated being an executive. I won't do it, again."

"But that's the perfect part of it," Hunt pressed on. "Paley remembers you, he likes you, and would be pleased to have you running our Hollywood programming department. Won't you at least consider it?"

"To tell you the truth, I'm burned out with television. I can't even stand to look at it. Irv Kershner, Walter Newman, and I have formed a partnership to do features. As a matter of fact we've optioned three books."

"Great!" Stromberg replied. "You can't find a better director than Kershner nor a better screenwriter than Walter Newman. So here's the deal I'm going to offer you. Clint Murchison is going to buy Paramount for $400 million and hire Aubrey to run it. It's all set. If you'll take this job I'm offering you, I'll guarantee you, Kershner, and Newman a three-picture deal! What could be better than that?"

"Sorry," I said again. "I'm not interested in being an executive and I'm hoping for an opening one day to teach full time at UCLA."

Stromberg stood up, more than a little annoyed. "Well, I can see your mind is made up," he said, "and I think you're making a big mistake, but what the hell, I tried my best. Thanks for coming over."

Throughout the brief meeting John Reynolds didn't utter a word. I had a strong feeling that he knew something neither Stromberg nor I did.

As we reached the door I turned to Stromberg. "Remember," I said, "you promised me a week's paid vacation in Puerto Vallarta."

"Okay," replied Stromberg, suddenly smiling, "you've earned it. You saved Sherwood's ass and he probably hates you for it."

Two weeks later, as my new wife, Marie Lovett, and I were flying back from Puerto Vallarta, we happened to pick up a foreign edition of the New York *Herald Tribune*. The front page headline read AUBREY FIRED BY CBS. The story went on to add that Hunt Stromberg Jr. had also been fired by William S. Paley, as had CBS's vice president, business affairs Hollywood, Frank Rohner, all on the same day. Why Rohner was included in the CBS executive massacre was inexplicable to me. He seemingly had no connection with the shenanigans of Aubrey and Stromberg. As far as I knew, Frank was a highly professional, solid citizen doing his job, no doubt under difficult circumstances.

The day following our return from Mexico, I returned to my Television City office. No sooner had I settled in to read my mail than a short, intense, scowling man entered. He had a nose like a pickaxe, small glinty eyes, and the determined look of an executioner.

He introduced himself as Mike Dann, the new president of CBS Television replacing Jim Aubrey. A no-nonsense fellow, Dann got right to the point, "I came right down to your office to ask you a question: do you have any plans here at CBS?"

"None whatsoever," I replied.

"That's good," he replied brusquely, "because CBS has no plans for you." He walked out of my office, and I never saw him again.

The next day I was ordered out of my office and told I would now be headquartered in the San Fernando Valley at CBS Studio Center where I could develop my series ideas under my contract. Perry Lafferty, the new VP, summoned me to his office to let me know, in the politest possible way, that I was henceforth persona non grata. They couldn't get me out of the building fast enough. Though unstated, it was apparent that they regarded me as part of the old unsavory regime. Hence I had to go immediately. Maybe they thought I would spread cholera, who knows? I had left for a week's vacation in Mexico a hero and returned a pariah. I found it amusing but not surprising. They still had to pay me a year's six-figure salary. It was sweet revenge.

My secretary and I reported to Studio Center to a suite of empty offices. There was no one else in the building. Even though my friends at Television City assured me that no project I developed would ever see the light of day, I hired two writers to write scripts for a projected one-hour series called *Oklahoma Run* about the settlers who poured into that territory to homestead land. This watershed event was a background of my family history—my grandparents, uncles, and aunts had arrived in the Territory a few months after the opening gun in 1898 and set up shop in tent cities.

One of the writers I hired was my friend the veteran screenwriter Bill Bowers; the other was a former CPN office-mate of mine, John Dunkle. Dunkle had been among the best of the *Gunsmoke* writers. He turned in a first-class teleplay.

Alas, Bowers remained Bowers. He came into my office for story conferences and told Hollywood story after Hollywood story, and in a matter of some weeks he failed to come up with a script, even though I had liked his story idea very much. My follow-up phone calls to Bowers were met by his usual warm conviviality and good humor—but no script. Weeks passed and I pressed on. Finally, Bowers delivered a shootable script. I also sent the new management at CBS a pilot script of *Oklahoma Run* I'd written for ABC some years earlier, the rights having reverted to me, plus the Dunkle and Bowers teleplays. Now I had three scripts for the series delivered to CBS.

Alas, my friends at CBS had spoken the truth. Every script or series idea I presented during the following year received an immediate flat "not interested" response. The new management made it clear they regarded me as part of the Aubrey–Stromberg axis and wanted nothing to do with me or any of my projects. I wondered if Perry Lafferty knew that I had been offered his job and turned it down. Meeting with him to receive the rejection face to face, I got the strong impression he was relishing dismissing me out of hand. But maybe I'd been in "the business" too long to be objective.

When I reported the first series rejection to my agent he laughed, "Just hope nobody ever actually films *Oklahoma Run*. That's the third network you've sold this series to, and you'll probably sell it again before you're done."

Unfortunately for the new CBS management team, they were stuck with me for another year after Stromberg and Aubrey picked up their second-year option. Having been exiled to purgatory in the Valley, I spent much of that year shopping on CBS's money and writing spec screenplays.

In 1988 Sherwood Schwartz's book *Inside Gilligan's Island* was published. Sol Saks phoned me, "You'd better read it," he insisted. "It contains a lot of crazy stuff about you."

I had had a bellyful of Gilligan, and I thought I could pretty well guess what Sherwood had to say about me. But, in preparation for my own book, I thought I ought to read it.

The first third of the book describes in minute detail the extraordinary struggles Sherwood had getting his pilot made and, finally, getting it on the CBS network schedule. But then the book mixes fact with fiction, outrageous, vindictive fiction. His vilification of me had not a shred of truth in it. Most surprising of all is Sherwood's rearranging of his memory in the most extraordinary way. He claims *Gilligan's Island* was on CBS, and already a big hit, when I "plotted" to usurp his role as producer. Somehow my arrival is listed on the Web site as in the *fifth year*. As you have just read, when I arrived Sherwood had not even settled on a location for the series, nothing had been shot, and he had only one script approved for production. Sherwood had worked so very hard to complete the sale of his pilot, it now appeared he was totally unprepared to actually get his series on the air. He was frozen at the helm. It was only then, after repeated warnings of his rapidly approaching airdate that CBS *demanded* I take over his series. Sadly, he took bows for producing all the episodes, including the thirteen I alone produced that successfully launched his series. Meanwhile, according to his account I was "plotting" to take over his series and "plotting" to change his characters. It's sheer hokum. In addition, he describes my meetings with writers as his own. Somehow "Wrongway Feldman" becomes *his* favorite, when in fact he had nothing whatsoever to do with it. I feel sorry that a writer of his undeniable talent had to stoop so low. But this, after all, is Hollywood. And I was grateful to be done with it.

In March of 1995 *Time* magazine printed a large photo of Sherwood Schwartz lying, his head on his elbow smiling proudly, in front of a set meant to represent *Gilligan's Island*. Sherwood was wearing his bronzed "Skipper" cap. The story beneath the photo could not have pleased the veteran comedy writer. The bold headline announced, in rather large letters, THE INVENTOR OF BAD TELEVISION. Ginia Bellafonte's article skewered Schwartz for both his big hits, *Gilligan's Island* and *The Brady Bunch*.

Obviously Sherwood had no idea the photo would appear over such a negative headline. How did he react? I have no idea, but my educated guess is that he did what Hollywood denizens have been doing in the face of bad reviews since the very beginning: he probably laughed all the way to the bank.

I am of course aware that legions of *Gilligan's Island* and *Brady Bunch* fans hugely enjoy these series. To each his own, as it should be. But in a democracy, we all have a right to express our own opinions.

12

Bewitched . . . Plenty Bothered and Bewildered

In the spring of 1966 my agent informed me that he had received an offer from Harry Ackerman, vice president of Screen Gems, for me to produce the third season of the half-hour sitcom *Bewitched*. It was already the reigning hit of television, debuting at number two in the ratings and remaining in that slot for an entire year. It was the only sitcom capable of knocking out James T. Aubrey's murderer's row of top-rated cornpone sitcoms.

I remembered Harry Ackerman from the days when he was vice president of programming at CBS Radio, Hollywood, a job I was to occupy a couple of years after he departed for television. What little contact I had had with Ackerman had been agreeable. He was a gentle man with a reputation as being honorable and trustworthy.

When I told him that I felt I had had a bellyful of producing television programs, he added that the offer included a guaranteed "pay or play" clause for me to direct an episode. "Pay or play" was a standard industry term meaning that in the event I didn't direct an episode, I would nonetheless be paid for it. Foolishly, I let that carrot seduce me. Half my income was going for child support, which suited me just fine, even though it meant I had to maintain a strong income. Also, *Bewitched* was the only offer I had on the table. Like it or not, this was medicine I had to take to stay afloat financially.

I knew little about the show other than my friend Sol Saks had written the pilot and it was highly regarded in the industry. *I Married a Witch* had been a Paramount hit movie of 1942, starring Frederic March, Veronica Lake, and Susan Hayward. But Sol Saks had come up with a fresh approach to the premise. He developed the comedic situation with a family of characters, most particularly the witch's mother, Endora, played with great gusto by the redoubtable Agnes Moorehead. It was Saks's creation of the mother as a meddling know-it-all superwitch along with the comedic talent of Elizabeth Montgomery and co-star Dick York that had catapulted the series to the highest ratings in ABC Television's history.

Yet I had learned that hyphenate Danny Arnold, one of television's best comedy writers, had departed the series in its prime as had his successor, comedy-writer producer Jerry Davis. I didn't know either of these highly regarded hyphenates personally, so I didn't feel comfortable phoning to ask them why they quit the show when it was on top, or if they were fired. Both Arnold and Davis could write circles around me in comedy. I wondered why I had been chosen. Nevertheless, it was a good credit to add to my portfolio. After giving it a lot of thought, I decided to try my luck with the series.

When I reported for work at the old apartment building across the street from the Columbia Pictures service entrance to the lot, I was returning to the site of my first job in television, eight years earlier.

I was greeted in my new office by William Asher, husband of star Elizabeth Montgomery and a successful director in his own right. Asher was a hyphenate of a different stripe, a director-producer. He had directed episodes of *I Love Lucy* and other hit TV comedies, as well as several low-budget features such as *Bikini Beach, Beach Blanket Bingo,* and the like. Asher was one of many restless Hollywood professionals who, like nomads, drifted from job to job, always delivering competent, if not inspired, work. They could come in on short notice and do a reliable job. Considering the speed at which the medium used up talent, these folks, while rarely reaching star status, were the backbone of the industry. Asher and I had a lot in common.

After Danny Arnold quit the series, Asher had settled into the producer's office as his own while temporarily filling the producer function until the new man reported for work. He introduced me to Ruth Flippen, our story editor, a petite, dour blonde with years of experience in comedy, and Dick Michaels, an enthusiastic, handsome young man who would be my assistant. Flippen was married to character actor Jay C. Flippen. I was struck by her seemingly deep-seated cynicism, unrelieved by her attempts at witty sarcasm. For whatever reasons I could not guess, it was quickly apparent this was a rather somber atmosphere in which to produce comedy.

Asher took me across the street onto the Columbia Pictures lot to meet the cast on the *Bewitched* set. He introduced me first to his wife, who was more attractive in person than she was on film. She had a slender, lithe body, long brown hair, and an exceptionally low-key manner. For a woman who had no overt physical sexuality, Montgomery exuded a subtle sensuality. She was cordial, even pleasant, but I sensed a hidden agenda without having a clue as to what it might be. I also suspected that Montgomery had a rich but dark and perhaps disturbed inner life. For whatever the reason, I was uncomfortable in her presence. It was immediately clear, however, that the discomfort was mutual. Often on the basis of unspoken disconnections, in the whimsical world of Hollywood, jobs don't pan out. I knew immediately that this would be one of those.

Montgomery was the daughter of the highly popular 1930s movie star Robert Montgomery. Although he was most famed for his ability to play light comedy (*Here Comes Mr. Jordan* and others) and was noted for his light touch in screwball comedies, he had won an Academy Award nomination for playing a psychotic killer in *Night Must Fall.* Following his distinguished acting career, he went on to host and produce one of the most successful of the great New York–originated live TV anthology series, *Robert Montgomery Presents.* His daughter, Elizabeth, had developed her considerable acting skills while making regular appearances on her father's program. Even among the cornucopia of the golden age New York live TV dramas, his series stood out for it's quality and originality.

In a Hollywood community many regarded as politically liberal, Montgomery was a staunch conservative Republican.

Agnes Moorehead, I thought, had no hidden agenda whatsoever. She let me know right off that she was a grande dame and was to be treated accordingly. She was a friend of the Ashers. Word had obviously reached her that it was her performance as Endora that was a key element in the show's success, and she apparently wanted to make certain everyone involved in the series knew it. Moorehead had a particularly interesting history. She had been a highly successful radio and stage actress with Orson Welles's *Mercury Theater.* She had appeared as Citizen Kane's mother and in minor or major roles in all of Welles's films, notably *The Magnificent Ambersons,* and had frequent guest-star appearances in such series as *The Twilight Zone.* However, nothing she had done had suggested her comedic talent for playing the over-the-top, wicked-witch, mother-in-law Endora in *Bewitched.*

Watching her perform on our set was to see a master of her craft at work. She routinely did her often wildly outrageous scenes in one take, then soon after the director said "cut," she swiftly and silently swept off into her dressing room at the other end of the stage. She apparently needed privacy. There was no levity in Agnes Moorehead and no nonsense. One got the understanding that she did what she was paid to do, and that was the end of it.

During my year producing the series I don't believe she and I exchanged more than a passing nod. As best I could tell, she spent every moment she was not on camera in her dressing room with the door closed. The crew also tread lightly around her. There was something mysterious in her reserve. In an industry known for its extraordinary informality, Agnes Moorehead on the set was generally called Miss Moorehead (our star was Liz or Elizabeth, as she preferred). I could not help but wonder who the private Agnes Moorehead really was. It was clear, however, that most of us who worked with her were seeing only the tip of the iceberg. When you encounter these larger-than-life actors in your own role as a producer, you learn to give them as much space as possible, the less contact the better.

On the other hand, Dick York, who played Samantha's husband, greeted me warmly. His was a friendly, open-faced greeting, but there was pain in his eyes. York had badly injured his back in an accident. He played his role superbly with exceptional comedic timing, yet he did it while frequently performing in excruciating pain. Yet, I never heard the actor utter a word of complaint. He remained amiable and eager to please. Between takes, York lay against a slant board propped against the soundstage wall. He often looked longingly at his co-star. However, it was immediately obvious she was annoyed by his attention. For whatever reason, Montgomery clearly did not like her co-star.

Having graciously introduced me to all of the key players as well as the important crew members, Asher excused himself to return to the office. Shortly thereafter, Montgomery took me aside. In a sotto voce conspiratorial voice, she said firmly, "I don't want your assistant ever to set foot on this stage, *ever.*"

I had just met my assistant, hence to my puzzled look she added, "Your assistant, Dick Michaels, I do not want him ever to set foot on this set. Is that clear?" Her emphasis suggested the young man had committed an egregious offense.

"Would you mind telling me what he's done to offend you?" I asked.

"It's none of your business," she snapped. "Just keep him off our set, understood?" My initial instinct upon meeting her was reinforced. The lady and I had plenty of chemistry, but of the negative variety.

When I returned to my new office, I found Asher sitting in the producer's chair behind the desk. "Terribly sorry," he said quickly, as he got up and took a seat across the desk from me. I asked him why his wife felt so strongly about Dick Michaels.

"I have no idea," he said. "Liz does stuff like that. It's just her style. However, I suggest you tell Dick to stay away. Who knows, by next week she might change her mind. You'll like Liz once you get to know her. By the way, we're taking you to lunch today."

I called Dick Michaels in to ask him the cause of Montgomery's edict.

"What did I do to offend her?" he replied with genuine consternation. "I have no idea, Liz and I have always gotten along very well. It's a mystery to me." And Michaels readily agreed to stay away from our show's soundstage.

During the cast's lunch break, Asher and I walked across the street to the soundstage where we picked up his wife and walked through the lot to the corner of Sunset and Gower. Columbia Drug Store was a unique establishment in Hollywood, a small unpretentious shop. Only by wandering through the narrow aisles could a customer discover a half-dozen small booths in the back where lunch was served from the small kitchen. It was like having a private dinning room.

They were an odd couple. Asher, short, stocky, bald, built like a middle-weight wrestler; Montgomery, tall, lean, very attractive. They seemed congenial enough, though quite obviously Asher was the more affectionate of the two. Clearly he was very much in love with his wife. Montgomery kept her feelings to herself. I was disappointed I could not warm up to her.

As Montgomery, Asher, and I entered, she explained to me, "They have the best brisket I've tasted anywhere in the world." It was the most animation I had seen from her. When someone is that guarded they have secrets. It was disquieting to realize, that first day on the job, that Montgomery and I would have difficulty working together. In her own low-key way, it was obvious that Elizabeth Montgomery controlled this series. Her husband, for all his undeniable talent, was cast in the awkward role of front man, when in fact he was anything but. His pride must have been taking a beating. Love does strange things to a man.

While we ate the superb brisket, Asher briefed me on the series, telling me which of the many guest characters ("relatives") seemed to work best. It was an excellent, generous briefing for a new man on the job. Montgomery said little, deferring to her husband. She was a reserved woman, yet once again, I felt she had a hidden agenda. Gradually I became aware that the purpose of the lunch was for the star to size me up, and clearly she was not favorably impressed. Later, when I inadvertently learned some of her secrets, they came as a complete surprise to me and also, no doubt, to her husband.

That afternoon Harry Ackerman, our executive producer, summoned me to his office. I had first met Ackerman at CBS Radio when he had been vice president, programming, and I had been a CPN staff writer. He was a highly regarded, quiet man, soft spoken, unimpressed with himself. After warmly welcoming me to the show, he got to the point. "Bill Asher wanted to take over as producer of the show, but privately Liz told me to tell him no. So I played the heavy. Actually," he added, "Asher had produced a script of yours and liked it. So he accepted you as a compromise. Liz had no opinion about you one way or the other, but she went along with it." He quickly and unconvincingly added, "However, I'm sure the two of you will get along fine, once you get to know each other. By the way, Asher is going to direct as many episodes as he can; you can fill in other directors as you need them." I came away from the meeting unhappily recognizing that my position as middleman between husband (director) and wife (star) with different agendas was going to make for a difficult year.

As we met with writers, Bill Asher always "just happened" to be in my office preparing to direct the next episode. Soon it became clear that Asher was determined to be the de facto producer and I was hired to be his front man. He had a point to prove. While I added suggestions from time to time (a few of the same comedy writers who came in with ideas had also worked on *Gilligan's Island*), Asher let me know in the most courteous possible way that it was his series. He would, however, welcome my ideas. As uncomfortable as it was being the ersatz producer, at least I could make it a point of having as few encounters with his wife as possible. It was becoming clearer by the hour that this was not the way I was willing to spend a year of my life.

Asher and I had a brief history together. As producer of the *Jane Wyman Fireside Theater* he had bought the first teleplay I had ever written, back in the 1950s. It was an adaptation of my radio play "Pawhuska," loosely based upon my Aunt Laura's life in Pawhuska, Oklahoma Territory, which I had written, produced, and directed for CBS Radio.

During my first meeting with Asher, I had been delighted to learn that he liked the script and asked for no rewrites. I explained that I had never been on a soundstage and would very much like to watch them shoot the teleplay.

"Sorry," Asher had replied, good-naturedly, "this director does not allow writers on the set. Sounds crazy, but that's the way it is. And no 'dropping in' on the set."

I learned early in my career that the egos of some directors are so fragile they can not bear to share the show with the writer of the script. Frank Capra, John Frankenheimer, and John Carpenter, on a grander scale, were among the scores of big-name feature film directors who steadfastly maintained—in the face of all evidence to the contrary—that credit for the completed film belonged solely to them, never mind the writers, actors, cinematographer, composer of the score, set decorator, wardrobe designers, editor, the crew of highly skilled technicians on the set, the countless experts who are largely responsible for the needed preproduction work . . . not to mention the producer who, in all likelihood, initiated the project in the first place and selected many of the key people actually responsible for the completed film (including the director). The auteur theory on its face is so ludicrous that it would be laughed out of existence but for the relentless self-promotion given it by the Directors' Guild of America. In any event, I was deeply disappointed with the episode for the *Fireside Theater* (I had written a Western parody, but it was directed as a dead-on serious traditional Western). I doubt if my being on the set would have changed any of the many wrongheaded decisions this particular director made. Thus I learned, with my first filmed script, the lowly status of the writer in Hollywood. *New York Times* film critic John Crosby dedicated a column to lambasting this particular show, focusing on the writer as "somewhere in Hollywood a writer sits suntanning himself by his swimming pool" or some such. Thus I also learned that when the TV show or feature is poor, it is the writer's fault. When it's good, it is the work of a brilliant auteur director.

Apparently, Universal Studios was not as displeased with the show as John Crosby and I were. They later hired former CPN staff writer Kathleen Hite to write a sequel as a pilot for a potential series. (For seven hundred dollars Universal had bought all rights to my script and the characters. Henceforth, I was out of the loop.) Universal never contacted me during any of this, but as far as I know Hite's teleplay was never produced

Asher made it a point to be present at every *Bewitched* story conference. There was not a large pool of hard comedy writers in Hollywood from which to choose. Professionals define hard comedy as comedy that makes the reader of the teleplay laugh out loud. The ability to write laugh-out-loud scripts is one of the rarest talents in the world, hence the same writers moved from show to show, always in demand. I'd guess that out of the Writers Guild current membership of close to ten thousand, a miniscule percent can write a script that can make the reader laugh out loud. These talented people do not necessarily write jokes, they write characters caught in often painfully difficult situations and it is their pain and frustration that most often generates the laughter. To paraphrase both F. Scott Fitzgerald and Chaplin, "Show me a tragedy and I'll show you a comedy." Chaplin once told an interviewer that it was the snowbound, starving Donner Party, reduced to cannibalism when trapped in the mountains en route to California, that inspired him to write his great comedy *The Gold Rush*.

Because of the ongoing scarcity of outstanding comedy writers, beginning writers who can demonstrate a gift for writing hard comedy will command million-dollar-a-year contracts with TV-sitcom production companies. That is why today all sitcoms are written by staffs of comedy writers, obviating the problem of everyone scrambling to grab the few hard comedy writers from the small pool available. The lack of outstanding comedy writers is made obvious every night on television's many witless sitcoms. In sixteen years of teaching screenwriting at UCLA to scores of writing students, I ran across only three who could write laugh-out-loud comedy. The apocryphal story of the old, dying actor consoling his weeping young acolytes is apt: "Don't worry about me, lads. Dying is easy, comedy is hard."

That Asher chose to impose himself on the story conferences was only mildly humiliating. I liked and admired his dedication to the series, I was at a place in my career where the niceties of a title were meaningless, and I had nothing to prove to anyone, least of all to myself. I knew my limitations; foremost among them being that I can not write hard comedy. If he wanted to produce the series to prove to his wife he was the man for the job, by all means, go ahead. I deferred to him with ease. He was, indeed, the best man to produce the series. I just had to figure out a way to work somewhere else until this situation passed.

Another basic reason I accepted deferring to Asher was that I had not seen many of the shows and was unfamiliar with the series' past episodes, whereas he and his wife had been creatively involved with *Bewitched* from the beginning, taking a great deal of the credit for creating the concept in the first place. True or not, the Writers Guild of America, which decides all writing credits for all American-made television programs and motion pictures, had awarded sole writing credit on *Bewitched* to Sol Saks.

Asher was, nonetheless, a consummate pro and, as I settled into my bizarre role, I began to enjoy watching him work.

The season progressed smoothly, I made my peace with it, and made whatever contributions I could, which, as it turned out, were welcomed by Asher. Liz forgot her edict about keeping Dick Michaels off the set, and within a few weeks he moved on and off the set whenever he needed, without consequence. As Dick gained Montgomery's approval, he became comfortable enough to bring his very pretty, blonde, young *shiksa* wife and child into the office for proud introductions. He presented himself as the portrait of a devoted husband and father.

I made it a point to learn how and why *Bewitched* worked so well. Sol Saks had told me that in creating the series he kept running into a key problem: if all his leading character, Samantha, had to do was twitch her nose to gain fame and fortune for herself and her husband, there would be no conflict. Finally, after struggling for some time, he hit on the idea of Samantha's mother, the mother-in-law superwitch, who would plague her daughter's life, demanding she use witchcraft. Samantha resisted because she did not want to emasculate her husband with her witchcraft. Once Saks added this key mother-daughter conflict he told me he knew he had a pilot script that could launch a series. Every day on the set I could see his creation performed by a superb cast of actors who were nonpareil in their ability to play comedy.

As Paul Lynde played the effeminate Uncle Arthur even the crew could not resist cracking up. Lynde would wander off the set staying in character after the camera stopped rolling. Marion Lorne was delightful as the confused and forgetful Aunt Clara, a modest, adorable woman on and off camera. Her performances in the classic early TV series *Mr. Peepers* were indelible in my mind. Unlike the *Gilligan's Island* set or others I had worked on, there was no horsing around, no jokes or wise cracks on the soundstage except by Paul Lynde.

The *Bewitched* set was a model of quiet probity, without bickering, animation, or joy. The tone of a set is always created by the star. Although everyone involved in the production much admired Elizabeth Montgomery's talent and her work ethic, it was obvious they were careful not to cross her. I came to see her as a forbidding figure, bearing wounds I could only imagine.

Alas, poor Dick York could merely lie motionless in pain against his slant board and look longingly toward his co-star. It seemed clear to me that York was in love with Montgomery, and this annoyed her. For whatever reason, Montgomery clearly did not like her co-star. Was it his weakness? I wondered. She stayed clear of him except when they played scenes together. I never saw them exchange even the most casual dialogue off camera. They left the set and immediately moved into distinctly separate worlds. He never complained about his physical ailments, but once in a while following a scene you could catch a glimpse of the pain written on his face as he hobbled his way back to the slant board. I found myself fascinated by this dynamic. It was a little drama going on in the midst of one of the most popular comedy series in the history of television. Actually, I gave too much notice to this minor subplot. There was a much bigger hidden drama going on that escaped my attention. I was not to discover it until some weeks after I had left the show. When I did, I couldn't have been more surprised.

On Thursday evenings, I gladly left *Bewitched* behind and followed my heart's desire happily teaching a course in film production for USC's Film School. I wanted to teach writing, but Irwin Blacker held down that post at USC. Although Blacker had heart problems, chairman Bernie Kantor made it clear he wanted no other screenwriting teacher on the faculty, no matter how ill Blacker was. Blacker was, in fact, an outstanding teacher.

UCLA's Department of Theater Arts, Film, and Television had no openings, but my friend Larry Thor from CBS Radio days, then professor and chairman of their screenwriting program, told me he would be interested in me teaching in his program if and when an opening occurred.

I had quickly put aside the notion of directing an episode of *Bewitched.* I was becoming increasingly aware that my primary goal was getting out of television altogether. Standing around twelve hours a day on a film or television set as directors so often did was not for me, especially since it usually consisted of endless waits for lighting adjustments between setups.

I never mentioned the directorial clause in my contract to anyone. When my agent mentioned it to me, I told him not to pursue it. Bill Asher was directing more and more episodes, quite successfully. He was obviously the best director the series ever had. Meanwhile, as front-man producer I spent my weekends at home writing stories I hoped would sell to feature films or become pilots for TV series other people could produce. Writing and selling a pilot script is the big payoff for a writer. As long as the series runs, the original writer continues to collect significant royalties. I knew with the instincts of a veteran that this particular assignment was going nowhere for me. As I had throughout my career, I resorted to the one skill upon which I could consistently rely: writing.

I came up with a treatment for a comedy about an American Airlines stewardess, which I called *Pie in the Sky.* It was based on a true incident involving a plane the airlines sent around the country to pick up various members of their crews who were stranded by a strike. The man in charge was the director of stewardess personnel. The whole rescue operation turned into a total comedic disaster, as it had in real life.

My agent was highly enthusiastic about the treatment I handed him. It seemed that Disney was looking for a comedy in which to star his client Rock Hudson. He was certain *Pie* was it and rushed the treatment out to Hudson, certain he had a quick sale.

The next day I picked up my home phone to hear my agent yelling, "What the hell did you do to Rock Hudson?"

I was dumbfounded. Although he lived next door to me, I had never met him nor even had a passing conversation with the actor. My agent wasn't satisfied with my answer.

"He claims you phoned the city to complain about his garbage cans being too close to the curb. Whether you did or didn't, he's enraged and I'll give you his comment: 'I will not read anything written by William Froug, not now, not ever! Tell him he can shove this story up his ass!'"

Of course, I had never complained to the city or anyone else about Rock Hudson's garbage cans. I'd never noticed them and had no idea where they were. But I'd been in the business long enough to realize that the truth was irrelevant. My agent's enthusiasm went limp, *Pie in the Sky* faded into also-ran status, never to arise again. It was becoming increasingly clear that feature films and I were not on speaking terms.

While in New York on business one weekend (I was partnered with Encyclopædia Britannica to produce *Critics at Large,* a pilot for a panel show to be hosted by Mortimer Adler and designed for television's then so-called Sunday afternoon "intellectual ghetto") I attended a small cocktail party held in a rather typical New York apartment. Perhaps thirty people were packed into a tiny living room, all either smoking or loading up on beverages from our host's ample bar set up on a small table in the living room. We were elbow to elbow, the noise was almost deafening.

A small man suddenly appeared before me, dark wavy hair, drink in hand.

"Monsieur Froug?" he inquired in a thick French accent, "you are the producer of *Bewitched?*"

When I confirmed he had found the guy he was looking for, he gave a little nod of his head, "Please, sir, if you don't mind, Monsieur Truffaut would like to meet you, I will bring him right over."

"Francois Truffaut?" was all I could finally get out, and to his nod I added, "Wants to meet me? I would be delighted." The small Frenchman disappeared into the mob.

Of all the New Wave French filmmakers I had come to admire, Truffaut was number one with me. His films spoke to the heart of the human condition, with maturity and compassion. He was a humanist in the best sense of the word. Like many European directors, Truffaut wrote the screenplays for his films, hence he was the first film critic to promulgate the auteur theory. He did not take into account that America's filmmaking tradition was as totally unlike Europe's as were our films.

The small man reappeared accompanied by another short, well-dressed man with dark wavy hair. I recognized Francois Truffaut.

He shook my hand and greeted me in French and continued speaking French with considerable enthusiasm. His interpreter broke in, "Francois wants you to know that he and his family watch *Bewitched* every week, it is their favorite American television series. And he wants to know what Agnes Moorehead is like to work with. Do you have any problems with her?"

I assured him we had no problem whatsoever with Moorehead, that she was a consummate professional, always showed up on time, knew her lines, and never caused additional takes.

Satisfied, Truffaut and his interpreter drifted back into the mob.

Asher always attended the *Bewitched* dubbing session, which didn't surprise me but did annoy me. As we played back the final rough cut, the laugh track engineer, at his keyboard watching the projection room screen, would fill in any of a number of prerecorded responses usually gleaned from live TV sitcom audiences. *I Love Lucy* was the laugh engineers' favorite source of "borrowed" laugh tracks. This process was known as "sweetening." Specialists in this field acquired a collection of almost every possible audience response—gasps, shock, stunned silence (yes, that is a sound), awe, and laughs of every size and quality, from belly and boffo to snicker and even reluctant-to-laugh. All of these were connected to the laugh track engineer's keyboard, which was not dissimilar to a court stenographer's transcribing machine but larger. The engineers who "played" their instruments were masters of their machines, unerringly cueing in just the right response. Their store of canned laughter remains the backbone of most TV sitcoms. Even sitcoms performed live before an audience usually have their sound tracks later enhanced to fit the taste of the producer (or sometimes the network) before they are broadcast.

I was uncomfortable with the entire process, and made more so by Asher's directions to the engineer to amplify whatever reaction he'd keyed in. The show was a big hit year in and year out, so who was I to argue with the man who had been part of *Bewitched* from the beginning?

My solace came at home nights and weekends as I wrote my new film treatment. I was totally caught up in my story. The magic of writing is that for a few hours you get to enter an alternative reality. The characters become so real they talk to you ; they write their own dialogue. It must be the same kind of escape actors feel when they really get into a role. There is no drug that can give you a high like it. A good story would drive me as much as I was driving it, which is always a welcome sign. I was writing a World War II action melodrama I called *Gutbucket*. Although totally fictional, I used my own experiences as skipper of a subchaser to launch the action-adventure piece. The writing went well; in a few weekends I completed a 110-page treatment for a feature film. It was far too long, but I decided to worry about that later. I gave it to my agent, who was enthusiastic about it. Within another month I had notes for a second screenplay.

My timing, as it turned out, was serendipitous. As the *Bewitched* season neared its end, I was called into a meeting in Harry Ackerman's office where Bill Asher and Elizabeth Montgomery were waiting. Ackerman was stooped over his desk, quietly munching on graham crackers between sips of milk.

"Ulcer," he muttered and resumed munching as I sat down. I knew my fate on the show was at least one of the topics of conversation. As I entered, Montgomery was speaking conspiratorially to Ackerman, "We've got to get rid of *him*," she said quietly with no attempt to conceal her annoyance. It was an order from a woman who didn't like revealing that she gave the orders that must be followed. After they left I asked Ackerman who "him" was.

"Dick York," Ackerman replied. "I don't know why. I can't talk her out of it. York is more important to the series than she's willing to admit. Asher tried to convince her she was wrong, but she was adamant. She wants him fired."

I was dumbfounded. Dick York was superb as Samantha's husband. His comedic timing was impeccable, and they appeared to work well together. Still, I had learned not to try to make sense of Elizabeth's edicts.

"When Liz makes up her mind," Ackerman continued, "there's not much you can do about it. Asher will try to get her to rethink it, but I'm inclined to doubt he'll succeed. She just doesn't want York on the series, period."

"Now," he continued, "I'm sorry to tell you that we've decided not to renegotiate your contract for next season. Bill Asher has convinced Liz to let him produce the show."

"Good. He's been doing it all season," I replied, "and honestly, Harry, the job didn't work out for me, either."

"What are your plans?" he asked me with genuine concern.

"I just got off the phone with my agent," I replied. "He has sold my film treatment to Walter Mirisch, with a two-picture deal for me to write and produce two features at United Artists, as soon as I can report for work. The money is equal to a year in television, and, boy, do I want out of this medium."

Ackerman rose and pumped my hand in warm congratulations. As I left his office, I allowed myself the luxury of thinking I was free at last from television. A fool and his optimism are perfect companions.

Bewitched was nominated for an Emmy that season (it had been nominated and had won various Emmys in previous seasons), which meant if it won again, as credited producer I was obliged to accept the award. Asher and Montgomery insisted I sit with them at the Emmy ceremony. While the winners were announced, I nervously decided if the show won, I would accept the award "on behalf of Elizabeth Montgomery and William Asher." Ironically, in that event I would be accepting an Emmy I didn't earn, eight years after I had not been allowed to accept an Emmy I did earn. My fears were groundless. It didn't happen. *The Monkees* won.

Elizabeth Montgomery succeeded in getting rid of her co-star, Dick York, who was replaced by actor Dick Sargent the following season. It was the death knell for the series. It lasted another two seasons to declining ratings and was canceled. *Bewitched* continues to thrive in reruns for which my friend, Sol Saks, must surely be giving thanks.

A couple of years later, one of the *Bewitched* writers told me that Elizabeth Montgomery had left Asher and run off to Hawaii with Dick Michaels. True or not (Asher and Liz later divorced), it made perfect sense to me.

13

One Subchaser Missing in Action

In the summer of 1970, I reported to work on the Sam Goldwyn lot just off Santa Monica Boulevard and Formosa, in Hollywood where the Mirisch Company kept offices and made many of their films. The Mirisch brothers were revolutionizing the way Hollywood made pictures. Walter, Lawrence, and Marvin Mirisch realized they didn't need to own a studio in order to become major players in Hollywood and produce a full slate of features. They merely leased space from Goldwyn and put a welcome sign out for the best moviemakers in town. They promised a hands-off operation. Creative people who came to the Mirisch Company were free to create, and in short order some of Hollywood's finest signed up.

This new independent film company quickly became the most successful operation as the old big studio system began to crumble. The Mirisch Company danced circles around MGM, Universal, Fox, Warner Brothers, and Columbia. Their movies racked up record box-office grosses and, while they were at it, gathered in Oscars and Oscar nominations by the bushel basket, turning out hit movies like *Some Like It Hot, The Great Escape, The Magnificent Seven, In the*

Heat of the Night, The Thomas Crown Affair, Irma La Douce, and *The Pink Panther* series.

They released their cornucopia of classics through United Artists. Keeping a firm eye on the budget (Marvin's department) and their overhead to a minimum they conquered Hollywood as no independent before or since.

Walter Mirisch had embarked on a new plan. He wanted to make ten World War II movies in the one-million-dollar-per-picture budget range. In the 1960s this was not the ridiculously low budget it would be today. With wise selections of scripts and casts of new people, Mirisch knew he could use these vehicles to build for the future. He bought *Gutbucket* as one of those vehicles.

You will perhaps understand my thrill when I drove onto the Goldwyn lot to meet Walter Mirisch, who, after the recent death of his brother Lawrence, had become producing head of the company.

When I entered Walter Mirisch's office, it was like hallowed ground to me. I was going to work where Billy Wilder made his movies as did John Sturgess, I. A. L. Diamond, Blake Edwards, and so many other of Hollywood's most creative filmmakers.

Although I'd worked at all the most famous studios during my checkered career in television, driving onto the lot that first day was a new and altogether thrilling experience. I had never allowed myself the luxury of believing I was qualified to enter the world of feature filmmaking. Even as I parked and went looking for Walter Mirisch's office, I had an uncomfortable feeling that I was sneaking under the big tent at the circus without buying a ticket. I felt I would soon be discovered and thrown out. It would have taken my father fifteen years to earn what the Mirisch Company paid me for *Gutbucket.* Nothing would have thrilled him more.

When I introduced myself to Walter Mirisch, I knew this was, indeed, a world apart from television. The ambiance in his office was serene, easy-going. His secretary, Jessie, looked more like an attractive middle-aged schoolmarm than a bustling, pert, young Hollywood secretary from the studio pool. There was no TV production frenzy, no secretaries rushing pages to mimeo or to the soundstages, no agents or actors crowding the waiting room eager to get in for an appointment. The phones were not ringing off the hooks. It was quiet, peaceful, relaxed. In Hollywood, wonders never cease.

Walter, a lean, good-looking man with a gentle smile, greeted me as I entered his office. He was a man of quiet self-assurance who exuded goodwill. I knew I was even luckier than I had imagined.

"I like your story very much," he said, as he greeted me. "I think it will make a very good picture. We've arranged an office for you in our writers building, and you'll find our small dining room close to your office. The food is quite good and inexpensive. You're welcome to lunch there whenever you feel like it."

"How soon do you want the screenplay?" I asked, still running on television time.

"Why, whenever you're ready to show it to me," he replied, "we're in no rush."

I couldn't believe what I was hearing, it was like some great healing balm washing over me. "Shift gears," I told myself, "slow down, it's okay."

"I think your only problem," said Mirisch, "is you've got a lot of story there. I imagine you're going to want to trim it down to get a two-hour screenplay out of it. However, write it at whatever length feels comfortable for you and we can always discuss cutting it later."

This was becoming a more and more miraculous experience. When had I ever said to a writer "whenever you're ready"? Never. But Mirisch clearly meant it. I checked into my new office, a small, spare room; a desk and a typewriter, no secretary, nothing on the walls (what a concept!), and went to work with a new and exhilarating sense of freedom.

The writing went as smoothly as had the treatment. If you have a driving action line you're always going to be ahead of the game. I merely had to start the story engine, and it took off on its own. That's the advantage of the action-adventure genre. To me it's the easiest kind of story for a screenwriter because it is inherently visual and character is secondary.

I was writing a fictional account of a twenty-one-year-old captain of a PC-class subchaser on patrol off Majuro Atoll in the Marshall Islands, whose ship makes contact with a submerged Japanese sub.

The captain orders his ship to General Quarters (battle stations), making a by-the-book attack run, in preparation for dropping depth charges. The sonar man reports the sub is on a course setting in the direction of Tokyo Bay. The skipper sends a message to CINCPAC (Commander in Chief, Pacific) in Pearl Harbor. He receives an astonishing reply—don't lose contact, but delay attack until further orders.

The action then cuts to CINCPAC headquarters in Pearl Harbor, where we learn that, during a nighttime raid on Majuro Atoll, a small force of Japanese commandos had gone ashore and captured an American admiral involved in planning the coming assault on the Japanese homeland. CINCPAC decides to send a destroyer squadron to the scene with a bold attempt to rescue the admiral; they don't think the young skipper can handle this job alone.

I played out my story intercutting our captured admiral being interrogated by the Japanese aboard their submarine and CINCPAC, then back to the inexperienced subchaser skipper on his first combat mission. The adventure is played against a time clock (always an excellent device for a screenwriter): trying to rescue the admiral before the sub reaches Tokyo.

As I wrote, I felt my pulse quicken; the chase had me charged with excitement. As the days went by, I was reliving my own routine days as skipper of the peacetime *PC 800*. That experience being a young commanding officer at sea gave me special insight into what my fictional skipper was feeling. I knew it was working well.

I went to lunch in the small Mirisch dining room (there were perhaps two rows of about a dozen four-seat tables divided by an aisle). I found myself seated next to a table occupied by Billy Wilder and I. A. L. Diamond who were seated facing one another over lunch. To me, these master screenwriters were two of the greatest stars in Hollywood. They collaborated on the screenplays for some of the funniest films in Hollywood history: *Some Like It Hot, Fortune Cookie,* and *Irma La Douce* during their ten-year collaboration.

I was struck by the oddity that during my many lunches seated at the table next to them, I never saw or heard these screenwriting giants utter a word to each other. I imagined it was during these silent lunches that they worked on their screenplay problems. Obviously they did their talking in their offices.

In four weeks I presented my screenplay to Walter Mirisch and went back to my office to sweat out his response. By mid-afternoon the next day I was summoned to his office. As I entered he was grinning. "Excellent script," he said. "We're going into production with it just as soon as we get the navy's cooperation. They're going to love this screenplay. Meantime, I've taken the liberty of setting up a preproduction meeting for you with our unit production manager, assistant director, and casting director. Finding a leading man who can play a twenty-one-year-old and is strong enough to carry a picture is not going to be a piece of cake. I think you're going to have difficulty bringing your picture in on budget, but we'll talk about that after the experts break it down. Your meeting is scheduled for tomorrow morning at nine on Stage Three. Is that okay for you?"

I sputtered some sort of answer, but my insides were doing a big-time celebration, the blood was rushing to my head: "We're going into production . . . is that okay for you?" Was I imagining what I was hearing?

"I'm delighted," was all I could manage. I phoned the navy's Hollywood PR officer and scheduled a meeting.

Our preproduction meeting went well. As we sat around the conference table on our soundstage, the discussion centered on how many days we would have to shoot at sea. Our unit production manager (UPM) had been busy breaking the script down into the scenes that could be filmed on a soundstage, which would save us a lot of money. Filming at sea is among the most expensive undertakings there is in the world of moviemaking. The UPM felt we were in a tight squeeze to make the picture for Walter Mirisch's goal of one million dollars. In fact, he rather doubted it.

"We can adjust the screenplay so there are more interior scenes, we can shoot on our soundstage and fewer exterior scenes at sea," I told him, knowing it was an easy fix that might make a great deal of difference in our budget. We had routinely done it on *Adventures in Paradise.*

"Sure," he replied, "but no subchaser, no film"

On that score, I had no doubts. How could the navy turn down a story in which a young, inexperienced commanding officer outwits an experienced, enemy sub commander at his own game? There was enthusiasm and encouragement from my production team, which made for an optimistic prognosis. Film crews can work miracles when they are dedicated to making the film work. We were in luck on one front: Walter Mirisch was willing to go with an unknown in the lead role. Later that day, he called me into his office to tell me he'd heard the meeting went well and was confident that, with the acquisition of a subchaser, we could make the film on budget. As I was about to leave he handed me a screenplay, saying, "Read this when you get time. It's a new Billy Wilder comedy going into production. I'd like your opinion."

I was flattered, indeed. That night I read the screenplay for *The Apartment* and dropped by his office the next morning to tell him my comments. As I handed it to him, I said, "It's brilliant, Walter, truly brilliant, but it's not a comedy."

"I know that, and you know that," he replied, smiling, "but we're advertising it as a comedy. We'll let the audience decide what it is."

The following week I got a call from the navy's Hollywood PR officer, asking me to come in for a meeting. When I arrived in his office he was holding the script, "I like your story very much. Very authentic. Obviously you were in antisubmarine warfare. Were you skipper of a PC?" I nodded affirmatively, watching his face turn cloudy.

"I'm sorry to tell you that I got a flat turndown from Washington. We can not give you Navy cooperation in making your movie, and we won't lease or loan you a subchaser."

"But, why?" I asked, flabbergasted. "It's great PR for the navy, and you yourself said it's authentic."

"Except for one detail, which is at the heart of your screenplay. No United States Navy admiral has ever been captured by the enemy. That is totally unacceptable. I wish I could help you out. I explained to my boss that this is a work of fiction, and it dramatizes how well our young officers can function under pressure. But, I hit a stone wall, and there's no appeal. You're going to have to make this movie on your own, without any help from the navy. I'm terribly sorry, if that's any consolation, and I'm sure it isn't."

I was crestfallen. When I reported back to Walter Mirisch he shared my reaction but it turned out he had a backup idea. He was not prepared to let this screenplay die without exploring every possibility.

"The Peruvian Navy bought several of our subchasers after the war, why don't you check with them? "

It turned out the Peruvian Navy had scrapped most of their PC-class subchasers a couple of years earlier. (Actually these little ships had been obsolete even before they went to sea. Japanese submarines could outrun us when surfaced.) When I reported back to Mirisch, he sympathetically pronounced the last rites. *Gutbucket* was dead. That screenplay, like many thousands of others bought but unproduced, sits in the files in a warehouse somewhere.

I had an idea for a second feature project. While browsing through the Beverly Hills Public Library one afternoon, researching a *Gunsmoke* script I was writing, I came across a little booklet titled *The Last Raid of the Daltons*. It was a remarkable account of the Dalton gang's foolhardy attempt to simultaneously rob two banks, which were directly across the street from each other, in their own hometown of Coffeyville, Kansas. The last of the old Western outlaw gangs, they planned the daring raid in broad daylight, in front of scores of townspeople who all knew them as neighboring farm boys. I was struck by how and why these robbers, led by the Dalton's youngest son, Bob, had attempted such an idiotic act.

But I had a much earlier interest in the Daltons. One day, back when I was a teenager visiting my grandfather, I got him talking about his life in the Oklahoma Territory shortly after the last of the Oklahoma Land Runs in 1903. Grandpa had opened a little clothing shop.

"I sold some boots to one the Dalton boys one day," he said offhandedly. He remembered very little about them except they were from nearby Coffeyville, Kansas. When they came to town the farmers sometimes gave them a real hoedown. Music, dancing. "You see," he explained to me, "the Daltons made trouble for the railroads and nobody liked the railroads. So they were kind of heroes, in a way. They treated all of us very nicely, even though they were a rowdy bunch." So the seed had been planted; I had a personal hook into Frank, Grat, Bob, and Emmett Dalton.

The Daltons' story probably had noodled around in my unconscious for years without my realizing it. "It was cooking," as I liked to tell myself. One day it announced to me that it was ready to be written.

My friend Mimi Roth was head of United Artist's story department. I told her my idea, and she arranged for me to meet with several high-level executives of the company. I told them my story treatment for the Daltons' last raid. They liked it and made a deal with my agent for me to write the screenplay. They agreed to pay my research expenses to Coffeyville to search the public records and the newspaper files. When I got to Kansas I was able to interview the last living eyewitness to the actual raid, a ninety-plus-year-old woman.

The Daltons had been marshals at one time before becoming outlaws or "on the dodge" as the locals termed it back then. I read how the Dalton boys boasted they were cousins and descendants of Jesse James, which they fervently believed even though it was untrue. In my focus on detail, I had missed this lie that was the key to the story. These guys wanted above all else to be even more famous than their imagined cousin. It was really the foundation for a fresh look at these notorious outlaws, but I used it in an inconsequential way.

With my tape recorder in hand, I recorded much of my information at the actual scene where the raid had taken place. I visited the Dalton museum and saw photos of their bodies next to the townsfolk who had killed them, standing proud as big game hunters with trophies of their kill. In death the Daltons had succeeded in what they set out to become: famous like their imagined cousin Jesse James. The more I researched, the more excited I became. Even though many movies had been made about them, I knew I had the real story and I could dramatize a fresh approach.

I returned to Hollywood with 150 pages of typed notes and a rusted railroad spike I found next to the Daltons' graves. I put it beside my IBM Selectric, as a good-luck charm.

But, somehow, the more I worked the more lost I became in the minutiae of the details I had unearthed. When I was finished about ten weeks later, I turned the screenplay in to United Artists. I feared that it wasn't right, but I didn't know how to fix it. I was too deep in the forest to see the trees, yet I hoped against hope that it was better than I thought it was.

A few days later Mimi Roth phoned to tell me they had decided to pass. She didn't think the story was focused and that there were too many irrelevant scenes. I was let down, of course. In reexamining the screenplay I realized the problem. I had overloaded my mind with details of the Daltons' lives. It was interesting history but poor drama. Mimi was right. I had buried myself in the minutiae of their lives.

My two-picture deal was dead. Lacking an opening as a full-time teacher at either USC (I was in my sixth year of part-time teaching at USC's Film School) or UCLA, like it or not, it was back to television. Over the next few years I freelanced scripts for a few series— *Paper Chase, Quincy, M.E., Big Hawaii, Charlie's Angels, Judd for the Defense,* and several others, but I did not want to go back to producing series unless it was financially necessary.

The lesson every writer has to learn is to get back on the horse that threw you. I turned to my keyboard for another ride on Hollywood's bucking bronco, never knowing how long my next ride would last. Hollywood is not a place for people looking for a steady job or a weekly paycheck.

14

So You Want to Be in Pictures?

One evening after my USC class was over, one of my students approached me. Thin, emaciated, skin too pale, he looked like death lurking. He said his name was Dan O'Bannon. His cheeks were sunken, his color pallid, his eyes dull. He handed me a screenplay and asked if I would read it.

I assured him I would and asked him if he was ill. "I haven't eaten in two days," he replied, his voice quiet as a tomb. "I have enough money for dinner tonight and that's it."

I took his script and asked him to call me the next morning. When I got home I started reading *The Devil in Mexico* by Dan O'Bannon. His dialogue was often brilliant, but his storytelling skills were quite poor. Still, this was a young talent the likes of which I had not seen in years. This kid could really write.

When he phoned the next morning, I invited him to come out to my house for lunch. He gratefully accepted.

As soon as he arrived he asked for some food, not trying to hide his embarrassment. I took a package of hot dogs out of the fridge and, without waiting for me to warm them, he ravenously wolfed them down. I could not convince him they would be better heated.

As he ate, I asked him the history of the screenplay. He had shopped it around but could not get an agent to represent him. Nobody liked the script. He didn't know what to do. He had to get a job, but he was dedicated to making a career for himself as a filmmaker, no matter what. It is this "no matter what" quality that is often the difference between the highly successful and the also-rans, especially in Hollywood.

O'Bannon explained that he suffered from a rare disease that produces severe abdominal inflammation and accompanying pain. Doctors had told him it was inflammatory bowel syndrome, and it was genetic. His mother had bequeathed it to him along with her cruelty, according to Dan. There was no cure, merely palliative treatment for the excruciating pain when the attacks came on. For O'Bannon, poverty and pain were nuisances he would endure as the price of success.

"Every dime I can scrape together goes to pay doctors," he told me, with some bitterness. But he hoped to get an agent with this script and maybe someday even sell *The Devil in Mexico*. I told him what I thought was wrong with the script and how I felt it could be fixed. It needed a major rewrite. He explained he'd put so much time in on it he had neither the energy nor the enthusiasm to make the considerable changes I'd suggested, though he heartily agreed with all of them.

"Why don't you do it?" he asked me. "It'll be like a new script, anyway. We'll share credit."

I had such a clear idea of how to restructure the script and rewrite one of the two major characters that I agreed, telling him it would take me several weeks.

"I don't care," O'Bannon replied, "take all the time you like; it's not going anywhere the way it is."

The next day I began my rewrite of O'Bannon's script. He had written a fictionalized account of the disappearance of the famous writer and newspaper man Ambrose Bierce. Bierce had attained national prominence for his short stories ("An Occurrence at Owl

Creek Bridge," among others) as well as many books and articles. He became known for the bitter and cynical tone of his writings, especially *The Devil's Dictionary*, published in 1906. Having tried mining for gold, writing a newspaper column, and whatever else struck his fancy, Bierce headed off into Mexico in 1913 to find and interview the then-infamous bandit Pancho Villa. It was presumed but not confirmed that Bierce was killed in Ojinaga, Mexico, in 1914.

O'Bannon's premise was that Bierce actually caught up and rode with Villa. His screenplay was essentially the dialogue between a cynical old man (Bierce) and an idealistic but ruthless revolutionary (Villa). Dan had written Bierce brilliantly, the bitterness and cynicism of the old man was so vivid that the character had to be Ambrose Bierce brought to life. Unfortunately, O'Bannon was totally lost in his attempts to creative a believable Villa. He had written a comic-book Mexican made worse by his inclusion of mock-Mexican spellings in Villa's dialogue. The other problem was the story didn't go anywhere. My job was to research Villa and bring reality to his character as well as invent some complications to build a second act. I felt we needed a third character, and it would generate more dramatic tension if that character was a woman.

I decided to create a female reporter from San Francisco who had followed Bierce. The old writer had been a well-known newspaperman in San Francisco, in one of his many incarnations. I had very little work to do rewriting Bierce. O'Bannon had etched him so perfectly I had only to stay in his tone for new scenes and dialogue.

When I finished the script I gave it to O'Bannon, who was delighted with it. After my agents at the William Morris Agency read it, I received a call from the head of their motion picture department raving about the screenplay. "I'm sending it out today to some of our top stars who I think are right for it, if that's okay with you. Omar Sharif is hot right now coming off *Lawrence of Arabia;* we've got offers for Elliott Gould following *M*A*S*H,* and we're looking for something for Peter Ustinov."

The agent was talking about three of the biggest names in motion pictures at that time. Would I argue?

Within a week or so I received a call from him advising me that Peter Ustinov wanted to meet with me to discuss *The Devil in Mexico;*

he wanted to play one of the two major roles. He was staying at the actress Elke Sommers's home in Coldwater Canyon and asked if I would drop by the following afternoon around three for a chat.

When I arrived I heard loud mariachi music blaring on loudspeakers inside the house. I knocked loudly and the door was opened by Ustinov wearing a serape and a sombrero, with castanets in his hands.

"Come in, my boy!" he shouted, grandly, "I'm just getting warmed up for the part!" He went swirling off into the living room. After finally turning the music down so I could hear him he said, "Love the script, definitely want to do it."

"Which part did you have in mind?" I asked him.

"Bierce," he replied, "by all means, he's the juicer role. Let's let Sharif or Gould do Villa." I gathered this meant he and the William Morris Agency had already wrapped this up as their package: their writer, their stars.

That was the first and only time I was ever to see Peter Ustinov. It was also the beginning and the end of *The Devil in Mexico*.

After a couple of weeks of silence I phoned William Morris.

"Oh, Peter is shopping it around," I was told. "Don't worry, he loves the screenplay. It's going to get made."

More silence followed as the weeks went by. All I got from the head of the motion picture department of the William Morris Agency was "Don't worry. Peter is running with it. He's determined to get it made."

One day I got a phone call from a friend working in development at a major studio. "Loved yours and O'Bannon's screenplay. We were interested in it, but Ustinov says he's attached as both actor and director. He's a terrible film director. But he said he's got the screenplay under option so we had to pass."

I phoned my agent and relayed this report, keeping my anger low key. He responded with surprise, "We didn't know Peter was doing that, we'll tell him to stop. You're right, of course, he has no option on your material."

Before the sordid episode was over, I had heard the same message from several friends. Ustinov was not only telling people he came with the package as the director but that he had the screenplay under option.

The Devil in Mexico died a quiet death. Ustinov, highly acclaimed actor, playwright, and sometimes film director, had struck out too many times in the latter capacity for Hollywood to accept. I later learned it's not uncommon for enthusiastic actors, directors, or producers to go out and try to sell screenplays they don't own or even have under option. Writers are powerless to stop them.

There's an odd postscript. I was visiting the Fox lot sometime later when I saw Beau Bridges; we had met when I was working on the Goldwyn lot.

"Listen," he said, "I just want to tell you I read your script while I was shooting on location in Mexico. That Ambrose Bierce screenplay. I loved it."

"What was it doing in Mexico?" I asked.

"Peter Ustinov was down there, showing it to everybody, including me. Great script."

Some years later, in 1989, Gregory Peck and Jane Fonda starred in *Old Gringo.* Peck played Ambrose Bierce and Jimmy Smits was Pancho Villa's second in command, but he was clearly a Villa surrogate. Jane Fonda played a school teacher. The script by Aida Bortnik and Luis Puenzo was based on a novel by Carlos Fuentes. Their story was about Bierce coming to Mexico to find Villa. Their premise was identical but their story went in a different direction. Good ideas are like microbes, they're naked to the eye but how mysteriously they travel! Did Dan O'Bannon start this sudden interest in Bierce meeting Villa? He may have; we will never know. When I mentioned it to Dan he replied, "Tsk! Tsk! Carlos, naughty boy."

Not long ago I was having dinner with my good friends Mimi Roth and her husband, Leon, a USC professor and former producer. "You know," she said, "I always wanted to make *The Devil in Mexico.* I'm sorry my management passed on it." It was a comment out of the blue, about a screenplay she had read almost thirty years earlier.

Dan O'Bannon finally found his voice and Hollywood found Dan O'Bannon. He wrote the blockbuster *Alien,* then *Blue Thunder, The Night of the Living Dead,* and *Total Recall.* Sometimes O'Bannon worked alone, sometimes in collaboration.

One evening I attended a screening of USC student films along with a few of my students. The main feature, *Dark Star,* was a science-fiction comedy written by Dan O'Bannon and co-starring O'Bannon. It was directed by his fellow student John Carpenter, who had also been in one of my USC evening classes. O'Bannon had helped build and design the extraordinarily clever sets. At one point in the film O'Bannon, playing an astronaut, moves toward the camera into a tight close-up and says, "I should tell you my name is not really Sergeant Pincheck. My name is Bill Froug." What a hoot for the audience, many of whom were or had been my students.

The last time Dan and I shared a meal, he drove me to a Chinese restaurant near the Fox lot in his brand new Cadillac. Our visit a couple of years after that, however, was not celebratory. It was when I interviewed him for my book *The New Screenwriter Looks at the New Screenwriter.* He was hooked up to a morphine drip while agitatedly pacing his UCLA hospital room. The intestinal inflammation that had intermittently plagued him with severe pain all of his life had struck again.

O'Bannon continued to write. Writers write because they can't *not* write, they don't waste time thinking about what sold or what didn't. Regardless of the outcome, they put the seat of their pants back down on the seat of the chair and keep writing. It's really not a choice. It comes with the territory.

Irv Kershner, Walter Newman, and I had continued having our dinners every Thursday evening at Musso-Frank restaurant on Hollywood Boulevard. Each of us had pet projects we thought were feature material. Each of us put up a little money, optioned a couple of lesser-known books, and hoped lightning would strike. We were still looking for ways to work together on a project.

The problem with our plan was that each of us was in demand in different areas of the business. Newman could get a high-paying screenwriting job any time he wanted, he had only to notify his agent, Leonard Hanser, that he was ready to work. Kershner was rapidly building a big career as a feature film director. And I was in demand as a television hyphenate. We agreed that although each of us was free to take an outside job, we would try to function as a unit, if the opportunity presented itself.

Soon lightning struck. Kershner got a call from a New York fan and business associate of his named Mort Mitofsky. Mitofsky was dubbed "the Angel of Broadway" by the New York papers because he was the key backer of David Merrick. Merrick was far and away the most successful producer on Broadway during the fifties and sixties (*Lullaby of Broadway, Carnival, Fanny,* and *Hello, Dolly!*). Merrick was also called "the Abominable Showman" because of his sometimes ruthless behavior.

Mitofsky had put together a deal with Philip Yordan, the screenwriter, producer, playwright, novelist, and head of Samuel Bronston Productions located in Spain. Bronston had recently completed a big-budget historical epic based on the life of El Cid, the eleventh-century Spanish hero who drove the Moors out of Spain. Yordan had co-written the screenplay. Charlton Heston and Sophia Loren starred in it, but the film did not fare well with either the critics or the box office.

Yordan and Bronson had the idea of using the sets of *El Cid* to produce a movie based on the best-selling novel *Dear and Glorious Physician*. Mitofsky had a firm offer from Yordan, on behalf of Samuel Bronston Productions, for Kershner to direct, Walter Newman to write, and me to produce their new film. When Kershner presented the offer to us at our next dinner meeting, we quickly accepted. Mitofsky instructed Kersh and Newman and me to come to New York to sign the contract. Yordan was paying our expenses. Newman said, "You guys can tell them I'm in," declining to join us.

Mitofsky had offered to put us up at the Hampshire House hotel where he lived. We arrived the night before the date set for the signing. After taking us out to dinner, we saw one of the Mitofsky-backed plays and then walked home, down the center of Broadway, now a snow covered, empty-of-all-traffic street. There had been a heavy snowfall the night before. The city was briefly a ghost town. The quiet was eerily intoxicating. We strolled the deserted streets, experiencing a silent night in New York City. It was a magical moment. In a jovial mood, we sang fragments of Broadway show tunes, fantasized about our upcoming life in Spain, and tossed a snowball now and then. Our laughter echoed off the walls of the buildings.

"Don't forget," Mitofsky said as he left us in the elevator, "we sign the contract at ten in the morning. By the way, you guys are invited to breakfast in my suite."

As I snuggled into bed that night I dared to tell myself, "This is real, this is incredible, this is not television."

After a celebratory breakfast, Kersh and I strolled down Fifth Avenue, basking in the sunshine and the magnificent crisp morning air feeling heady and talkative about what fun we were going to have in Spain. We let our fantasies run wild.

As we crossed the street we passed a newsstand from which screamed a six-column front-page banner headline on a morning paper: SAMUEL BRONSTON FILES BANKRUPTCY.

Mitofsky came walking briskly and somewhat breathlessly up to us, "I just got a call from Yordan," he said. "The meeting's called off. No picture. You guys might as well go home."

Mitofsky later asked me to stay over that night to have dinner with David Merrick. "He wants to go into pictures," Mort said. "I told him he's nuts."

"Do you think I'll tell him anything different?" I asked him.

Nonetheless, Merrick and I had a pleasant, conversational dinner, during which I doubt I told him anything he didn't already know, except perhaps the extent to which agents controlled much of Hollywood. I flew back to L.A. the following morning. To his credit, Yordan eventually reimbursed us for our expenses.

15

One Last Fling

That summer of 1971 I received a call from my agent telling me that Allen Courtney, the president of MGM Television, had a commitment for an ABC Movie of the Week he wanted me to produce. All he had to show me was a one-page treatment by a New York writer, Lewis John Carlino.

Carlino's story was called *In Search of America.* It was about an upper-middle-class American family who buys an old school bus, refurbishes it as a mobile home, and sets out with their teenage son to travel the back roads of America. Their first stopover was at a Woodstock-like rock festival where the son meets a pretty teenage girl. He falls in love with her, only to learn she has been diagnosed with leukemia. The theme of the story was how each member of the family, especially the son, copes with the harsh realities of life, including premature death.

I was fascinated with the possibilities inherent in the concept and agreed to produce it. Courtney phoned to tell me how pleased he was and that Carlino would be in town in a few days. He would set up a meeting for us.

Courtney and I met for breakfast at the Beverly Hills Hotel where a hippie in bell-bottomed jeans, long hair, and beads joined us. The moment Carlino began talking it was clear this was not a pose. Carlino was the real thing. He lived on a farm in New Jersey with his wife and three children. They grew most of the food they ate. Carlino had won an Obie Award for his off-Broadway one-act plays and had written the screenplays for *Seconds, The Fox,* and *The Brotherhood.* His career as a writer, begun in the early sixties, was beginning to shift into high gear.

We talked enthusiastically about the possibilities open to us from his premise. Carlino was willing to develop the story any way it struck our fancy. He wanted to explore his coming-of-age theme against the backdrop of the whole family's eagerness to share their son's experience as they began their odyssey in search of America.

Born in New York City of poor Sicilian immigrants, Carlino still held the excitement of his parents' sense of discovery in a new land. Carlino had hitchhiked across much of the United States and was eager to move out of the East Coast and into the home he was building in Colorado, "the frontier" as he called it. There was nothing phony or pretentious about this guy. He had been there and done that. I knew I liked Lewis John Carlino and his genuine enthusiasm for life.

Courtney saw the chemistry between us and suggested I fly back to New York where we could continue our discussions and work out a story outline for ABC's approval.

A week later Luigi (as he liked to be called) and I were holed up in the Plaza Hotel talking story when we received a call from Courtney. "I told ABC about the chemistry between you two and how you've progressed with your story. You have a green light to write your outline. Oh, and there's one minor thing. The girl must not die. ABC won't have it any other way. No use arguing with them; their approval is contingent on it."

Surprisingly, Carlino was agreeable. However, I felt a large part of the dramatic underpinning had been cut from the story. In any event, we were back to square one. The structure we had been building no longer worked. More seriously, ABC had removed the theme of the story. In television you learn to roll with the punches or you find another game.

Luigi and I decided to treat ourselves to the most elaborate lunch available in New York, sampling dishes from several Italian restaurants where Carlino knew the exceptional quality of the food, indeed, he was a connoisseur of fine New York restaurants. By the time we completed our luncheon orgy, we had worked out the story and, sadly, my time in New York was finished. There is nothing in this world that can equal a few days in New York City on an open-ended expense account.

When I returned from New York I learned MGM had set up the production through Four Star Productions, an independent production company located in Beverly Hills, and when I reported for work I was greeted by my old friend David Levy, vice president of Four Star. Levy and I had been founding members of the Caucus for Producers, Writers, and Directors. Although David was a card-carrying Republican and I a devout liberal, we had somehow meshed comfortably in spite of fundamental political differences and often vociferous but reasoned disagreements.

My first order of business was to await Carlino's teleplay, which arrived much sooner than I expected. Except for being a bit short, he had done an excellent, if not inspired, job. I phoned him and suggested a few minor changes and the addition of a couple of scenes. Meanwhile, I went about the business of hiring a director.

I decided to hire Paul Bogart as director. We had never met, but I much admired his work on PBS as well as his gift for directing comedies like *All in the Family.* It was an unusual choice, but I figured he would bring depth to the project. After getting ABC's approval, I sent him the script.

Paul and I met in my office a few days later and discussed casting at length. Trying to find a teenager who could carry the film was our core problem. Casting the parents was easy. I had worked with Vera Miles on previous shows and felt she would bring warmth, beauty, and talent to the role of the mother. Miles was a goodwill ambassador for all actors; she was a consummate professional with a cheerful personality, which brightened every set to which she reported. She had been a John Ford and Alfred Hitchcock favorite, playing the female lead in several major films and was a longtime favorite of mine. Paul Bogart suggested Carl Betts for the father, an excellent choice. Betts had played the husband in *The Donna Reed Show.* A handsome, thoughtful actor, he had an innate likeability that allowed him to connect with audiences. Four Star called their agents and confirmed both Vera Miles and Carl Betts were available.

I had remembered Carl Betts for a more personal reason. He had played the title character a season or two earlier in a very good lawyer series, *Judd for the Defense,* produced by Paul Monash. Monash had hired me to write a script for the series; he liked it and brought me back to write a second. Though I never saw the episodes, Monash told me they had played well.

For the young girl we both liked Tyne Daly, a beautiful and gifted young actress who, as it turned out, would later become one of the two leads in the police drama series *Cagney & Lacey.* For the kid our teenager would hang out with at the rock festival, we both liked Sal Mineo.

After all our featured players were set, Bogart came up with the fresh idea of Jeff Bridges, younger brother of Beau and son of the universally liked Lloyd Bridges, as our teenager. Jeff had had very little exposure as an actor, so we asked him to come by the office for a reading. He left with the part.

Our big problem with *In Search of America* was the budget. We had only ten days to shoot the TV movie. Carlino's story called for the family's first stop to be a rock festival on the magnitude of Woodstock. Paul and I got a print of the film *Woodstock* and sat together watching with awe and a sense of intimidation. There was no way we could touch the ambiance or the drama of that remarkable event. But a rock festival was at the epicenter of Carlino's screenplay.

On our location, we looked for ways to convey Woodstock on a very limited budget. At Warner's ranch in the San Fernando Valley, we found a rock outcropping with trails leading in and out where, in our imagination, the big event was actually happening off camera. We decided the family would park on the outer fringe of the festival and thus limit our exposure to celebrating throngs. The key would have to be hiring as many extras as we could afford to move in and out of the family's campsite so we could get a sense of what was going on close by. It was a cheat made necessary by the enormity of the event itself, juxtaposed with our limited budget.

The shooting went smoothly. Jeff was perfect for the part as were Miles, Betts, and Mineo. After the first couple of days of shooting, we discovered our film was running a little short. Overnight I added brief scenes for Vera Miles and Carl Betts. If all actors were as professional and accomplished as these two, a producer's life would be almost easy.

The dailies looked good and we finished right on our ten-day shooting schedule. Personally I felt the story lacked heft by the exclusion of Carlino's original theme—that of the boy having to deal with his emotions arising from the death of someone his own age, in this case a young girl with whom he was involved. But when networks tell their producers and writers to jump, all too often we respond, "How high?"

Returning from our location to the Four Stars offices one Friday afternoon, I ran into the actor Anthony Quinn just outside my office rushing off somewhere. He grabbed me. "I'd like you to produce *Across 110th Street*," he said. "How about it? Meet me in the basement projection room of the Beverly Hills Hotel tomorrow noon. I've got some film to show you."

"Thanks," I replied, "but I'm in the midst of producing a TV movie; I'll be tied up for the next month or two."

"Never mind that, my friend, I'm talking big screen. A real movie, not this television shit. It will take me a while to set up the deal anyway. Meet me tomorrow at noon. Beverly Hills Hotel basement projection room. We'll have some fun with this picture."

The actor's enthusiasm was obviously genuine and his excitement charming. I agreed to meet him at the hotel.

When I arrived Quinn was seated comfortably, munching on a huge club sandwich and being fawned over by two gorgeous, voluptuous, young women in G-string bikinis.

"I took the liberty of ordering without you. I hope you don't mind," said the star, taking a hefty swig of beer. "Order some food. Come on, it's Saturday, nobody works on Saturday, have some fun. Girls, pay some attention to my friend; he's going to produce my new film!" Quinn was full of grandiosity, laughter, and good cheer. In my mind's eye I figured he was playing Henry VIII. When room service came I ordered iced tea. It was obvious this actor was going to be in charge and possibly he was looking for a lackey. I wanted no part of it.

I never knew if Quinn recalled that I was a close friend of his sister, Stella, and her husband, screenwriter Martin Goldsmith. The three of us had visited the actor in his home some months earlier, and he had taken me on a personal tour of his outstanding art collection as well as showing me some of his own work. It didn't strike me as odd in the least that he made no mention of our earlier meeting in his home; probably because he had no recollection of the incident. Stars tend to live in the moment, which is usually a nanosecond.

Within half an hour, I'd finished my iced tea and left. I wasn't going to stick around for the royal performance. It was not a question of my being a prude or making a value judgment. Saturdays were too valuable a day off to waste on an actor's ego. Besides, I was knee deep in *In Search of America.* Quinn later found another producer, got a good screenplay by Luther Davis, and made the movie. Perhaps I missed an opportunity, but I couldn't be two places at once, though I often felt while working in television that somehow I was doing just that. Tempting as other work might be, I had to find a teaching berth.

During the weeks of preproduction on *In Search of America,* my agent and I often had lunch together at a small Italian restaurant on Beverly Drive just across the street from the Four Star offices. Joe Verdi, the owner, took a liking to us, dropping by our table to suggest specialties of the day. When business was slow he asked if he could join us in our booth. Our friendly encounters led to an unusual proposition.

"Listen, you guys," he said one day, lowering his voice, "you're special with me, so I'm going to let you in on a special deal. Each of you give me a check for five hundred dollars and tomorrow when you come in for lunch, I'll give each of you eight one-hundred dollar bills. All strictly legal, I guarantee you."

We declined, but got a good laugh out of it after we left the restaurant. After all, this is Hollywood. Anything can and does happen, often.

Joe Verdi repeated this strange proposition the next time we came in for lunch, always followed by, "It's legal, strictly legal. Trust me, I wouldn't do anything to hurt my best customers, would I? Come on, guys, I've got a business here, I'm here every day for years and I'll be here tomorrow. I'm not going anywhere, believe me. Why would I risk doing anything illegal? Am I going to run off with your checks? I don't think so."

After lunch we talked about what Verdi's con was about but could not come up with an explanation. He had offered none except to assure us of its legality. We believed him but were mystified. We were both certain Joe Verdi was not dealing drugs. So the next time we came in to lunch we each gave him a check for five hundred dollars. The following day he came to our table and counted out eight one-hundred dollar bills in front of each of us, adding, "By the way, guys, today's lunch is on me."

What scheme was he working? We hadn't a clue. The best we could come up with was that perhaps he was selling unlisted stock, but we had no evidence to support our theory. We kept our three-hundred dollar profit and never discussed it again, nor did Joe ever offer us another one of his "strictly legal" deals again. However, we continued to enjoy his excellent advice on luncheon specials.

The point of this little tale is that everybody in Hollywood has a hustle: the payoffs can be enormous and the possibilities are always sky high. It is no coincidence that popular actors are called stars. It's an apt metaphor.

When we showed the finished rough cut of *In Search of America* to the young ABC executive in charge of this project, he hit the ceiling.

"Where's the rock festival?" he angrily demanded of Paul and me. "Are you guys so cheap or so dumb you didn't know this story was supposed to take place at a rock festival?" His anger set a new and awful benchmark for me. In all my years of producing television series I had never received such a bawling out. We were flabbergasted, rendered speechless by the surprise attack. Later both of us agreed, here was a sad case of a young man carried away with his authority.

In Search of America played well, if not outstandingly, on ABC's *Monday Night at the Movies,* but I was quite disappointed with it. At one time, there were serious discussions about this concept becoming a pilot for a series, but we did not have series commitments from the major actors, so that idea was discarded. That young ABC executive was just the shot I needed to remind me to never, ever produce television again. Unfortunately, nobody had ever told me to never say never.

Soon thereafter, Carlino moved to Los Angeles to be nearer his rapidly increasing movie work; he even bought a beautiful ranch house in Mandeville Canyon. He had divorced his wife and married Jill, a pretty, red-haired British script supervisor whom he'd met while directing *The Sailor Who Fell from Grace with the Sea* for which Carlino had also written the screenplay. Every holiday Luigi and Jill prepared magnificent feasts, which they shared with their friends. I was delighted to be counted among them.

He sold several original screenplays, inviting me to the screening of the rough cut each time there was a new Carlino film to see. We also attended a performance in a small Los Angeles theater of his one-act plays. Carlino went on to adapt and direct *The Great Santini,* which won Academy Award nominations for Robert Duvall and for supporting actor Michael O'Keefe.

Carlino bought a huge black Honda motorcycle, complete with rack and matching black suitcases. He and Jill would take off for weeks at a time seeing the country. They biked through the deserts, up California Highway 1, along the Pacific shore, and up to San Francisco. Life was an unending series of thrills for them.

For a couple of years he was on a roll, every word he put on paper seemed to find an eager buyer. Then gradually, his star began to fade. Almost as astonishingly as his huge successes had lit up the Hollywood firmament, his career slowly descended. Tragedy seemed to be coming at him from all directions. His only son, Lewis John Jr., was paralyzed for life by a tragic dive off the end of a pier into water he didn't realize was shallow; his ex-wife and his daughters were diagnosed as terminally ill with breast cancers. Understandably, Carlino did not handle his and his family's decline well. He got involved with drugs. Then one day he told me he and Jill were moving to Tiburon on San Francisco Bay. I wrote to his forwarding address and, when I received no response, I tried phoning only to learn the phone had been disconnected; he had left only a post office box forwarding address. Nonetheless, as my new books on screenwriting came out, I sent him copies with instructions for forwarding. There has never been a response. My friend had become the screenwriter-director who fell from grace with the industry.

After *In Search of America* was broadcast, I received a phone call from an old friend from my CBS Radio days, Larry Thor. In addition to his professorship at UCLA, Thor had been a CBS announcer and had played the lead in one of radio's best-written mystery dramas, *Broadway Is My Beat* by Mort Fine and David Friedkin.

Thor, an Icelander by birth, possessed one of the best minds I'd ever encountered. His highly intelligent and insightful analysis of films and screenplays made him an excellent teacher, even though he was not himself a screenwriter. He phoned to tell me UCLA had an opening for a screenwriting teacher and to offer me the job.

"It only pays ten thousand dollars for the year, and it's full time. You'll have to teach four courses, and it's only on a one-year trial basis."

He was surprised how quickly I said yes. My business manager, David Licht, with whom I had been associated for over twenty-five years, thought I was insane. "But what are you going to live on?" he asked, while expressing his incredulity.

"There's always my IBM Selectric," I answered. "When all else fails, it's always hot to trot."

As I walked onto the UCLA campus, I felt a thrill totally unlike anything I'd ever known in movie studios, even MGM. This was not the world of Let's Pretend, this was for real. Even the air smelled smarter. There were students bustling around the sculpture garden, rushing in and out of buildings. I had a sense of being at home at last. I knew beyond a shadow of a doubt that this is where I belonged and this is where I was going to stay.

When I met with Thor in his UCLA office, he explained that screenwriting teacher Alexander Mackendrick, who had directed the classic Alec Guinness comedy *The Man in the White Suit,* had resigned. "He was sick to death of reading student screenplays," Thor explained, chuckling, "but that's one of the most important parts of our job." Thor told me I could start January 1 and showed me to my future office just down the hall from his. Mackendrick had already packed up and left. I looked forward to settling into my post as a lecturer at UCLA, confidently content, sweetly secure, and far from the madness of Hollywood, or so I thought.

Offering what turned out to be a farewell gift from Hollywood, I received a call from an actor who had been a guest star on one of my shows. He invited me to a beach party at his Malibu home and asked me to bring along a beautiful young actress who had played second lead in a CBS hit sitcom of the sixties. I'll call her Lola Buford. Lola was a beautiful blonde in her late thirties, just a touch over the hill to continue playing ingénues. "She wants to meet you," the actor told me, then added, "why in the world she would want to do that, I wouldn't know."

My brief marriage to Marie was now, unfortunately yet not surprisingly, history. As an unattached, middle-aged, reasonably attractive, divorced male, it was not an unusual offer. I jotted down the date and the lady's address and phone number.

When I arrived to pick her up, I was surprised by how youthful and beautiful her face and figure were. Showbiz had not ravaged her as it does so many young actresses who fall short of their dream of stardom.

As we drove out Pacific Coast Highway she began to talk about her years at CBS-TV and her series. I was happy to note she held no bitterness or remorse over the cancellation of her show. "Time to move on," she said, airily. "That Jim Aubrey is some kind of head case," she added, "what a trip that was."

I decided the lady was in the mood to talk and I was in the mood to listen, so I remained silent.

"He took me down to Acapulco for a weekend with him and his friend, Greg Martindale, the lawyer. Greg had his own girl. I thought I knew what I was in for, some drinks, some sex, some laughs, what the hell. But honestly, there's no way I could have expected what I got from James T. Aubrey. We're in the hotel room and we're both buck naked. As we jump in bed, suddenly Aubrey grabs me by the arm. 'You're going to have to lick my ass.' He says so quietly that I felt a chill go over my entire body. I was speechless.

"'You hear me, don't you?' His voice was ice cold and just above a whisper. 'You're going to have to lick my ass. Don't worry, it's nice and clean. And get your tongue up in there.'

"'I won't. No way, no how.' I answered. I thought, is this really happening?

"'It's the only way I can get off,' he insisted. 'If you don't, I'll break your arm.' His voice was nasty, threatening. I was getting very frightened.

"His grip on my arm tightened and he began to twist it, slowly but firmly. It was very painful," she continued. "He was letting me know he had the strength to do it." She paused to take a breath, as the memory of it seemed to overtake her.

"I knew there was no point screaming. We were in a suite with Greg and his girl. They must have known what was going on; he and Aubrey were buddies.

"'Get busy, lady,' Aubrey says, 'I haven't got all day.'

"I swing around and stuck my finger in his eye. He jerked back. His grip loosened for a moment and I broke loose, grabbed a big beach towel, and ran out of the room.

"I stayed at the poolside bar, wrapped in that towel until Greg came down much later and told me to get dressed. We flew home that evening; the weekend was over. Can you believe that guy?" she asked me.

"I've read allegations that he'd broken a girl's arm in Miami or something like that."

"Unfuckingbelievable," she said, "but it actually happened to me."

Once we entered the star's large rambling beach house on the sands of Malibu, it was clear this was going to be an unfuckingbelievable night. There were scores of people, a few of whom I recognized, crowded at the long old Western-style bar. Along the bar were trays neatly loaded with marijuana joints, small boxes of a white powder I assumed to be cocaine, plus the usual assortment of whiskey bottles on glass shelves behind our genial host, the bartender.

"Come on in and light up or we've got booze, you name it," he called cheerfully, after taking a hit of whatever he held in his fingers.

Marijuana at a party was not news to me, but I had never seen it and other drugs displayed so abundantly and opulently. I was an infrequent, recreational user of marijuana, but I had no desire to try anything beyond grass, and wasn't about to begin now.

My date and I each reached for one of the conveniently rolled joints, lit up, and inhaled deeply. When I next looked around, she was gone, somewhere lost in the throng. I was out on the beach alone being attacked by a monster dog who loomed over me like King Kong. I was shaking in terror, stumbling to get back inside before the monster dog ripped me to shreds.

Nothing I'd ever smoked had hit me so hard. I was on a bad trip to end all bad trips. I was terrified. Hallucinating wildly, I made my way back inside, flopped down into an empty chair, and held on to the arms of it for dear life, trying desperately to outlast the nightmare that had overwhelmed me on the beach.

Thus the party passed or I passed the party. I was finally able to ask my host what I had been smoking.

"Great stuff isn't it?" he replied, chuckling. "Got it in this week from Mexico. Acapulco Gold."

I vaguely remember driving my date home. It was the first and last time we saw each other, and my first and last date with Acapulco Gold. Both were too heavy-duty for this Arkansas yokel. I could not wait to run and hide in the safety of academe.

16

Free at Last

In January 1971 I reported to work at the University of California, Los Angeles, as a lecturer in the Department of Theater Arts, Film, and Television.

Walking onto the campus from the mammoth parking structure to McGowan Hall where my office was located was a ten minute stroll past bulletin boards jammed with messages and announcements. Students hurried past on their way to classes, whirling leaves in their wake. Straight ahead of me was the famed UCLA sculpture garden, an outstanding collection of some of the great art of western civilization. I knew someday, somehow, I was going to figure out a way to hold a class in this inspiring setting. I hadn't even reached my office to report in for my first day, yet my mind was already busy spinning dreams of teaching the best screenwriting classes ever. Though I was on a one-year trial appointment, I hadn't the slightest doubt that here was where I was going to spend the remainder of my work life.

I reported to Professor Larry Thor's office, just down the hall from my new office. Though Thor and I were both CBS Radio graduates, neither of us wasted a moment in rehashing the past. Like me, Thor was excited about being a teacher. Though we came to UCLA by entirely different routes, we understood that this was where we had each hoped our destiny would take us. Thor explained that as the new guy on the block I would be teaching four screenwriting courses: two courses of beginning screenwriting and two graduate courses.

"What's the difference between beginning and graduate courses?" I asked him.

"Whatever you want it to be," he replied. "I usually fit the course to the student instead of the other way around. Give them whatever they need and as much of it as they can handle. Incidentally, you probably won't find any students who want to learn how to write television; I never have and neither has anyone else here. Tells you a lot about the medium, doesn't it?"

Professor William Menger, a stocky, heavy-set man with long strands of hair combed over his completely bald pate, wandered into my office to welcome me. Menger was the third member of the screenwriting facility. He was a novelist with no screenwriting credits. Unlike Thor, Menger was a rather shut-down character. It was clear from the start that he stayed pretty much within himself. He had the corner office down the hall from Thor and me, but as I was to soon learn he spent most of his time in it behind a closed door.

That first day Thor and I went to lunch at the north campus cafeteria, which was packed with chattering students. The many tables outside were filled. There was an infectious air of excitement and a zest for life that you could find nowhere else but on a university campus. In the noisy cafeteria all conversations were carried on by exuberant shouts. Even as I write this, these many years later, the memory evokes in me a deep longing to return to UCLA, to magically start all over again from that very first day. I knew at once that I had found my rightful place in the world.

Larry Thor was among the most articulate and intelligent people I've ever known and certainly the most warmhearted and giving of souls. Students flocked to his office (his door was always open) just to sit on the floor at his feet and listen to him converse on any subject that suited his fancy. He could casually offer insights into what made a great screenplay as no screenwriter I have every met.

Thor was a quiet, thoughtful man with a big-hearted openness to life while still maintaining an enduring skepticism about the attitudes and mores of the society around him. He often came to the office with remembered headlines or feature stories from the day's paper, adding ironic comments that could get students and teacher alike laughing. The absurdities of everyday life were the source of most of his humor. He used them to engage his students in fresh ways of looking at life. He reminded me of the great humanitarian and humorist Will Rogers.

Thor invited me to his home for lunch one Saturday afternoon. He lived with his second wife, Jeanne, a radio actress, in a rambling, weathered old beach house on Escondido Beach, a few miles north of Malibu. After lunch, we wandered up the beach and found a spot for bird-watching. A tall, pleasant man with a wide smile ambled up. He looked familiar but I couldn't quite place him.

"Mind if I join you guys?" he said, sitting next to us as we both welcomed him.

"Hi," he said to me, extending his hand, "I'm Bill Rogers."

"Bill's my next-door neighbor," Larry told me, "we like to watch the action out at sea. Sometimes we catch a whale spouting, sometimes a few cruising sharks or seals nearby. But always plenty of bird life."

Will Rogers Jr. was very much like his father in looks, voice, and mannerisms. "I know you," I suddenly found myself saying to Rogers, "I voted for you once."

"Thanks," he said with a grin, "my Dad warned me to stay out of politics. 'No place for a honest man,' was the way he put it.

"There's another thing my dad said that nobody seems to get right. Everybody says he said, 'I never met a man I didn't like.' But what he really said was, 'I never met a man I didn't like, and neither did my wife.' They always leave off the last part, which is what made it funny."

"I loved your father," I told him, "my whole family loved him. My father even named his store 'Rogers' after your Dad. I'm not sure that was a tribute, since my Dad went bankrupt during the Depression."

"Everybody loved my dad," said Bill Rogers, after a thoughtful pause. "And so did I. He never should have gotten into that damned plane. But he loved flying . . ."

I had felt an uneasiness about Thor hiring me at UCLA. It was a nagging feeling he was merely repaying a debt of gratitude for an unusual incident between us some years earlier. I had no way of knowing how the impact of my firing him from the radio show he had created and was scheduled to star in would play out. I knew how deeply he felt about that show, but I had taken the only course of action available to me. If he held a grudge, he certainly gave no hint of it. But it had been a memorable and ghastly moment in his life as well as mine.

Alas, Thor had shown up on recording day almost too drunk to walk, his cheeks spotted with tiny, bloody razor nicks from an obviously sloppy shave. He demanded to be let into the studio to moderate his show. His speech was slurry beyond comprehension and I had no choice but to turn him away. When he fell to the floor, sobbing, I called a security guard to take him across the street to a small coffee shop, fill him with coffee, and stay with him until he was certain Thor was sober enough to drive home. I dismissed the cast and the engineers and went over to join Thor and the guard. It had been a huge embarrassment and humiliation for my friend. We never spoke of the incident or his show again.

I thought of that horrible afternoon as Thor and I were finishing our first UCLA lunch.

"You know," he said, as if reading my mind, "I owe you a great deal. You really saved my life."

"How so?" I asked.

"That day I showed up drunk and you kicked me off my own show was rock bottom for me. I'd been drinking for a lot of years, but like all drunks I was in denial." He suddenly laughed. "Didn't you know, the favorite pastime of us Icelanders is getting drunk. What else are we going to do during our nine-month winters?

"I'd never been so humiliated in my life," he continued. "But, as things turned out, it was the best thing that ever happened to me. I went to an AA meeting the next day and I've been going to AA meetings for sixteen years. Sixteen years clean and sober. So, I owe you big time."

"Is that why you hired me?" I asked.

"Don't be ridiculous. Do you know how often we get the chance to hire a man with your credentials? Especially to come in here to teach on a temporary basis, for the lowest salary the university can offer?"

Suddenly my doubts were gone. I had obviously been wrong. The decks were swept clean, as far as I was concerned. The rest was up to me.

I soon discovered the faculty of the theater arts department was divided not only into theater faculty and film faculty but further divided into subspecialties. If you were a student who majored in making films, you were in the film production program with a specific faculty. If you wanted to study animation or critical studies, or screen/television writing, each area was taught by specialists in their field. While there was friendly camaraderie among most of the faculty, there were few crossover courses. It sometimes seemed that students were not merely in different majors but in different schools, and theater arts majors were in a different world altogether. We had almost no interaction with them. There were few courses that gave students much information outside of their specific area of interest.

The filmmaking faculty had early on decided theirs was the only aspect of the program that was meaningful. Therefore, the four film production teachers had effectively taken over the faculty meetings. They had abolished the niceties of *Robert's Rules of Order,* and others spoke at their sufferance. We screenwriting teachers were generally regarded as harmless eunuchs, certainly not as important contributors to the filmmaking process.

During faculty meetings Thor, Menger, and I generally sat silently in the back of the room, sometimes reading student scripts, rarely paying much attention to the filmmaking teachers who, by and large, had made no films themselves. They even prided themselves on their lack of experience in the much-despised world of "commercial" films for which they had unspeakable disdain. At one of my first faculty meetings, a film production teacher stood up to proclaim, "film, as we all know, is the director's medium. Screenwriters are, by and large, carpenters who follow the director's instructions." I was so inflamed by this ridiculous nonsense that I was determined to mount a counterattack in one way or another.

I went home that evening and immediately wrote a proposal for an interview book, listing the best screenwriters working at that time in Hollywood as my subjects, along with some brief introductions of them. I included an introduction making the case for screenwriters. I called the book *The Screenwriter Looks at the Screenwriter.*

Thanks to the generosity of my friend, film critic and historian Arthur Knight, I sent my proposal to his agent in New York. Agent Betty Anne Clarke responded she liked the idea but thought it would be a hard sell; still, she would do her best.

Unlike me, Thor and Menger were unfazed by the put-down of screenwriters. "Same old bullshit," was Menger's response. Thor was more philosophical, "It's sixties claptrap, the truth is they actually just hand a kid a camera and walk away."

After some of the filmmaking students discovered what it would cost them to make their obligatory student film in order to graduate, they frequently came running to one of the three screenwriting teachers to switch their major to writing. We required a complete original final-draft screenplay as the ticket for admission into our program. If they had no screenplay to show us, we rarely obliged. When I arrived at UCLA we were averaging over one hundred and fifteen applicants for fifteen openings in our screenwriting program, which I attributed to Thor as well as to the industry's continuous demands for new screenwriters.

Teaching four courses, I had more than thirty students writing feature-length screenplays. The constant onslaught of pages kept me reading night and day and at least one day every weekend. No wonder Alexander Mackendrick had resigned. Larry Thor had twenty-five students in one of his seminars. When I tried to convince him he was not doing a service to himself nor for his students, he only laughed. "If a kid wants to learn screenwriting, we're here to teach them. Besides, the only way to learn to write is to write. As long as we demand writing, they'll learn. Maybe they'll learn in spite of us."

Every time I passed Thor's office with its open door policy, I saw students sitting on his couch or on the green shag rug at his feet. His

279

was a Socratic style of teaching, inviting questions that led to in-depth discussions. Students sat in rapt attention as the Icelander analyzed screenplays, not only theirs but those of films currently playing in Westwood, the "village" on the southern border of our campus.

My first two quarters of teaching at UCLA passed at light speed. The heavy reading load was made lighter by the high quality of writing my students were delivering. I was amazed to discover their level of writing was not very different from what I had seen from the Writers Guild members working in the freelance market.

Just before the school year ended, Larry Thor advised me the faculty had voted to renew my contract for the coming year. I've often wondered whether they would have been so agreeable to keeping me on had they known the storm of protest I would be creating in the coming school year. I doubt it.

17

Hollywood, UCLA

I had learned in my first year that USC's Film School and UCLA's Department of Theater Arts film school were as different as night and day. While equally outstanding in the education they offered students, their fundamental approach could not have been more opposite. USC cultivated close ties with Hollywood and the entertainment industry. UCLA eschewed any connection with it. For obscure reasons lost to history, UCLA wanted no part of "commercial" filmmaking. They were teaching *art.*

Ironically, if UCLA film school graduates, such as Francis Ford Coppola, became Hollywood luminaries, the same teachers who disdained the entertainment industry now frequently boasted of their successful graduates.

During the summer, Larry Thor and I talked during afternoon walks at his home on Escondido Beach, especially about revising UCLA's screenwriting program. Thor agreed that students were getting short shrift when there were twenty or thirty of them in a seminar. But the university would not allow us to significantly reduce our admissions, and the demands for enrollment in our screenwriting program were steadily increasing.

Thor, generous to a fault, said he hated the idea of turning away any kid who wanted to be a screenwriter. He would take as many as thirty students in one of his seminars. But I felt that working with six students in a seminar, each assigned to write a feature-length final draft screenplay every quarter, would create something closer to one-on-one tutorial instruction and demand more writing. University policy had set six as a minimum but had no official maximum figure. Though Thor and I agreed to disagree, he never tried to dissuade me from my position.

What I believed was largely responsible for the increase in demand for our courses was the growing tendency of the studios to go into "development" deals with writers. With the studios always desperately searching for material, they had come up with the idea of putting many screenwriters in "development," paying them Guild minimum for their scripts at the front end, with a much larger payment if their screenplay ever went into production. The growing new philosophy was to develop ten or twenty screenplays with hopes that one of them would land a big-name star or a big-name director and find its way into production. One young studio executive boasted to me that he had two hundred screenplays in development in hopes of bringing one to film. Many studio executives I met would ask me for a first look at our program's best students' work. I told them my first choice was to find our outstanding writers an agent, which was always the students' primary goal. When our screenwriting awards were handed out at the end of the school year, we could expect as many as a half-dozen agents attending the ceremony introducing themselves to the winners. While we welcomed Hollywood professionals' interest in our students' work, we understood that in the majority of instances these brief introductions led nowhere except to disappointment for the students. While everyone in Hollywood professes eagerness to read the work of new screenwriters, the ugly truth is that very few of these eager-to-read people ever actually read the scripts submitted to them. They are actually read by readers on staff who submit a one-page synopsis and an evaluation of the script.

Former screenwriting students with talent who had written at least one of what was called a "show script," or "calling card script," would happily settle for development deals. They could live for months on the up-front money (often twenty or thirty thousand dollars or more) while their reputation became established as a proven professional who had sold material. Having sold a script, they were eligible to join the Writers Guild of America, West. Many of these former students lived from year to year off the income generated by development deals, without ever having one of their scripts made into a movie. Ironically, students with great show scripts would often sell other scripts they'd written without ever selling the show script. Several students with a half-dozen screenplays written while at UCLA would later tell me, "I sold the worst one first." A wise student never stopped writing, building up a small arsenal of screenplays. Getting into the marketplace was tough, but staying there was tougher still. As we all knew, the only way to develop as a writer is to write and then write more and more. It's a simple axiom that applies to all would-be artists: musicians, dancers, painters, composers, actors, directors, whoever. There is no shortcut.

In spite of the abundance of highly talented writers, we also had a fair number of students who had no grasp of the fundamentals of screenwriting. I suggested to Thor that we institute a required beginning screenwriting course that would deal with the basics of structure, character development, theme, dialogue, and selecting a compelling story. I had taught such a course the previous summer at USC, where I continued to teach one night a week.

Thor liked the idea very much and told me to plan on it; he would clear the way with our department chairman, Wally Boyle.

The following fall, I was astonished to discover our small lecture hall at Melnitz was packed to overflowing. More surprising yet was that many of the students who had signed up were production majors. In talking to them they explained that, although they were convinced film was a director's medium, they felt this beginning writing course would be valuable.

As it happened, seventy-five students showed up for that first class, with about another dozen standing in the rear of our packed small lecture hall. I solved the problem by making my dream come true. I took the entire class out into the sculpture garden where I conducted my lectures followed by Q-and-A sessions. In my first class meeting two students held up their hands to announce they'd decided to become filmmakers after seeing "An Occurrence at Owl Creek Bridge" on *The Twilight Zone.*

Thor was delighted at this unexpected turn of events. He even attended some of my lectures. William Menger, as expected, remained in his office behind his closed door. The feedback from the students was excellent, especially from the production students. I had really arrived as a teacher and I knew it.

During our spring quarter I found a notice in my box to attend an emergency meeting of the faculty the following afternoon.

Our long, narrow conference room on the first floor was packed. Professor Bill Adams, one of four members of the production faculty, called the meeting to order and got right to the point by slamming his fist down on the table with full force. "It has been brought to my attention that Bill Froug is teaching Hollywood screenwriting!" he shouted angrily, sounding like I was spreading the black plague. "God damn it," he yelled, "UCLA is not a fucking trade school! I personally won't have it!" The room erupted into a crescendo of voices, mine was quickly drowned out. It was clear the sentiments were overwhelmingly against me.

Another film production faculty member, noting his agreement with Adams, quickly called for a vote. In response to the question of whether my introductory course should be taught at UCLA, the heavy majority vote was no. I was ordered to complete the course for the present quarter and thereafter it would not be offered to students.

I was especially disappointed that Larry Thor was not present. I knew he could have turned the whole subject into the farce it was, and thereby silence Adams with humor, as he had often done before. Adams had established himself in faculty meetings as a bully and firebrand, whose angry, sometimes loud statements turned our meetings into chaos. They often descended into shouting matches.

The production faculty, the " gang of four," as they were sometimes unaffectionately called, were holdovers from the sixties when teachers were not supposed to actually teach anything and the students were assumed to learn by osmosis. Though not youngsters, industry people like myself and Larry Thor were a new breed of motion picture industry professionals with years of hands-on experience coming into film schools to actually teach students to become whatever they wanted to become—writers, directors, actors, photographers, producers, animators—or train them for any field that helped them achieve their aspirations.

We were not about to be deterred from our determination to teach, in spite of the production faculty's seeming determination not to teach. "Just point the camera and shoot, and it will be beautiful, because you are beautiful," one production faculty member was reliably reported to have told his filmmaking students.

One evening, my friend, writer Pat Falken-Smith, phoned and asked me if I would like to join her for an evening of bridge with famed director Don Siegel and his wife. Although I was not an avid bridge fan, I very much enjoyed Pat's company and I wanted to meet the great director whose work *(Invasion of the Body Snatchers, Madigan, Coogan's Bluff, The Killers)* I admired.

On the way over to Siegel's house, Pat told me that Don's wife was Doe Avedon, the ex-wife of and model for the noted photographer Richard Avedon, as well as the title subject of the movie *Funny Face.*

We were greeted at the door by one of the most striking women I had ever seen. Doe Avedon, a slight figure with huge eyes, was stunning. I had difficulty taking my eyes off her.

The bridge game was uneventful until Siegel made a remark about the director being the auteur of the films he directed, adding disparaging remarks about the role of screenwriters in general. Pat and I objected to Siegel's snide remarks and his belittling attitude toward writers. Pat had been a reader for Screen Gems when I first met her and now was a staff writer on *General Hospital.* We both knew that without a screenplay no narrative film could exist. Given blank pages, the director had nothing to auteur. Though we both admired Siegel's work, we were certainly not going to let him get away with his ego-driven claims of authorship. Siegel's wife watched passively with her astonishingly large, beautiful eyes.

"I'll prove it to you," he suddenly said to me. "I'm just finishing a new feature, *Charley Varrick* with Walter Matthau. You choose your best students, and I'll let them read every draft of every script as well as every memo I wrote to every writer involved in the picture. Then they can see who the real auteur of the film is."

It was an offer I couldn't refuse, and I immediately added a stipulation. "After my select group of graduate screenwriting students has read all the material, you've got to promise to screen the film for them and do a Q-and-A with them afterward. Agreed?"

"Absolutely," Siegel responded. "We'll have the screening at Universal followed by the Q-and-A in my office. The picture will be finished in about a month. Sound okay? By the way, there are three different drafts of the screenplay, and I have no idea how many pages my notes to the writers run."

By the time he'd finished his proposal, I knew exactly how I wanted to structure the seminar I was going to suggest to UCLA. Siegel and I were delighted to confront the issue, each being certain we were on the right side.

"Your kids are in for some serious reading time. By the way," he added, "I have one condition: I want to read every student paper. I'm confident I'll prove my point."

As a screenwriting teacher I knew I had struck gold.

The next day I went to the chairman of UCLA's Department of Theater Arts, Film, and Television and requested permission to make this project a two-credit graduate seminar in screenwriting. He readily agreed.

Then I set about selecting six of my best graduate students. There were more volunteers than I could accept. I'd discovered that six is the best number for a serious discussion group as well as a question-and-answer session. I phoned Siegel's office telling his secretary we would need seven copies of the material he was sending over.

The following week heavy boxes of material labeled *Charley Varrick* arrived in my office from Universal. Each student's assignment was to read and evaluate all of the material and compare it to the finished film, especially as it related to Siegel's claim he was auteur of the film. "Was he?" I asked them. "If so, how so? If not, why not?"

True to his word, Siegel phoned to give me the time and date he would be available to run the picture followed by the Q-and-A. Per our agreement, our students would not discuss the material until after we'd read everything he'd sent us, seen the film, and met with Siegel. Following all this, my course assignment was that each student had to turn in a paper on the film, an analysis of the written material, and an evaluation of Don Siegel as auteur of this film.

We gathered at Don's office where he escorted us to a studio projection room. Following the screening we were instructed to return to his office for the Q-and-A. The seven of us watched *Charley Varrick* in silence, each of us examining the film in the context of the assignment. We walked back to Siegel's office in silence.

Don had placed a high stool for himself in the center of his small office so we could all circle him for an intimate Q-and-A. During the ninety-minute discussion that followed, the students were guarded in their comments. It seemed obvious they had reservations about the movie but did not want to embarrass the director. If Siegel felt any of that negative feedback, he certainly kept it to himself.

It was a good session. A lot of questions were directed to Don as to why he had made the script choices he did and what his goal had been from the origin of the project forward. Siegel fielded the questions like the consummate professional he was. When we had run out of time he took me aside and said, as the students were filing out, "Don't forget, I want to read those papers, all of them."

When the papers were turned in, I was not surprised to discover that none of my six students liked the film; neither had I.

But what did surprise me was how strongly they felt about the direction Siegel had given the writers in his memos to them. "Sure," one of them wrote, "he was the auteur, all right. He took a story that was not very good to begin with and consistently made it worse. When it comes to blame for this lousy movie, it almost all falls on Don Siegel."

Although the opinions were markedly individual, the unanimous agreement was that *Charley Varrick* was a poor movie, made worse by Don Siegel's written instructions to the writers. Peter Bogdanovich had written the first screenplay, which we all agreed was pedestrian. The subsequent screenplays, while markedly different following Siegel's instructions, were not made better because of his orders to the screenwriters. A couple said Siegel ruined whatever chance the story had.

While I agreed with them in general, I had a problem they didn't. I was under an obligation to show their papers to Siegel. I had felt telling them this up front would have prevented them from honestly answering the questions I'd assigned them.

After about a week, Siegel phoned requesting I send him copies of the student papers. I stalled, making whatever excuses I could to avoid the inevitable disaster.

Another week passed and he phoned me at my UCLA office again. This time I tried another tactic: the half truth, the last refuge of scoundrels.

"They're all in, Don, but, honestly, they're not favorable. They didn't like the film and blamed it on the writing."

He was completely satisfied with my explanation. "Sure," he snapped back, "I understand. I don't need to read them. What the fuck do they know, anyway?"

Charley Varrick failed with the critics as well as the box office. Everyone in Hollywood knows the two judgments are frequently unrelated.

Over the following few years I was gradually seeing less and less of Larry Thor in his office or in meetings, and I was growing concerned. We had fewer lunches together. Uncharacteristically, his office door was kept closed. When I next saw him I asked if there was something wrong. He laughingly assured me he never felt better but perhaps had been working too hard. From time to time Thor was offered minor roles in films, usually as an officer in the military or sometimes as a police officer. He was what was called a "day player." Actors in these roles could pick up as much as five hundred dollars for a few hours work. It was understood if you were a full-time teacher, you had to find outside jobs occasionally to augment the meager salaries.

I received news from Betty Anne Clarke in New York that she had sold my book to Macmillan, having found an editor who championed the cause of screenwriters. The money was minuscule but most welcome.

There were storm clouds gathering on the distant horizon, but I could not see them. Before our summer break, the faculty had approved my employment for a third year as an assistant professor 3, with a salary increase. I was now able to limit my teaching to only three seminars plus directed studies courses with outstanding writers.

Although my Hollywood agents regarded me as somewhere on a distant and uninteresting planet, I was determined to find more free-lance television writing gigs to allow me to live on my UCLA salary.

As luck would have it, I found the perfect writing assignment for a full-time college screenwriting teacher. I received a phone call from Jack Beck, former news director at KNX-CBS Radio. We had known each other only in passing during our radio days. He was now heading up a television wing of Time-Life Films and was gung ho to do a drama series commemorating the upcoming two-hundredth anniversary of the American Revolution. He had a deal with a U.C.–Santa Barbara professor who was coming out with a new three-volume history on the subject. Advance copies of the manuscript would be available for his writers. He offered me a firm commitment of ten thousand dollars for a one-hour teleplay, which was above the Writers Guild minimum at that time. The kicker was he wanted me to dramatize the origins of the American Revolution in a one-hour script! I eagerly accepted the offer. It meant I would spend my summer reading this new history of the American Revolution, as interesting a way to spend a summer off as any I could imagine.

The professor's manuscript turned out to be lively, modern, and excellent reading. Beck called to tell me Time-Life had a commitment available for a second script on Benjamin Franklin and, since I had agreed to write the first episode of the American saga and could not do both, he suggested I designate another writer for the second episode. The deal would be the same.

I chose my good friend David Rintels, an excellent writer who had already won an Emmy Award and been nominated for a second. While fascinated with history, Rintels was not sure he was comfortable writing historical drama. Nonetheless, he accepted the assignment.

I turned in my one-hour teleplay. Beck congratulated me on a job well done. He wanted no changes and asked me to keep on Rintels's case.

Rintels, as it happened, was also busy writing his one-man play,

Clarence Darrow, which would later become a hit on Broadway starring Henry Fonda. He told me he had written some scenes for the Franklin script. He was unhappy with his work to date and wanted me to convey to Time-Life that he felt he couldn't do an outstanding job and would not turn in a mediocre one. He said he would appreciate if they would let him off the hook.

Beck was agreeable because the sales department at Time-Life Films had advised him that they found no ad agencies or any potential sponsors interested in dramatizing the American Revolution. What the sponsors wanted, he was told, were musicals, comics, fireworks, entertainments, anything but the American Revolution itself. For all I know, my script lies in the Time-Life vaults. I have a faded copy of it in the garage.

My book *The Screenwriter Looks at the Screenwriter* had been published by Macmillan in 1972 to dismal sales. The *New York Times* had, however, printed my introduction in its entirety on the front page of their Sunday arts and leisure section, which probably impressed the faculty as much as the book itself. It certainly was a consolation prize to me. I was promoted in a big step up the academic ladder to associate professor, which put me on tenure-track and reaffirmed what I had known from the first day. I was where I wanted to be, doing what I wanted to do. Best of all, it meant no more television series production.

But I was seeing less and less of Larry Thor. One day I invited him to my apartment for lunch. I had finally decided hinting about the subject was useless. My friend was far too intelligent for game playing.

"Larry," I finally said, "one of my students told me he saw you take a vodka bottle from your filing cabinet. Are you drinking?"

"Me, drinking?" he chuckled, "Why, I celebrated my nineteenth AA birthday last week. I'm clean and sober. Your student was wrong."

After Thor left I was somehow not reassured. Denial is the single most deadly weapon of the disease of alcoholism. Denial kills. I had lost more than one friend to alcoholism.

In 1973 a phone call to my UCLA office resulted in a moment of sweet revenge, rare for anyone working even on the fringes of Hollywood.

Harris Katleman, whom I had not seen since my *Philip Marlowe* disaster, called with a most unusual offer for a hyphenate who had been out of the business almost three years.

"I'm with MGM Television now," Katleman said, adding, "Jim Aubrey is now president of MGM. You remember, Jim, don't you?" Katleman said with a sardonic laugh. "We're making a pilot of the Hepburn-Tracy movie *Adam's Rib,* and we have an excellent script by Peter Stone. And I want you to produce it."

"I'm out of the business," I told him. "I'm a full-time teacher."

"I know all about that, but this is a one-week job. We've got this great script, a great director, Peter Hunt, who directed *1776,* there's really nothing you have to do. By the way, we've got Blythe Danner for the Hepburn part and Ken Howard for the Tracy part. It's all set."

I vividly remembered Katleman as the guy who had given me two hours to pack my stuff and get off the MGM lot fourteen years earlier. I had realized at the time he was only following Mark Goodson's orders and I held no grudge. I simply didn't want anything to do with the business I had happily left behind.

"Then what do you need me for?" I replied.

"Look," he said, his voice losing his usual happy bullshit pitch, "MGM wants you, you're acceptable to ABC. Come on, I'll pay you ten thousand dollars for one week's work. You can practically phone it in."

Suddenly I was seriously interested, "Ten thousand and no commitment to produce the series?" I countered.

"Okay, okay, I'll messenger you the script today, you'll like it," he replied. "We've got an office waiting for you at MGM. Report to work Monday morning."

The first thing that struck me upon returning to the Culver City lot was that the entire studio had a coat of fresh, light gray paint. It was as if the embalmer had prepared the studio for burial, which, everyone in the business knew, was only a short time away. The studio had been purchased by a Vegas multimillionaire named

Kirk Kerkorian in 1969. Hollywood quickly surmised the MGM library of film alone was worth the purchase price, and the land itself was worth more than the purchase price. Today, wall-to-wall condos and apartments desecrate the back lots of the hallowed ground upon which the romantic and largely unreal image of Hollywood's America was created. Nonetheless, I was surprised by the waves of nostalgia sweeping over me as I walked into the MGM entrance once again. I was unprepared for the depth of my connection with that magnificent studio's movies as well as those frantic years trying to feed the insatiable appetite of the television tube. I was back at my old stomping ground, new coat of paint notwithstanding. It seemed to me appropriate that James T. Aubrey, the living embodiment of the superneat, immaculate, superclean Ivy Leaguer, would begin his MGM reign by giving this enormous studio a fresh coat of paint. The place hadn't looked so tidy since it was built five decades earlier.

The *Adam's Rib* pilot director, Peter Hunt, a plump, young pink-faced guy, greeted me in my new office with a welcoming smile and a hearty handshake. Wasting no time we ordered a studio car and driver (the Teamsters Union will not permit a producer, director, or actor to drive his or her car to seek out locations for future filming or even to commute to film locations during shooting). By the end of the drive we'd found the exact locales we needed. I spent the rest of the afternoon in one of the many posh projection rooms in the basement of the Thalberg Building watching *Adam's Rib,* MGM's 1949 movie starring Katharine Hepburn and Spencer Tracy. It would be a tough act to follow.

The following day Peter Hunt and I read several actors and chose the other members of the cast. After we'd finished, Hunt told me he'd set up a screening of his movie *1776* for me that afternoon. Peter Stone, a writer with many outstanding feature-film credits, had written the book for the musical as he had our excellent pilot script for *Adam's Rib.*

Sinking deeply into the luxurious, cushioned maroon leather chairs, alone in the theatrical-sized, big-screen screening room in the basement of MGM's Thalberg Building, I flicked the switch and asked the projectionist to roll the film.

Unlike the actual American Revolution, *1776* started with a blast of music followed by the Founding Fathers cracking jokes and dancing all over the place as choreographed. I soon sank deeper into the chair and fell into a sound and blissful sleep. Two hours later I was awakened by the projectionist telling me he had to go home.

While we were shooting, I visited the *Adam's Rib* set downtown in City Hall where we were filming a couple of scenes and chatted with one of our stars, Blythe Danner, who was holding her new baby. I can therefore claim that I am among the first men in America to hold superstar Gwyneth Paltrow in his arms. I had briefly known Gwyneth's father, Bruce Paltrow, a delightful, highly intelligent fellow, and one of our outstanding hyphenates who created, wrote, and executive produced both *The White Shadow* and *St. Elsewhere.* In my judgment both series belong in television's hall of fame.

When we saw the first day's dailies of *Adam's Rib,* we knew we were on the right track, but we also knew, as superb as both our lead actors were, neither one had that charisma or indefinable magic we call star power. Katharine Hepburns and Spencer Tracys are rarer than honest studio bookkeeping. Walking down MGM's main street to my office later, I saw Jim Aubrey, lean and handsome as ever, standing in a doorway chatting with Katleman. I waved and continued on. It appeared he had been hired to become MGM's funeral director.

When the answer print was shown to MGM and the network, everyone was delighted. Harris Katleman had been right. An orangutan could have produced it. It was a classy pilot, for which I could take little credit. What pleased me most is that I had not missed a class nor failed to read a single student script while working on it.

By the end of the day Katleman was in my office as I was packing to leave.

"ABC loved the show," he said with even more enthusiasm than usual. "They bought it on the spot, and they've promised us a great time slot: Friday night 9:30, just the audience for a sophisticated comedy." Pausing to take a breath, he added, "Of course I told them you'll produce the series."

I just sat staring at him. "Why? You know I'm teaching at UCLA."

He chuckled, "Sure, but I told them I'd talk you into it, when you hear the kind of numbers I'm offering. Eighty to ninety thousand dollars for the first year, and increases all along the way. Besides, you can do it in your spare time, teaching a few courses surely doesn't take that much time. You'll run over to UCLA, teach a course, and come back and knock off the series. Piece of cake."

"No thanks, Harris," I replied, "I am a teacher first, last, and always. Producing television series is simply not on my agenda. Not now, not ever again, end of story."

He simply couldn't believe what I was telling him. He kept jabbering away about the money, the great opportunity, yadda, yadda, yadda. I simply walked out of the office and went home. As I drove home I felt a deep satisfaction that I had gotten a tiny bit of revenge on the guy who had abruptly ordered me out of my MGM offices fourteen years earlier. Peter Hunt took over as producer of the series. Unfortunately, it had a short run. I've never seen it. My best guess is that Danner and Howard, though both first-rate actors, simply didn't have the charisma to excite audiences. Ironically, Blythe's daughter Gwyneth has become the star her mother was not. Yet, for my money, though Gwyneth has the great looks she is not nearly the actress her mother is.

Many years later, the Museum of Broadcasting sent me a certificate that reads, "*Adam's Rib-Premier* has been accepted into the permanent collection of the museum of broadcasting, April 1989."

With the publication of *The Screenwriter Looks at the Screenwriter,* several professors of the film production faculty came forward to congratulate me for making the case for screenwriters. Evidently, writing about Hollywood screenwriting was approved but teaching it was verboten. I had published rather than perished.

The following year, I was named chairman of the screenwriting program, a thankless job entailing little more than signing off on students changing their major or completing their work for a degree.

In the spring of 1975, my two television agents at William Morris, Bill Haber and Rowland Perkins, asked me to lunch.

I liked both of these gentlemen enormously. We'd socialized frequently, even played some pretty rotten tennis together. We'd lunched countless times, but from Haber's voice I knew this lunch was different. Something important was in the wind.

"We have some exciting news," Haber said, even before we ordered.

"Some of us from the William Morris Agency are going to open our own agency, and we want you to come with us," Perkins said.

"C-a-a-a-a," said Haber, drawing out the sound, "Creative Artists Agency. We're honoring our clients with the name of our new company."

Perkins rattled off the names of the five agents who were leaving to form CAA. They were some of the top younger people in the Beverly Hills Morris office.

"Here's the deal," Haber continued, enthusiastically, "we're going to ask a few of our best clients to come with us so that we can package them. We will bring you our best writers, best directors, and we'll build a television production company around you, like we've done for several of our clients. Maybe we could build you into another Aaron Spelling."

It was the sound of fingernails on blackboard to me, yet I hated to take the wind out of my good friends' sails. Still, there was no avoiding it. "I'm not interested, guys, I'm a full-time teacher at UCLA and love it, but I'm always open for a teleplay job." They were speechless, until Haber took a breath. "I didn't believe you'd pass up a chance like this," he said. "What are they paying you, paper clips?"

"Come on, Bill," Perkins added, "we know you love teaching, but we're talking about the possibility of real money here. Creative Artists is going to be big, really big, and we'd like you to come with us."

The packaging business was bigger in television than in features. An agent could couple a hyphenate with a star and sell the "package" to the studio or network and collect a 10 percent fee on top of the entire budget for each episode of the series. Thus, a series with a million-dollar-per-episode budget would earn the agent a $100,000-per-episode commission for the length of the first run. Agencies like Ashley-Famous, International Creative Management, MCA (in its glory days known as "the octopus" of the entertainment industry, since they packaged so many series, representing many of the top stars in the business), and William Morris were achieving commissions that reached into the millions every year for every new series they sold. At one point Ashley-Steiner (later to become Ashley-Famous) had four or five of their series in the top ten. Thus the goal of Creative Artists Agency was to create packages. Commissions on individual salaries were relatively meaningless. In fact, if you were part of one of their packages the agencies took no individual commission. Their commission for the series was coming off the top. It was California law.

Later during our lunch I repeated my request that their getting me an occasional freelance teleplay assignment to augment my teaching income would be most helpful, but they were not interested.

"There's just not enough money in it," Haber said. "We could spend as much time getting you a script assignment as selling you as a package, maybe more."

At the time the going rate for one-hour episodic teleplays was $4,500. Their commission would have been $450. It was hardly worth the paperwork even to a start-up company, especially when compared to the potential income from selling one of their packaged series. Hyphenates with a hot series idea and a star to go along with it were worth millions. It was their ability to demand and get these off-the-top package fees from the studios and networks that made talent agencies the most powerful force in Hollywood.

When CAA first opened its doors in 1975, Haber's wife, Carole, was answering phones. Theirs was an incredible success story. Surprisingly, it wasn't television packaging alone that launched them into orbit. Among the five William Morris agents who left to form Creative Artists Agency was one Michael Ovitz, head of their theatrical film department. It was Ovitz who burst off the launching pad like a rocket, signing up major stars and major directors, building the greatest powerhouse agency since the days when Lew Wasserman was king of Hollywood, heading up MCA back in the late forties and fifties.

Until Ovitz left to become second-in-command at Disney, CAA was the undisputed command central in Hollywood. Ultimately, both Haber and Perkins sold their shares of the empire (worth fortunes, no doubt) and moved on to different venues.

Ovitz symbolized the rise of the super-agent, often more powerful than any single studio head. Extremely creative, bright, shrewd, and aggressive agents had rushed in to fill the void left by the old studio powerhouses. Hollywood, like sports in America, became the kingdom of the agents.

I returned home from UCLA early one afternoon to a ringing telephone. It was Larry Thor. His voice was desperate.

"Bill! Bill!" was his plaintive cry, "I'm having a heart attack! I'm having a heart attack!"

"Where are you?" I asked,

"In the hospital! Hold on, the nurse wants to talk to you."

The nurse's voice came on, "Mr. Thor can't talk just now, we're quite busy trying to help him. Call back in a couple of hours," she said, and hung up.

I did as told and reached the same nurse a couple of hours later. "How's Larry Thor?" I asked.

"I'm sorry to tell you Professor Thor died about an hour ago," she replied.

"I should have told you he's an alcoholic; maybe he was having DTs?" I said, already feeling guilty that somehow I had not helped him as much as I should have.

"We knew," she answered. "We usually list these deaths as heart attacks."

For a long time I explored my actions to try to find out if there was something I could have done to help my friend. No matter how I replayed the events of the previous five years, I could not find the moment when what I said or did might have prevented this tragic outcome. I didn't know it in those days but I have since come to understand that among its symptoms, alcoholism is a disease of isolation. Certainly during the past two or three years prior to his death, Thor had been coming to school less and less often; I had noticed he began reading student screenplays while seated alone watching student films. Gradually he had slipped away from his friends, from the school, and from students he loved, until he was gone.

To this day, I've never stopped missing Larry. He was a man who would have been missed by very many people had they known him. But he followed too faithfully the advice I heard him so often give his screenwriting students: "Guard your secrets."

In the end he practiced precisely what he preached, and it led to his death.

With the death of Larry Thor, and with more applications for our screenwriting program than we could handle and increasing yearly, I was required to recommend another teacher to replace him, as soon as possible. Our department chairman, John Young, suggested Lewis Ray Hunter, his former student and a UCLA Theater Arts graduate student. Hunter, with whom I had worked when he was an NBC executive, eagerly accepted the job.

Soon after Hunter's arrival, Bill Menger told me he planned to retire at the end of the following school year. I next recommended Richard Walter, Arthur Knight's teaching assistant at USC's Film School. Although I had considerable doubts, in the end I felt I owed it to Arthur, who had started my career as a teacher. Before they arrived, I reorganized the UCLA screenwriting program, replacing the previous graduation requirement of one final-draft thesis screenplay with a new, much tougher policy demanding one screenplay from each writing student each quarter; a total of four final-draft scripts as a requirement for their degree. It was a quantum leap forward. Writers in our program were going to have to write, and write some more, and keep writing in order to graduate.

With John Young's approval, we also instituted a policy of six students per seminar, eliminating the thirty and more students in a graduate-level class. I had come to understand over my years of teaching that, in the final analysis, the best way to learn to become a screenwriter is to write screenplays, with the aid of as much one-on-one feedback as time allows.

As we reshaped our program to meet the ever-increasing enrollment applications, UCLA reshaped its attitude toward Hollywood. Reluctantly, our film faculty came to recognize that there was nothing inherently wrong with students being taught by professionals to become professionals themselves. It was okay for students to go to work in Hollywood and make a living, especially those whose extraordinary success brought credit to UCLA. Times were changing dramatically. There was a growing, albeit reluctant, awareness that professional Hollywood producers, actors, writers, directors, cinematographers, and filmmakers from all of the arts and crafts had invaluable expertise, as well as vital financial support, to contribute to UCLA. It was a huge step for UCLA to accept Hollywood. In this respect they were light years behind the University of Southern California's vaunted film school. No longer unwelcome as "commercial" filmmakers, many Hollywood people became eager to participate as part-time teachers at UCLA and have continued to be an exciting part of the faculty. Belatedly, UCLA finally recognized the importance of our Department of Theater Arts, Film, and Television, and upgraded us to the School of Theater Arts, Film, and Television. It was far more than a face-lift. The sixties were behind us. We had officially arrived.

Years after I retired, Professors Hunter (a dedicated and outstanding teacher) and Walters (a choice I later regretted) gave an interview in which they stated that UCLA's screenwriting program had had a difficult time attracting screenwriting students until they joined the faculty. It was breathtaking *chutzpah,* even by Hollywood standards.

18

Fun and Games in TV Land

In the spring of 1975, I was eligible for two quarters of sabbatical. By parlaying a spring quarter with the following fall and including the usual summer quarter hiatus, I was able to put together nine months of free time. Along with two other couples, my girlfriend and I booked passage aboard a barge for a cruise through the canals of the south of France. The trip was for only two weeks, but it was to be my first nonworking vacation since I had started working in Hollywood. Freelance hyphenates can't afford vacations. April is the hiring month as production companies staff up new shows for the coming fall season. Summer is preproduction time, the busiest months of the year. As retail merchants' years are determined by their Christmas season, hyphenates' years are often determined by their ability to land a staff job in April. Thereafter they are left to the increasingly chancy and diminishing freelance job market.

In calculating the cost of our European barge trip, it was beginning to seem likely that I had underestimated the expense. The answer was, as it had been throughout my career, if I could land one teleplay assignment on a TV series the trip would be paid for.

By chance I had read in the *Hollywood Reporter* that Universal Studios was starting preproduction on a new Jack Webb series called *Mobile One.* The veteran actor Jackie Cooper would play the lead. And best of all, the producer of the series was my old friend Bill Bowers.

Bowers greeted my call with more enthusiasm than I could have imagined.

"By all means, I want you to do a script for our new series, how about coming over to my office this afternoon?"

As it turned out Bowers's new office was on the Universal Studio lot in North Hollywood, the only major studio where my career in Hollywood had not taken me.

Universal had constructed a small building for Jack Webb's Mark VII Productions on the lot.

When I entered Bowers's office, he rushed to the door to greet me warmly. "So glad you called," he said. "I was just about to call you."

"I want to do a script for your show, pal," I told him.

"Oh, you're going to, of course, but there's a little job I want you to do for me first."

I didn't like his huge grin or the comic tone in his voice. Something was not kosher, but I didn't have a clue to what was coming.

"You see, I sold this series idea to Jack Webb. It's about this reporter who drives around L.A. in a mobile unit reporting stories for our all-news radio station. Sound familiar? It's based on that cute gal reporter you're living with, Joy Nuell, except that I changed her to a guy. Jackie Cooper is going to play the lead, and he's going to be terrific. But, there's just this one teeny problem. Jack loved the idea and sold it to ABC, on condition that I produce the series, but, hell, I don't know anything about producing television. And that's how you fit in."

"Oh, no, Bowers," I hastily cut in, "I'm done with producing television, I only want to sell you a script before Joy and I head off to Europe for the summer."

"No problem," said Bowers, "part of the deal with ABC was that I would stay on as producer of the series."

"So you'll agree to a one-script assignment, right?"

"Well, yes, and no. Jack and I talked it over, and we came up with the idea that everything would work out just fine if you'd agree to be our story editor. It was Jack's idea."

"We're leaving for Europe in June. But I've got plenty of time to write a script before I leave."

"Come on, Willie," he pleaded, "just thirteen weeks. That's all I'm asking for, just help me get this series started and you're free to go."

"We're leaving in June," I responded.

"But you haven't heard the really good part," Bowers blithely continued, as though I hadn't spoken, "$1,500 a week, thirteen weeks, plus $4,500 a teleplay. As a matter of fact, you can write as many as you like while you're working with us. I figure that's about $25,000 for the thirteen weeks work; I suppose they don't pay teachers that kind of money, do they? Let's go to lunch and talk about it."

By the time Bowers and I had finished lunch, I was planning how to gracefully tell my friends that I wouldn't be going to France with them. With two kids in college, and two more on deck, the decision (though I squirmed in making it) was not that difficult. Since I had "retired" from television, or so I thought, to become a full-time teacher, supporting my rather upscale lifestyle and providing an equally good lifestyle for my four growing children had become increasingly chancy.

I reported to work the next morning. Bowers was already ensconced in his office chair, his feet on his desk alongside a cup of freshly sharpened pencils, sipping coffee while regaling the secretaries of the Jack Webb organization with his tales of Hollywood. Bowers, when I coaxed him away from his audience, gave me the names of a couple of new young writers he wanted me to interview for the series. They had no writing credits, but Bowers wanted to give them a break. One of them, just out of college, had boarded at his home. I made appointments with them for the following day. Around five o'clock Bowers appeared in my office.

"I ought to tell you Jack Webb expects us to drop by his office at the end of the day to have a drink with him. Of course, he knows that I don't drink, so you get the job." To my lack of response, he added, "Look, he's a good guy but he's got nobody to talk to. It's the least we can do, okay?"

"Sure," I replied. And we ambled down the long hallway.

"Jack and I met when he directed my movie *The Last Time I Saw Archie* with Bob Mitchum. We hit it off and decided we wanted to do something else together, and *Mobile One* turns out to be it. He's a really good guy, you're going to like him."

I had long ago discovered that there was almost no one in Hollywood that Bill Bowers didn't like, and that the feeling was apparently mutual. I didn't imagine the man had an enemy in the world, despite his years of being, as he liked to claim, "the town drunk."

Entering Jack Webb's very large office was like a visit to San Francisco at the turn of the nineteenth century (Webb's career started in San Francisco radio). A huge mahogany bar ran the length of one wall, complete with brass rail and elaborate red velvet bar stools; giant white-handled beer dispensers stood at attention for the thirsty visitor. Behind the bar was an enormous gilt-framed mirror; red velvet curtains with dripping gold fringe framed the windows.

"Come on in, fellas," Sergeant Joe Friday said as we entered, "wrap yourselves around a drink."

Webb, seated behind a massive desk, pointed his empty glass toward the bar, "We have tap beer, three brands, every brand of booze your heart desires, and wine if you're a little skittish about the hard stuff. Help yourselves!"

It was immediately clear that Jack Webb, bloated and somewhat the worse for wear, had already amply helped himself. His fans from his *Dragnet* series would still recognize him, but they wouldn't be happy about it. Here was a man who had clearly used and abused his life.

"Of course you know I don't drink, Jack," Bowers said, "but maybe Bill can take up some of my slack."

"I'm strictly a two-drink man," I responded, defensively.

"Drink whatever you damn well please," Webb replied, clearly annoyed, "and if my booze isn't good enough, I'm at the Cock and Bull bar on the Strip almost every afternoon; you're welcome to join me there, it's on me. I'm glad you're helping us out on the show," he said as I settled into a seat across the desk from him. "It's not going to be an easy one. But I know Bowers will come up with something."

We made small talk for about fifteen minutes, and then beat a polite retreat.

As we walked down the hall Bowers repeated, "He's a good guy, he just has nobody to talk to. I think it'd be a good idea for us to drop in on him every afternoon before we leave for the day."

The following day our star, Jackie Cooper, dropped by our offices to inquire if we had any scripts to show him yet. An actor who began his career at age three, appearing in eight episodes of the *Our Gang* series, followed by the starring role in *Skippy* in 1930, for which he won an Academy Award at the age of eleven, Jackie Cooper was a professional's professional. He had starred in *The Champ* with Wallace Beery in 1931. By all accounts he had been the most popular child star in Hollywood. And now, forty-plus years later, it was easy to see why. Cooper was a man with no pretensions, no inflated opinion of himself, just an actor eager to do a good job. Cooper had gone on to star in television series, winning an Emmy Award along the way while producing and directing many of them. I liked him at once. As expected, Bowers sidestepped the question of scripts while managing to project his usual great good humor and assurances. The truth is we had no scripts, only a couple in work by Bowers's neophyte writers and the one I owed the show, plus Bowers had promised to write a couple. But on the surface of things we were not in bad shape.

Three weeks later, the situation hadn't changed. Every morning when I came into work, I discovered Bowers with his feet on his desk sipping coffee and regaling whatever audience had gathered in his office with his marvelous, albeit oft-repeated Hollywood stories. Sometimes he had one of his lined legal pads fastened to a clipboard in his lap, the unused sharpened pencils still in their cup.

"Ticonderoga number 2, the only pencil worth a damn," he told me one day. "Lemme show you what I've got." Bowers wrote in longhand on his lined yellow legal-sized pads, then he gave them to his secretary to type before editing. Many of the old-time screenwriters wrote in this fashion. He then read off some quite funny random lines for a proposed scene. "I haven't got the story worked out yet, but I'll get to it in the next couple of days. A couple of lines of dialogue often gets me started."

I was just beginning to realize the magnitude of the problem. Bill Bowers, with some forty feature film-writing credits, was still

William Bowers, the self-proclaimed "town drunk" and prolific screenwriter who wrote or co-wrote more than forty movies including the Oscar-nominated *The Gunfighter.* Bowers wrote and produced *Support Your Local Sheriff,* but he was lost in the fast pace of TV. (courtesy of Marge Bowers)

operating on feature-film time. Four good pages a week was a good week's work. A minimum ten pages a day was a television writers normal day. Bowers was in a different time zone altogether.

"I read your script last night, liked it," he said, "but you need to loosen up your dialogue. Look it over before you send it to mimeo. Good going. Let's shoot it."

I volunteered to help him solve his story problem, but instead he launched into another movie tale. I would confront him again and again about the problem of not having any scripts to shoot, advising him that the first work I'd seen from his young writers was not promising, if usable at all.

The preproduction weeks were slipping away. My pleas to Bowers to finish his script went for naught. "Don't worry about it," was his mantra. Webb's production manager began to make nervous visits to both his office and mine, and the network began calling, "When do we see scripts?"

Bowers's response was to insist that I join him and actor James Garner in the Universal commissary for lunch. Garner had starred in *Support Your Local Sheriff,* written and produced by Bowers.

James Garner turned out to be as charming, friendly, and down-to-earth as everyone who had ever worked with him said he was. He and Bowers swapped Hollywood war stories. It was clear that Garner was as fond of Bowers as everyone else. There was an almost childlike innocence to the aging screenwriter that, while driving friends and producers nuts, nonetheless was acceptable because of the endearing quality of his personality. He didn't have a mean bone in his body.

"How're you doing for scripts, Bowers?" Garner suddenly asked, "I hear you're having problems."

"No problems," I heard my friend reply, "we'll have them when we need them."

Scripts did, indeed begin to drift in. Bowers read them and pronounced them fine, "except they need a *teeny little bit* of rewriting," Bowers would add with a laugh. What they needed was a page one rewrite, top to bottom. But maybe my old friend had some tricks up his sleeve he hadn't told me about. In Hollywood miracles happen routinely.

When we saw the first dailies they were not good. Jackie Cooper was okay in the role but the problem was we hadn't figured out anything especially interesting for him to do. A reporter roaming around L.A. in a mobile unit might have sounded interesting in a pitch meeting, but on screen it was simply a bore. Bowers put as good a face on it as possible, "It's coming along, it just takes time to develop," he assured Jack Webb and our production manager.

The weeks went by seemingly at light speed. Jackie Cooper, the soul of patience, dropped by our offices from time to time to inquire about the status of scripts and left satisfied by Bowers's cheerful reassurances.

One day the inevitable happened. Our production manager rushed breathlessly into our office, "We've got nothing to shoot tomorrow!" The desperation in his voice was palpable. Bowers settled into his chair, calmly poured himself a cup of coffee, propped his feet up on his desk, and started scribbling on his pad, "Come back after lunch," Bowers said, "I'll have something for you."

I watched in amazement as the old pro thoughtfully scribbled whatever was coming to mind. Bowers at work was suddenly a picture of intense concentration When he finished he handed me a couple of pages, "What do you think?"

The material was witty, but the delightful dialogue went nowhere. When I gave him my comments he replied, blandly, "Tell our casting guy to get Sidney Miller to come in and do his drunk act. We'll put him on top of a billboard that reads, 'Don't Drink and Drive.' Have the sign be an ad for some fictitious memorial park, you know, like Forest Lawn. They put up those billboards all over town, every Christmas."

We shot it just the way Bowers had called for it. As I watched the filming I could not help but be struck by watching an aging Sidney Miller, the actor I had first seen almost thirty years ago escorting the pretty redhead from Little Rock on my extraordinary first night in Hollywood. I had come full circle, from beginning freelance writer to professor of screenwriting at UCLA . . . with countless showbiz stops along the way. It had been a tumultuous and unpredictable journey.

Mobile One died a merciful death after thirteen less-than-mediocre episodes. Quite simply, we had never figured out what to do with our premise. For that reason, all of our scripts had been equally poor, mine included. It wasn't simply Bowers's fault. A highly successful screenwriter, he was totally lost in television land. It was the result of deals made in good faith but based primarily upon genuine friendships. Countless motion pictures have failed for the same reason. When I returned to UCLA's sculpture garden that fall, it looked more than ever like the Garden of Eden.

As resolved as I was to teach, I was equally resolved to maintain my living standard while doing it. Fortunately, I received a call from the story editor on a new series called *Quincy, M.E.,* starring Jack Klugman. Quincy was a crime-fighting Los Angeles medical examiner who just happened to be a better sleuth than anyone in the entire Los Angeles Police Department.

I was invited to come out to Universal and pitch some stories for the series. I agreed, having seen one of them. My policy in freelancing television series was to reserve any serious thinking about the stories I was going to propose until I was driving in traffic on the freeway to the meeting. Somehow the conscious effort of driving safely helped free my unconscious mind. By the time I got to the lot, I usually had three or four notions I thought might be salable.

When I arrived at the *Quincy* offices, I was surprised to see the star lounging on the couch in white duck pants, a white sailor hat, beach sandals, and casual shirt unbuttoned to the navel. Apparently, he had just dropped by on the way to or from the beach. He was in conversation with the story editor, David Shaw, whom I had met briefly at a Writers Guild meeting and admired as a writer. David was the younger brother of the famous writer Irwin Shaw.

"What have you got for us?" said the star, as if to the vegetable salesman in a market. Asparagus had more warmth.

I went into my pitch. Klugman suddenly shouted, "Stop right there! I like that one, the Cesar Chavez story. I can see it now, we'll do a Mexican fiesta scene, we'll have a little mariachi band and I'll eat some hot chili peppers . . . owww!" He leaped to his feet and went spinning around the little office, fanning his open mouth, "hot, hot, hot," adding, "I love that Mexican food but, oh, it's so hot! Let's work on that one, and we'll have a mariachi band, olé!" he announced to Shaw and me.

With no prompting or participation from me, Jack Klugman paced the room dictating not only the story he wanted but also the scenes he wanted in the teleplay based on the story idea I had pitched. Within twenty minutes he finished with, "Good story, now go home and write it." Unlike Peter Ustinov and his Mexican performance at Elke Sommers's home, Klugman was not telling me how much he liked my idea, only how he wanted it written.

Driving back to Santa Monica on the freeway, I tried to piece together what there was about my story that had so ignited the star. I recalled that what I had come in with had no fiesta, mariachi band, or hot chilies. It had been the story of the search for the killer of a Mexican union organizer who had led a strike against farm owners. Klugman had gotten that part right. My idea had originated with a fictionalized Cesar Chavez character.

Over the following weekend I struggled to bring all the disparate ideas into some sort of structure. I could not fit a fiesta or a hot-chili-eating sequence into it. However, I completed a story and sent it to Shaw on Monday.

Whatever I had pieced together got approval from Shaw, the series producer, the network, Klugman, and whoever else needed to see it. The following week I was told to go to script.

I wrote a draft that was a much more personal story than I imagined it would be. I had wandered off my network-approved outline, as I am wont to do. When I turned it in, there was immediate reaction. "I like it," Shaw phoned to say, "but it needs work." The three most frequently heard words in the life of a film or television writer are "it needs work." Professionals learn to accept it as the price of admission into the business. Sometimes it means a few scenes changed; sometimes a top to bottom rewrite.

The following day the series producer phoned to say he hated it and Klugman refused to do it. They were throwing the script out. After he hung up, the phone immediately rang again, it was the producer's secretary. "I just want to tell you how very much I liked your script," she said quietly, obviously fearful she would be overheard. "It's a really wonderful script. The best one we've had here in a long time, believe me."

I thanked her, assuming she was performing the last rites on a dead teleplay. But after about another week, David Shaw phoned back. He had spoken to Klugman telling him how he wanted to rewrite my script. Klugman gave Shaw the go-ahead, saying he liked what he had in mind and would do it, if Shaw rewrote it. Unlike anyone else I've ever met in the business, David Shaw asked me if I would mind if he rewrote my script! It was an unheard of gesture and, of course, I told him I was delighted and hoped he would either take full credit for the script or at least agree to share credit on the episode. He did neither; he left me with sole credit. Thus, I received full residuals for the episode. However, the final-draft script Shaw sent, as required by the Writers Guild, was an excellent top-to-bottom rewrite of what I had turned in.

In the spring of 1978 the trade papers announced a new series titled *Paper Chase,* based on the book by John Osborn, about students struggling to get through Harvard Law School. The series focused on a law professor named Charles W. Kingsley Jr., to be played by noted actor-producer John Houseman. Who better to write a script about a college professor than a college professor? I made an appointment to meet the story editor and pitched a few story ideas, one of which he liked in particular. He gave me an assignment to write a story outline. The outline met with enthusiastic approval from the producer and the network, and I was told to write the script. However, the script ignited a ruckus no one could have predicted.

My story was about a law school professor who is accused by one of his female students of giving A grades in exchange for sex. Although it wasn't based on an actual case, we did have one UCLA film production professor whom the women students nicknamed "Hands." Though we felt we knew who the culprit was, young coeds feared reporting him, figuring their complaints would be ignored or they would be hassled by other faculty members. So none of the young women spoke out. Whether their fears were well founded or not, I did not know. There was an occasional scribbled sign on the bulletin board, "Women: watch out for 'Hands.'" Thanks to Hands, I had the basis for a *Paper Chase*.

But when the producers presented my script to their star, they reported that Houseman had flown into a rage, stating if they insisted on shooting the script, he would quit the series. I was not there to witness the tirade, but the producers gave me a blow-by-blow. Houseman had shouted, "No university professor would ever commit such an immoral, disgusting act!"

In order to calm their star they arranged for him to talk to John Osborn, the former Harvard law student and author of the book upon which the motion picture and television series were based. Houseman was dumbfounded when Osborn told him the problem of professorial sex with students was commonplace, even at Harvard Law. Houseman was mollified but still not happy.

The producers arranged for a dinner for all of us, including Houseman, in an upscale Beverly Hills restaurant. The subject of sex and university professors was never broached. I came to understand this was merely a hand-holding exercise to reinforce Houseman's stature as emperor of the series. Nothing more was said about the script. The story editor did an excellent rewrite (I had gone far off track in my first draft). Hausman played Professor Kingsfield in his usual imperious, impeccable style. I was told the show played well, but I've never seen it.

There is a simple explanation why some writers don't want to see the filmed versions of their work. There is very little possibility that the finished picture will equal the vision the writer saw in his or her mind's eye as they wrote the characters and the scenes. True, on rare occasions the finished product can surpass the writer's expectations, but those instances are so rare they are not worth the dashed hopes of the usual disappointments. Producers, on the other hand, see their product again and again ad nauseam, from dailies to first rough cut (the so-called directors cut) to final rough cut, through scoring and soundstage dubbing, and on to answer print, and finally as the work shows on television or in the theater. At long last, they are numbed by the experiences, sometimes feeling that the whole enterprise wasn't worth the time and effort spent on it.

In 1981, John Young, chairman of UCLA's Department of Theater Arts, Film, and Television had his secretary put a message in my box asking me to see him at my earliest convenience.

I very much admired Young, as most of the faculty did. He managed to stay on top of the sometimes bungling bureaucracy and handle the endless, almost terminally boring meetings and the faculty infighting with poise and equanimity. John Young was a slight, handsome, gray-haired gentleman with a keen wit and a pixie sense of humor. I routinely went to see him when I had problems with academic red tape. Young could finesse an antiquated regulation like no one I had known in the teaching profession. We had an easy, casual, enjoyable relationship; thus I was surprised by the formality of the request.

As I stood in his office across the desk from him, I knew before he spoke that he had something special on his mind. He picked up a piece of paper and glanced at it before speaking, "It is my job to advise you that the faculty has promoted you to the rank of full professor. The vote was unanimous."

He put the paper down and looked up at me with an impish grin. "I'm also required under faculty rules to report the essence of what was said during the discussion regarding your promotion.

"The faculty agreed, and I quote, 'You are the best screenwriting teacher in the world.' That, too, was unanimous." He began to chuckle. "Honestly, Bill, they said it and they really meant it, and I agree with them."

"That covers a lot of territory," I said. "How did they get to know so many screenwriting teachers?"

It was wonderful hyperbole and a long way from an earlier time when essentially the same faculty had unanimously demanded I cease teaching "Hollywood screenwriting." Times had indeed changed.

The difference was the change occurring in the industry itself. Making independent films was becoming commonplace. Movies (now called "films"), for better or worse, were less formulaic, more diverse, and a boom was underway for original made-for-television movies. Cable networks were dramatizing subject matter the networks wouldn't touch: abortion, interracial marriage, our racial divide. The marketplace was exploding. Graduates with talent had a cornucopia of opportunities open to them.

Most film schools were beginning to recognize screenwriting as much more than painting-by-the-numbers as some popular screenwriting books espoused. A new generation of screenwriters was experimenting with new structures, new ways to tell their stories. While the auteur theory had flourished in the sixties and seventies, by the eighties it was universally understood that a director did not necessarily have the original vision, or oeuvre as film critics like to call it, unless he or she had written the screenplay. However, the Directors Guild of America, a bastion of egocentricity, continued to insist upon the demonstrably absurd "a film by" director credit, as if there were not at least a few dozen other creative folks whose combined talents were responsible for bringing the story to the screen. The indisputable truth is that the screenplay is usually the oeuvre. The director's job is to interpret and present the writer's vision. Making movies is and always has been a collaborative effort. "One man, one film," as egomaniacal directors (never in short supply) like to boast, is ridiculous on its face. Production companies and studios were beginning to realize it begins with the written word, the screenplay. Every studio has come to understand the truth of the old axiom "If it ain't on the page, it ain't on the stage." The pages come from the writer; rarely the director.

As if to underscore that point, a few months later a well-dressed gentleman (brass-buttoned Brooks Brothers double-breasted blazer, oxford button-down shirt and old school tie) appeared at my office door, introducing himself as a representative of Danmarks Radio, the Danish government's equivalent to the BBC. He wanted to know if I would be interested in coming to Copenhagen the following summer to teach screenwriting to a select group of Danish writers. All my expenses would be paid plus a car and a first-class SAS round-trip ticket to Copenhagen, which I was free to exchange for an "apex" around-the-world ticket, with as many stopovers as I chose. Fighting the temptation to leap for joy, I told him I would have to see samples of their writers' work.

"We have about twenty eager applicants," he responded, "and I will see that you are sent samples of their writing. I know twenty is a bit much," he added, "so you can bring along another teacher if you like."

I immediately phoned my long-time friend Mort Fine who, with his partner David Friedkin, had written and produced *I Spy* for Bill Cosby. Friedkin and Fine wrote the screenplay for the 1965 classic *The Pawnbroker*. Mort, working alone, had written the feature film *The Greek Tycoon* for Anthony Quinn, and he had also been a key writer on *Kojak*. Mort and his wife, Bernice, already world travelers, were delighted by the prospect. After reading all the submissions from Copenhagen, I sent copies to Fine. We arranged for a Sunday breakfast at the Brentwood Hamburger Hamlet to discuss our evaluations.

As we sat in a sunny booth, we confessed to each other that we felt the submitted material was quite poor. In the tough Hollywood marketplace, these writers wouldn't have stood a chance.

Mort suggested we divide them in half, each taking ten. I insisted on sticking with my successful graduate class seminars of six. Fine, having little teaching experience, was happy to take the rest.

On cinco de Mayo, the day a few of us CBS Radio writers had once or twice driven down to Tijuana to celebrate at the bullfights, Mort and I were in Copenhagen, driving into the teeth of a raging blizzard with the temperature an even zero.

Each of us soon fell in love with our young students, all of whom were fluent in English, exceptionally bright, personable, and eager to learn.

Among the students in my seminar was a tall, pencil-thin, red-haired woman who was the poet laureate of Denmark; another was a young, good-looking member of the Danish parliament; there was a writer who had written Danish films; and other students who had Danish television credits. Danmarks Radio had included an attractive young woman who was their story editor. A more delightful and diverse bunch of students I can not imagine.

We immediately went to work on their stories. We focused on the need for dramatic tension in almost every scene and certainly in every story, which seemed totally foreign to them. Back at the hotel, after thawing in a hot bath for half an hour, I watched Danmarks

Radio's television. What I saw seemed to explain why we were brought to Copenhagen. Between each of their unbelievably boring programs there was a stationary camera fixed on a tank of tropical fish! These were the station breaks, only slightly more interesting than test patterns.

I met with the head of Danmarks Radio to ask why I had been hired. He gave me an unexpected response.

"For some time Danmarks Radio has been the only television channel available to our population. But more and more of our viewers are turning to European channels primarily to watch popular American programming. If that weren't disheartening enough, we have a new commercial second channel starting next year in Copenhagen. It will undoubtedly present reruns of the top American programs. We will be buried. We want you to teach our writers how you Americans do it."

It was the identical story I'd heard in Australia. Hector Crawford Productions had invited me to come to Melbourne one summer to write a couple of scripts for one of their television private-eye series. Like the Danes, the Aussies' scripts lacked the drive and energy we Americans put into our films and television. To me the single word "energy" expresses the difference between American forms of mass communication and all others. Australian television was, in fact, primarily American television reruns. Even though Crawford was the single most successful producer of Australian TV programming, seven of their top-ten series were American reruns and the other three Crawford-produced programs were poorly mimicked American shows. I was nonplussed. I did not like the idea of the world being dominated by American television because I did not respect much of American television myself.

Mort and I were invited back for a second seminar in Copenhagen the following summer. We eagerly accepted.

Eventually, one of my former Danish students, who became the left-wing leader in their parliament, denounced the idea that Denmark had to import American television writers. He demanded Danmarks Radio do a better job of developing indigenous Danish programming. Of course, he was right.

Later I learned that my red-haired poet laureate had been nominated for the Danish equivalent of an Emmy Award for her movie-
for-television developed in our class. Her story was about a young
woman who loses her battle against anorexia and dies. How very
Danish!

19

Only Sometimes a Happy Ending

There was a sense of dissatisfaction slowly building among Hollywood's contract hyphenates. More and more they were beginning to be treated like, well, writers. Many of them were getting no respect. An example of one of the causes of our resentment was a young actor named Robert Blake, a highly experienced former child actor with a multitude of credits as an adult. He had received excellent reviews for his work as one of the two young murderers in Truman Capote's *In Cold Blood.*

In 1975 Universal studios sold NBC on the notion of building a series around Blake. That the actor was physically quite short and known as hot-tempered and tempestuous apparently only made him more appealing. The series was called *Baretta* and was a spin-off from another failed detective series. Tony Baretta was a very unusual detective, a cop who lived in a run-down hotel and worked alone. His wardrobe consisted of T-shirts and jeans. (Blake had built his small body to perfection, and he liked to exhibit it.) Baretta's best friend was Fred, his pet cockatoo. When Blake reported to work, he established himself from the first moment he appeared on Universal's soundstage. He let one and all know that he was the star, and was to be treated as a star should be treated. Furthermore, he was going to personally ensure the scripts were up to his high standards.

But things didn't work out quite that way. As the scripts came in, Blake complained they weren't good enough. In short order he found a solution for the problem; he fired the writer-producer in charge. And when the new hyphenate didn't work out to his satisfaction, he fired him, too. And so it went. Tony Baretta was, indeed one hot-tempered cop. It was rumored that during production Blake was locked in the studio at night so that he didn't wander off and forget to show up for production the next day. I don't know if it was true or not, but I do know that in Hollywood, the more bizarre the rumor, the more likely that it is true.

Hyphenates seemed to come and go almost before they could unpack their reading glasses. Blake quickly became known as "Napoleon" or simply "the little tyrant."

In Hollywood, when a TV star wanted the hyphenate in charge fired, both the studio and the network usually asked "How soon do you want him off the lot?" In fact, it soon became obvious in television that whenever the star demanded a raise the studio or the network merely asked where he would like the money delivered and in what denominations. This was especially true at Universal Studios but it was true at the other studios as well. Stars always called the shots and still do.

Another actor famous for firing hyphenates was Peter Falk, the highly popular star of *Columbo.* Like Blake, it appeared all he had to do was threaten to take a walk and cadres of unctuous studio and network executives arrived on the set to reassure him he was king of the universe.

If hyphenates had never known it before, they were being forcefully reminded that the face on the screen was what television is all about. All the rest, stories, characters, locales, ideas, are so much window trimming. It's the close-up that counts.

What were hyphenates to do in order to salvage a shred of dignity, if not respect? The majority of us were under contract to the studios and/or the networks. Only a small minority of us owned our own companies. We were basically hired guns with no union to give us a voice. The Writers Guild could represent us only as writers since the NLRB had ruled that producer-writers were supervisors, employees or not, therefore ineligible for union representation.

Nonetheless, a small group of us banded together and formed the Television Producers Guild in 1957. We soon began to attract other hyphenates. Our membership grew rapidly, but management pointedly looked the other way. They were not interested in talking to us. What we lacked in numbers we made up for in zeal. We were going to get a union somehow, some way.

Back in 1950 some feature film producers had formed the Screen Producers Guild as a social club. They welcomed all producers as members. Much to their consternation many television hyphenates had joined. Soon, hyphenates equaled or outnumbered the conservative old-line feature film producers.

As one of the founding members and first board members of the Television Producers Guild, I suggested to our board that our best chance for recognition was to join the Screen Producers Guild en masse and try to change it into a union. Our board's vote was unanimous. We believed most hyphenates would follow our lead. In 1966 TPG amalgamated with the Screen Producers Guild and became the Producers Guild of America. It was a bloodless coup, a quiet takeover.

The old-time studio producers were appalled at what was happening to their social club but were powerless to stop it. However, at meetings they were invariably courteous and welcoming to these new producers from the other side of the tracks. One got the impression that they sensed the way the work world was going and, like it or not, it was going to television.

Now we had what we hoped would be a solid platform upon which to build if not a union, at least an organization that, by sheer force of numbers, could sit down with the Association of Motion Picture and Television Producers (AMPTP) and negotiate a minimum basic agreement.

AMPTP insisted that no matter what we called ourselves we were still a social club. They would have nothing to do with us. Our board meetings were unproductive, talkative, and frustrating. Yet our membership continued to grow. Hyphenates were on the march. We sensed ultimate victory. It was especially encouraging to sit at the table with producers such as Roger Corman (who rarely said a word), retired General Frank McCarthy (our secretary who had been General George Patton's aide and had produced the movie *Patton*), and David Dortort (our president and creator-producer of *Bonanza*). Our board was made up of industry heavy hitters, a mix of hyphenates and feature producers. We formed various committees and discussed industry issues, all aimed toward the final goal of recognition. Finally, we got the Writers Guild to meet with us. Inch by inch we were letting Hollywood know through the trade press that a new and unstoppable force was coming its way.

At each of PGA's meetings with the Writers Guild (which we writer-producers understood was our primary union), their lawyers were unequivocal in their opinion that as supervisors we could not form our own union. Furthermore, the Writers Guild could not represent or negotiate for us as producers, only as writers.

Lou Greenspan, the Producers Guild's executive director and an old union man, suggested we meet with the heads of the Hollywood branch of the International Alliance of Theatrical Stage Employees (IATSE, or "I-ott-see" as it is called by Hollywood). With eight hundred local unions in North America, it represents members in every branch of the business, including art directors, script supervisors, cameramen, set painters, sound and lab technicians, what have you. Roughly speaking, IATSE represents everybody involved in the physical production of the film. The crew, the stage hands, script supervisors, set decorators, and prop people are listed "below the line" on the budget primarily because their cost is fixed by union minimums. Writers, actors, producers, directors, and sometimes cinematographers are listed "above the line" because each of their fees can vary wildly, depending upon how much the studio and/or producer has budgeted for the film or series. Above-the-line costs are likely to be far higher than each artist's union scale.

This division was established many years ago to enable production entities to calculate the exact cost of the below-the-line expenses of a feature or television series before going into production. The above-the-line is a different matter and is generally the difference between a high- and a low-budget movie. It is always adjustable; below-the-line, on the other hand, has very little flexibility. Today, with star and director salaries in the multimillions, the cost of the above-the-line generally far exceeds the cost of the entire below-the-line on most film projects, be they features or TV.

I was a member of the committee assigned to meet with the heads of IATSE's Hollywood local. The meeting was short and cordial. "We can not represent you because you are supervisors, you hire and fire people," their executives told us. "However, we certainly wish you luck."

We were back to square one. The years and the meetings continued. Producers, especially hyphenates, liked to get together and discuss mutual problems as well as ways to win recognition. But we made no significant headway in our quest to improve working conditions, much less negotiate a minimum basic agreement such as those the Writers Guild and the Directors Guild had for their members.

The issue of producer crediting was a sore point for many of us. Anyone in a top position in the production company could put their relatives or their mistress's name on the finished product as producer, and they sometimes did. As the actual producers of a series or feature films, we were powerless to stop this insidious practice.

Meanwhile, the Writers Guild was getting plenty of complaints about hyphenates rewriting members' scripts, without giving writers a chance to do the rewrite themselves or even notifying them. I myself had been a victim of that practice several times. When a *Bonanza* I wrote was totally rewritten by the producer the night before shooting, I responded by registering a pseudonym, Frank Unger, with the Writers Guild. I then wrote the producer to use Frank Unger as my onscreen credit, as I was entitled to under guild rules, adding that the initials were a token of my displeasure about his last-minute rewrite. No surprise, he didn't speak to me for a few years. In the urgency of our production deadlines to meet airdates, even I was guilty of doing last minute rewrites (although I never took any writing credit). There was plenty of blame to go around.

The Writers Guild announced a special meeting for all concerned to discuss "the hyphenate problem." We met in a large room just above the old Writers Guild Theater on Melrose Avenue. David

Rintels, my close friend and a past president of the Writers Guild, and I were among those who shared a table at the front of the room. Almost one hundred members packed the big room. After several people had aired their views, Rintels rose to speak, explaining the problem the Guild membership was having and advising the group that this was a discussion meeting only. No specific action was planned; the Guild was open to ideas. He made his usual eloquent speech discussing the reality that we are writers first, producers second.

I responded that the situation was generally created by writers themselves who demanded producer credit before taking a staff TV job. The truth was that many of these hyphenates only delivered a shooting script, yet they were negotiating for such titles as supervising producer, associate producer, and the like. They were not involved in hiring a director, a cast, the editing, or any other of the many important functions of a producer. For many hyphenates "producer" was and remains a sham title.

Suddenly a man leaped to his feet in the back of the room and shouted at the top of his voice, "He's right, you hear me! The son of a bitch is right!" I recognized Mel Brooks even though we had never met. But Brooks was not yet satisfied that he had made his point. He picked up his metal folding chair and flung it down on the floor with a crash, shouting, "He's right, he's right, the son of a bitch is right!" He quickly strode down the aisle shouting the same message: "He's right, god damn it! He's right!" while slamming the empty aisle chairs to the floor. Metal chairs were crashing all around us as Brooks, shouting, strode toward us at the front table. In stunned silence, punctuated by a few puzzled laughs, the meeting immediately adjourned. We all filed out quietly.

Brooks came up to me and said, "You know, you're right about what you said, I mean it," then shouted again, "YOU ARE RIGHT!" I suspect the great comedy writer-producer-director-actor was just plain tired of listening to speeches. What better way to end a meeting quickly?

The Writers Guild continues to struggle with the hyphenate issue to this day, but the Producers Guild was slowly going nowhere. Our executive director unexpectedly died. As his replacement we chose Rosalind Wyman, a former Los Angeles City Councilwoman. Wyman claimed, with some justification, that she had been responsible for bringing the Brooklyn Dodgers to Los Angeles. Wyman was very much in favor of the Producers Guild becoming a union. She felt strongly that the best way to go about that was to seek affiliation with the Teamsters Union.

Although I agreed with her union sentiments, I found it hard to believe the Teamsters would walk a picket line for producers. Furthermore, it seemed to me the Teamsters Union and the Producers Guild were, on the face of it, an unsavory connection for the producers but not for the Teamsters. However, Wyman continued to lobby the board hard for meetings with the Teamsters. She claimed that Lew Wasserman, president and CEO of Universal Studios, had suggested we join the Teamsters. While I never questioned her sincerity, I found it hard to believe the once most powerful man in Hollywood would recommend such an alliance.

Meanwhile, I had accepted an offer to teach another screenwriting seminar in Copenhagen during UCLA's summer quarter. When I returned about eight weeks later, I received a call from Roz Wyman. She informed me that the PGA board had voted unanimously in my absence to begin talks with the Teamsters, aimed at PGA becoming an affiliate. She explained our constitution required every board member's vote to make the decision unanimous. If I voted with the rest of the board, it was a done deal. We would begin talks with the Teamsters. If I voted no, the issue would have to go to the full membership for a vote.

I voted no. Wyman was most unhappy, pointing out this would cause considerable time-loss and expense, the convening of the entire membership, and a lot of work for her. I responded that I had been down this road before with IATSE. Did the producers really want to be in the Teamsters Union? I thought the membership should make that decision. Displeased as she was she had no choice but to announce a special meeting to decide the issue.

My sole dissenting vote sent a ripple effect throughout the industry. The battle lines were drawn. The media, smelling blood, came at us full force. (For a few days the story occupied the front pages of *Daily Variety* and the *Hollywood Reporter*.) I received a letter from

Billy Sackheim asking me to sign his enclosed proxy so I could add my vote with his for explorations with the Teamsters.

I phoned Wyman explaining if Sackheim was able to put out a mailer to the entire membership, I also wanted our mailing list. She countered, explaining Sackheim had paid for his own mailing. I responded that I would do the same. She was forced to agree. I sent her a letter to forward to the membership along with a proxy explaining why I was opposed to Teamster affiliation. Both of our daily trade papers played the story as their lead piece with front-page banner headlines. Within a few days I received a phone call from Howard Koch, a highly respected, major feature film producer at Paramount. I knew him slightly.

"Bill," he said in a friendly manner, "you just have to be careful when you are coming out strong against the Teamsters. Use your head."

I did not take the call as a threat but rather as genuine concern from a guy who knew the town far better than I. Meantime, proxies began to pour into my mail box. I was hearing from feature film producers whose credits would fill a phone book, as well as many young guys who were primarily writers. I had no idea this issue would evoke so much response. Some letters contained brief, angry statements against producers allying with the Teamsters.

An NBC *Nightly News* reporter phoned and asked for an on-camera interview. The issue was beginning to take on a life that had the whole of Hollywood talking. I had not thought of it as such a big deal. Television journalists had paid little attention to the PGA before this conflict. The interview with two other PGA dissidents and myself was conducted at the Beverly Hilton Hotel the next afternoon, where the PGA meeting was scheduled to be held the following evening. It was brief and painless. When I saw it broadcast on the NBC's *Nightly News* I was shocked. In answer to the reporter's question of what the Teamsters Union could do for the Producers Guild, I had replied, "Some of our members claim we would win recognition as a union, get a minimum wage agreement, and the right to determine the producer's credit as the Writers Guild does, but I don't think so, and I don't agree."

However, NBC *Nightly News* broadcast my quote, BUT they lopped off the "but I don't think so, and I don't agree."

That night my phone began ringing off the hook with angry calls from those whose proxy I held. "But I thought you were against our joining the Teamsters Union?" was the essence of the messages. I explained to the callers what happened, and fortunately they accepted my answer.

The much-heralded meeting the following night was standing room only. We had never had such a turnout. Television news crews were clogging the doorway as I made my way in and took an aisle seat. The room was thick with smoke and the loud chatter of the argumentative crowd. I recognized some producer friends who angrily turned away from me. The crowd appeared to be pro negotiations with the Teamsters, and I was seen as what I was, the lone vote on the board who had forced this meeting. To many in the crowd I was the enemy.

After the banging of the gavel several times, the unruly meeting was called to order. Since the sole subject of the meeting was the approval or disapproval of negotiations with the Teamsters, the chairman immediately asked for a motion to start the discussion.

Speaker after speaker took the floor to support or oppose discussions with the Teamsters. It was hard to tell which way the vote was going to go. Finally, when the membership was pretty much talked out, someone called for a vote. Hands went up for yea and then for nay. It was too close to call, though both sides were shouting victory. The chair decided to order a hand count.

Suddenly Billy Sackheim stood up, "Mr. Chairman," he proclaimed, waving a fist full of paper, "I have thirty-seven proxies for opening discussions with the Teamsters union." There were cheers and applause. He sat down. It was my cue. Standing, I called out, "Mr. Chairman, I have fifty-one proxies *against* negotiating with the Teamsters."

Pandemonium broke loose. I was greeted by loud boos, waving fists, hisses, and a general uproar accompanied by expressions of disgust and disapproval. Several of my liberal friends I'd known for years waved down-turned fists at me as they scowled; I was not prepared for the ugly vehemence of those who disagreed. It was now obvious to one and all that I had entered the meeting with enough proxies to control the outcome.

But, on the whole, we all left without lasting rancor, or so I had hoped. Sackheim, however, came up to me as the audience was filing out to say, with considerable contempt, "I hope you're satisfied."

The following day the NBC reporter phoned me to apologize, saying that the network needed to cut twelve seconds off the interview, and he chose to lop off the entire point of my statement.

To their credit the Producers Guild of America never gave up their struggle for recognition for their members. In 1968 the PGA signed a collective bargaining agreement with all major motion picture and television companies as represented by AMPTP. The agreement created a Guild Shop, gave minimum wage, credits, and creative rights as well as pension, health and welfare benefits for ten years. The following year an activist group in the Writers Guild filed a lawsuit charging the PGA agreement a "sweetheart deal" with management. In 1972 the Los Angeles Superior Court ruled in favor of the PGA, and the Writers Guild activists appealed. In 1974 the Appellate Court overruled the Superior Court nullifying the PGA contract.

In 1984 the PGA signed a four-year autonomous affiliation agreement with the Teamsters Union. In August of 1985 the PGA membership voted to strike as sanctioned by the joint council of the Teamsters, but the strike was not implemented when it became obvious that Teamster Local 399 (Hollywood) would not support the strike. In 1989 the PGA terminated their affiliation with the Teamsters. The outcome was pathetically predictable.

Coming home to my apartment in Santa Monica one afternoon, I stopped off at San Vicente Foods, a relatively small supermarket where I was a frequent shopper. While browsing through the aisles, I saw a small, rotund woman in gray ballooning flowing robes, drifting silently, almost ghostly, past me. Her heavily bloated face looked familiar, but her eyes were slits hidden behind padded lids. There was only a hint of familiarity; I refused to believe my eyes. The young manager of the market nervously approached me. "Do you know who that is?" he whispered to me. I told him I was uncertain, having seen her only in passing.

"It's Ida Lupino!" he whispered. "She comes in once in a while, late in the afternoon, carrying a canvas sack. I hate to say this," he continued, "but I'm pretty sure she's stealing canned goods." Before I could reply, he hastily added, "I say, let her take what she needs. Ida Lupino, a bag lady! Incredible." It belatedly occurred to me that he was right!

I hurriedly left the market, but there was no sign of the bloated woman in the parking lot. I never saw her again. I hope against hope that the rotund ghostlike figure in the market surely was somebody else; the memories of the work we did together over the years still remain uppermost in my mind. But, as much as I rejected the idea, I knew it was Ida.

20

Scenes from the Life of a Teacher

Although I enjoyed my activist role in union politics, my primary focus was on teaching. One afternoon during my UCLA office hours, I answered a knock on my door to discover a liveried chauffeur, in shiny black boots, standing between two preteens in black suits, white shirts, black ties, like two bar mitzvah boys. They were Mel Brooks in miniature.

"Mr. Brooks asked me to bring his sons to you," the chauffeur said. "He'll be phoning you to explain."

Right on cue my office phone rang. The voice was instantly recognizable. "Hey, Froug," the gravel-voiced Mel Brooks said into my ear, "I want you to teach my kids screenwriting." I had discovered Brooks's normal voice is only slightly softer than a shout. When Mel Brooks speaks, he broadcasts.

"I can't, Mel," I replied, "unless they are enrolled in UCLA's screenwriting program."

"Okay, okay," Brooks replied, resignation in his voice, "I'll have to do it myself." And he hung up.

The battle for hyphenate recognition was by no means over. The PGA persisted. They joined IATSE, negotiated in and out of deals with the studios, signed contracts with studios who later reneged. PGA never gave up. Finally they began negotiations on their own with AMPTP, whom I suspect was fearful that sooner or later PGA would find a home and support from a bigger, stronger union. At long last, the studios decided to grant a pension plan and health-and-welfare coverage for producers working in theatrical films and prime-time network television. It had taken the new generation more than ten years, but they had finally made it.

The companies also agreed to negotiate restrictions of the producer credit to people who had actually earned it. Not even Hollywood could have come up with a happier ending.

Shortly before my retirement, the most unusual screenwriting student I ever encountered showed up during my office hours one afternoon. He introduced himself as Jeffrey Boam. He was there to plead his case for acceptance as one of my directed studies students. Boam was a bit older than other applicants, but he had the attitude of a young man who was going to become a successful screenwriter or die trying. As it turned out, he did both.

Boam gave me two screenplays to read as his tickets for acceptance. I read both and concluded he was not a strong writer; in fact, he seemed to have little talent for the work. When I asked him back to discuss my conclusion, he was unfazed. The agents who had seen his scripts had turned him down. It didn't deter him. He said no matter what I thought, he was going to be a screenwriter, so I might as well agree to work with him. I did not know until many years later when I read his introduction to my book *Screenwriting Tricks of the Trade* that he had decided to, as he put it, "target me" to be his teacher. *Tricks* was my answer to UCLA for having canceled my fundamentals of screenwriting lecture series over a decade earlier. That book contains the essence of the inflammatory Hollywood screenwriting that had been banned from UCLA. What's doubly satisfying is that this little opus remains among the best-selling screenwriting books of all time globally.

During one of our one-on-one sessions, Boam told me he wanted to write a screenplay about John Dillinger. I was not enthusiastic, reminding him there were already more movies about Dillinger than robberies he had committed. As with everything else about this remarkable young writer, he stuck to his guns. He assured me he had an entirely different approach. There was no talking him out of it.

Over the course of the quarter he came in with research he had done on Dillinger. Indeed, the material was fresh and fascinating. Nothing I'd heard or read about the infamous outlaw approached his concept. I told him to write a treatment for his proposed screenplay.

What he brought in was deeply disappointing. All this fresh material had been turned into a boring story. Worst of all, Boam realized it but did not know how to solve the problem. We talked at length, and he went home to write again.

By the end of the school year, Boam had turned in an incomplete and boring script titled *Johnny,* which is the name Dillinger liked to be called. When I expressed my disappointment, he had a quick response.

"Are you busy this summer?" he suddenly asked me. When I replied I had no plans he said, "How about taking a crack at *Johnny?*"

I told him I saw nothing I could save in his screenplay except the exciting personal history he'd learned about Dillinger. Again, he was not put off in he least, "I have an idea," he said. "You know everything I know about Dillinger. Take my research and write a new script."

Arguments were useless against a man with the determination of Jeffrey Boam. I agreed to do it.

That summer I took Jeffrey's notes and wrote a new screenplay in about three weeks. Every Friday afternoon he would come by my apartment and sit in the living room reading pages while I continued writing in my office in a back bedroom. The afternoon I wrote "Fade Out," I heard Jeffrey yell "Oh, no!" in the living room. I rushed in having no idea what had happened to him.

He was sitting on the couch holding one of the Hollywood trade papers. "Can you believe this?" He handed the paper to me.

On the front page of the *Hollywood Reporter* was a story headlined MILIUS FILMING DILLINGER. John Milius, a well-known screenwriter-director was starting production the coming week on a film about John Dillinger.

"We're doomed," sighed Boam.

"You're right," I responded.

Nonetheless, doomed or not, we now had a screenplay we both felt would have been salable except for this unfortunate coincidence. I gave it to my agent who confirmed the obvious; Milius's film made our script useless to features, but he liked it very much and felt he had a shot at a TV movie sale.

Those of us who ply our trade in Hollywood understand that sometimes ideas are simply in the air, nobody owns them until they are put on paper. There is not a great deal of thievery in the business; it's too risky, too time consuming, and it's unnecessary. Great ideas are as universal as thinking itself, but writers and their ilk (painters, sculptors, musicians, producers, dancers, directors, all creative folk) create something from them. Boam happened to have a much better idea than I thought he had, but John Milius simply got there first.

However, my agent did make a sale of *Johnny* to a well-established motion picture producer named Edward Lewis (of *Spartacus* fame). He had frequently partnered with actor Kirk Douglas. For ten thousand dollars Lewis bought a one-year option on our screenplay (Boam and I had agreed to share credit for the script) and apparently turned right around and sold it to NBC for a television movie for how much money I do not know.

NBC wanted a minor rewrite to fill in a bit more of Dillinger's background. Boam suggested I do it. The polish was to be included in the ten thousand dollar option price. It took me less than an afternoon.

NBC was happy with the result. That turned out to be the easy part. It was time for Edward Lewis to pay us the ten thousand dollars NBC had already paid him for the option. He refused. My agent demanded the money due, again Lewis steadfastly refused. Finally I asked my business manager, David Licht (also an attorney), to help me out. Talking to Lewis's attorney, Licht reported back the most extraordinary conversation. Lewis's attorney told Licht, "I will not make out a check for ten thousand dollars to someone I haven't met."

After months of stalling it was time to bring in the Writers Guild. They sent a telegram to Edward Lewis stating simply that unless the check was delivered to my agent by noon the next day, Edward Lewis Productions would be on the guild's "unfair list," meaning he could no longer employ any writer who was a member of the guild, which was every writer in Hollywood. The check arrived the next day.

Scoundrels, while not a significant portion of the Hollywood population, are not in short supply. Even the most visible and highly successful people in town sometimes vanish when it comes time to pay money due to writers. Unlike directors and actors, once the script is turned in, once writers have delivered their goods, they are no longer needed. Most of the other creative people involved in making a feature are embarrassed to have the screenwriter anywhere in the same county. They are living reminders to the director and actors that they did not, in fact, create the story, nor did the actors create the characters, contrary to their statements to the press. What may be the root of the problem is that actors basically resent writers putting words in their mouths. It's a totally understandable reaction.

During several recent negotiations, the Writers Guild of America, West (WGAW) has settled longstanding and difficult problems. Among the many issues was the writer's right to sit in on table readings of the screenplay (the first joint meeting of the cast) and actually visit the set and go on press junkets. At long last, WGA demanded and won the right for screenwriters to be unlocked from the closet. It was a singular victory, though the guild was unable to eliminate the director's vanity credit ("a film by John Frankensmith" or "John Frankensmith's *It's All Mine*"). Many directors' egos are vaster than space, aided and abetted by film and media critics who simplify their jobs by awarding director auteur credit whether the directors deserve it or not. (It saves the critics the bother of having to research who actually did what on a film.) Another issue the guild fought for was the elimination of late payment for writing services. No matter how financially secure the company is or how pleased the production entity is with the services of the writer, Hollywood history says that producing companies will routinely delay payment to the writer as long as they can stall, invent excuses, or dodge agents and business managers. The writer all too often gets paid only after the Writers

Guild threatens to put the company out of business. This is as true of the major studios as it is of the small independent production companies, perhaps even more so. The ugly reality is that writers are the untouchables of Hollywood.

The oft-told story about the ambitious starlet who was so dumb she fucked the screenwriter contains bedrock truth. It could be paraphrased as the studios are so dumb they keep trying to fuck the writers, but thanks to WGAW they rarely get away with it. Late payments and sometimes no payments at all are ongoing issues with the guild and continue to be a battle in every contract we negotiate. The bottom line is everybody in Hollywood wants to fuck the writer, and not for the writer's pleasure.

After graduating from UCLA, Jeffrey Boam's grit and determination eventually paid off handsomely. In 1978 he wrote *Straight Time*, followed by *The Dead Zone, Interspace, The Lost Boys,* and *Funny Farm.*

One day they were filming *Straight Time* on the beach in Santa Monica just below my apartment building. Jeffrey came rushing up to my apartment, fit to be tied. "Dustin Hoffman is throwing out my dialogue, he's improvising the entire scene! This is not what I wrote!"

I assured him there was nothing unusual about Dustin Hoffman's improvising lines, and it was merely one of the hazards of being a screenwriter in Hollywood. He left unhappy, but somewhat mollified. Nothing would stand in the way of this driven young writer, including talent or lack of it. He would succeed.

Boam so impressed director Richard Donner that Donner hired him to write *Lethal Weapon 2*, the first sequel to the enormously successful *Lethal Weapon*. Boam also received a writing credit on *Lethal Weapon 3*. The sequels were even more successful than the original. George Lucas hired Boam to write the hugely successful *Indiana Jones and the Last Crusade*, based on Lucas's story.

Warner Brothers signed Jeffrey to a two-year, three-million-dollar contract making him the highest paid contract screenwriter in history. *People* magazine profiled him, he was briefly lionized on television, he was a short-lived toast of the town.

But by the end of Boam's contract Warners had became disenchanted with his work, and his contract was not renewed. His last movie, *The Phantom,* was a failure, as was his television series, *The Adventures of Briscoe County, Jr.*

Boam's luck took a terrible turn in 2000 when he was diagnosed with a bizarre, fatal illness. His agonizingly slow death at a young age touched everyone who ever knew or worked with this most remarkable young man. Jeffrey's widow told me he was struggling with the vicissitudes of Hollywood and questioning his own talent during his final days.

Jeffrey Boam's career personifies the theme of this book. To paraphrase Rudyard Kipling: If you can meet with success and failure and treat those two impostors just the same, the victories and defeats of showbiz will leave you unscathed. However, if you are unable to get a handle on Kipling's wisdom, you will make yourself miserable working in Hollywood. Take a plane, go home.

Index

Index

Index

Index

Index

A RAY AND PAT BROWNE BOOK

Murder on the Reservation: American Indian Crime Fiction
Ray B. Browne

Profiles of Popular Culture: A Reader
Edited by Ray B. Browne

Goddesses and Monsters: Women, Myth, Power, and Popular Culture
Jane Caputi

Mystery, Violence, and Popular Culture
John G. Cawelti

Baseball and Country Music
Don Cusic

Popular Witchcraft: Straight from the Witch's Mouth, 2nd edition
Jack Fritscher

The Essential Guide to Werewolf Literature
Brian J. Frost

How I Escaped from Gilligan's Island: *And Other Misadventures of a Hollywood
     Writer-Producer*
William Froug

Popular Culture Theory and Methodology: A Basic Introduction
Edited by Harold E. Hinds, Jr., Marilyn F. Motz and Angela M. S. Nelson

Rituals and Patterns in Children's Lives
Edited by Kathy Merlock Jackson

Images of the Corpse: From the Renaissance to Cyberspace
Edited by Elizabeth Klaver

Dissecting Stephen King: From the Gothic to Literary Naturalism
Heidi Strengell

Walking Shadows: Orson Welles, William Randolph Hearst, and Citizen Kane
John Evangelist Walsh

Spectral America: Phantoms and the National Imagination
Edited by Jeffrey Andrew Weinstock

King of the Cowboys, Queen of the West: Roy Rogers and Dale Evans
Raymond E. White